The Complete

IDIOT'S

Next Step with the

INTERNET

by Peter Kent

alpha
books

A Division of Macmillan Computer Publishing USA
A Prentice Hall Macmillan Company
201 W. 103rd Street, Indianapolis, Indiana 46290 USA

For Mum.

©1994 Alpha Books
Part of the Complete Idiot's Guide Series

International Standard Book Number:1-56761-524-4
Library of Congress Catalog Card Number: 94-72613

96   95   8   7   6   5   4   3   2

Interpretation of the printing code: the rightmost number of the first series of numbers is the year of the book's printing; the rightmost number of the second series of numbers is the number of the book's printing. For example, a printing code of 94-1 shows that the first printing of the book occurred in 1994.

Screen reproductions in this book were created by means of the program Collage Plus from Inner Media, Inc., Hollis, NH.

Printed in the United States of America

Publisher
Marie Butler-Knight

Acquisitions Editor
Barry Pruett

Managing Editor
Elizabeth Keaffaber

Product Development Manager
Faithe Wempen

Production Editor
Phil Kitchel

Copy Editor
San Dee Phillips

Cover Designer
Karen Ruggles

Designer
Barbara Webster

Illustrations
Steve Vanderbosch

Indexer
Chris Cleveland

Production Team
*Gary Adair, Brad Chinn, Dan Caparo, Kim Cofer, Lisa Daugherty,
David Dean, Cynthia Drovin, Jennifer Eberhardt, Erika Millen,
G. Alan Palmore, Beth Rago, Bobbi Satterfield, Carol Stamile,
Karen Walsh, Robert Wolf*

Special thanks to Art Smoot for ensuring the technical accuracy of this book.

Contents at a Glance

This page unintentionally left blank.

Contents

Introduction

So you heard all the hype about the Information Highway, eh? You got online—and discovered it's actually a dirt track! If your experiences on the Internet are anything like those of syndicated columnist Mike Royko, you were disappointed. Royko spoke of the "fascinating knowledge that will come leaping out of your computer screen... assuming, of course, that you have the time, the patience, and the inclination to become a computer nerd."

Okay, so plenty of people are happy with the Internet. Some people actually *like* the command line, and take a perverse enjoyment in claiming that typing commands is better than using a mouse and those cutesy, little icon things. Most people feel trapped at the command line, though. They learned about computers in a graphical-user-interface world, but when it was time to check out the Internet, they found themselves back in a 1970s UNIX world.

Okay, So What's My Next Step?

In my last book about the Internet, *The Complete Idiot's Guide to the Internet*, I introduced thousands of people to the command-line Internet, the only type of access available to many users. I explained how to get rolling quickly in a complicated system, and how systems, such as FTP, Telnet, and WAIS, looked complicated but you could tame them with the right knowledge. Knowing how to use a system well improves the system—but it's still the same old system. So maybe you are ready for more.

In *The Complete Idiot's Next Step with the Internet*, we're going to take a step further, a step away from the command line and into the last decade of the 20th Century. We're going to start by learning how to improve what you already have: how to "talk" to people on the Internet, how to play games, how to use UNIX like a pro, how to use a new Gopher tool (Jughead), how to start contributing to the Internet's information resources, and how to find a program that will make e-mail easier to use.

You're also going to find out how to take the next step to graphical-user-interface Internet. You've been using a mouse for a few years, now—there's no need to throw it away when you get onto the Internet. You'll find that working with the programs described in this book is like working with a completely new online system. You're no longer on the Internet; you're on the Internet+. I'll show you the different programs available, so you can pick and choose just what you need to really make the Internet fly.

Who Are You?

I'm going to make a few assumptions about you. You already know a little about the Internet. You know what FTP is, how to use Telnet, why you'd want to work with the World Wide Web. You understand how to use e-mail, how to track down other users' e-mail addresses, and when to go to WAIS. If you don't have this basic knowledge, get a copy of *The Complete Idiot's Guide to the Internet*. It will turn you from an Internet-Idiot into an Internet-Nerd in a few easy steps. (Well, okay, it won't take you quite that far, but you will feel a lot more at home in Internet-land.)

I'm also going to assume that you are working with an IBM PC-compatible. While the techniques discussed in *The Complete Idiot's Guide to the Internet* are, in general, independent of the type of computer you are using, in this book, we're going to be looking at advanced Internet software that runs on the PC, mostly in Microsoft Windows. As you progress and start using the fancy software, you'll find that it's *platform dependent*, if you'll excuse the computer jargon. It's impractical to cover all types of computers in one book, so we're going with the PC.

What Do You Need?

The first part of the book deals with improving the setup you already have: you'll learn how to *talk* to people on the Net, how to use Internet games, and how to work with Jughead and ping. You can do all this with your current account. However, starting in Part II, we're going to be looking at software that won't run unless you have either a permanent connection to the Internet or a dial-in direct account (a SLIP, CSLIP, or PPP account).

(We'll go over this terminology later in the book.) If you have a dial-in terminal account—one that you use by dialing into your service provider's host computer using a communications program, such as Windows Terminal, CrossTalk, PROCOMM, HyperACCESS, or Qmodem—you won't be able to use the software described.

That's not necessarily a problem, though. Over the last six months, the price of both setting up and using a dial-in direct account has dropped considerably. You can set up such an account for as little as $35, perhaps less by the time you read this. And you can find service providers who charge the same hourly rate for dial-in direct accounts as they do for dial-in terminal accounts. If you don't have a permanent connection to the net through your company or school, you can get a dial-in direct account relatively cheaply.

So What's the Catch?

The catch, dear reader, is that to use a dial-in direct account, you'll have to use to SLIP, CSLIP, or PPP software. And such software can be a pain in the derriere to install. In fact, in March of 1994, *Boardwatch Magazine* complained that these programs are "uninstallable by humanoids."

Things change quickly on the Internet. The commercial software has improved dramatically in the last few months. You can get WinGopher, for instance, out of the box and up and running on the publisher's test server in ten minutes or less. Other commercial products seem to be cleaning up their act, too, improving installation procedures and documentation.

As for shareware and freeware, documentation remains poor—but you have this book, haven't you? I'll explain how to acquire and install Trumpet Winsock, for example, an essential component for any Internet shareware setup. And I'll take a look at a variety of other programs and provide a few pointers for easy installation.

How Use This Book

You know how to use a book, don't you? You have your table of contents, index, and stuff in-between. The stuff in-between divides into smaller stuff, like this:

Part I: Improving What You've Got   Talking, playing, working, and distributing information using an ordinary dial-in terminal or permanent connection.

Part II: The Freebie/Almost Freebie Route   This section will show you how to install software you can find laying around on the Internet, programs that are either free or close to it.

Part III: The Cough-Up-the-Dough Route   This section is a review of tempting commercial programs you may want to buy; you'll learn what they can do for you and the problems you'll have installing them (and how to avoid those problems).

Part IV: Quick & Easy "Pink SLIP": Using The Pipeline   Oh, did we mention there's a disk at the back of this book? You may have noticed. This section explains how to install the software; how to get online; and how to use The Pipeline's special Internet connection: a fast and easy way to get a graphical user interface running on the Internet.

The "Conventions Used in this Book" Stuff

I have used a few conventions in this book to make it easier to use. For example, when you need to type something, it will appear like this:

Type **This**

Just type what it says. In this case, it means, "type the word **this**." It's as simple as that. If I don't know exactly what you'll have to type—because you have to supply some of the information—I'll put the unknown information in italics. For instance:

Type **This** *filename*

I don't know the file name, so you'll have to supply it.

If I'm showing you something that appears on the screen, it'll appear in a special font, like this:

    This is on the screen.

If you want to understand more about the subject you are learning, you'll find some background information in boxes. Because this information is in boxes, you can quickly skip over the information if you want to avoid the gory details. Here are the special icons and boxes used in this book that help you learn just what you need:

Skip this background fodder (technical twaddle) unless it truly interests you.

There's help when things go wrong!

These notes and tips show the easiest way to perform some task.

Easy-to-understand definitions for Internet terms let you "speak like a geek."

Someone Else Owns This Stuff

Look, you know that some of the things I'm going to mention in this book are owned by someone. That means they own the copyright. So copyrights for all products are owned by, er, the person who owns them. In other words, "commercial names of products from manufacturers or developers that appear in this book are registered or unregistered trademarks of those respective manufacturers or developers." You know, the usual legal stuff.

Acknowledgments

Many thanks to Gilles Vollant, who helped me figure out the crazy LaserMaster/Win32s problem. To the many faceless tech support people and company representatives who put up with me. To all the shareware, freeware, and public domain software developers on the Internet who've done such a fantastic job of creating new tools. To Faithe Wempen, who has cleaned up three of my books. To the various staff members at Alpha Books, who I've never seen but who manage to get books out at breathtaking speed. And to my wife and kids, who haven't had much of a summer.

Part I
Improving What You've Got

If you've read "The Complete Idiot's Guide to the Internet" (you really should, you know), you've learned most of the basics about working and goofing off on the Internet. However, there's more. I didn't have time or space to cover everything, after all. Now I'm going to explain more useful stuff, such as how to "talk" with other Internet users, play games, use neat-o UNIX tricks, and work with Jughead.

I'm going to take you a step further. I'll explain how to take on another role, that of information provider; I'll show you a few simple methods you can use to distribute information. I'll also show you how to improve your e-mail system by installing a Windows program. And I'll prepare you for the next step, the leap into the graphical user interface Internet. It's a whole other country.

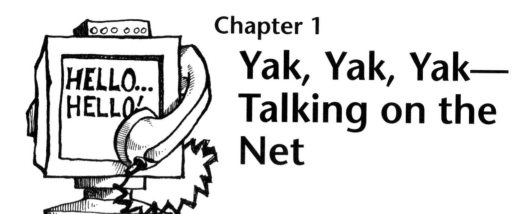

Chapter 1

Yak, Yak, Yak— Talking on the Net

In This Chapter

- ☛ Understanding the difference between **talk** and **chat**
- ☛ Using **talk** and **YTalk**
- ☛ Using **write** and **wall**
- ☛ Using the **IRC** chat systems

Do you have too many hours in your day? You do everything you need to do by lunch, and you're at loose ends for the rest of the day? Have you exhausted all the time-wasting techniques you learned in college? Are you looking for something new?

Welcome to *chatting* on the Internet: a step above newsgroups and e-mail. Sure, those are okay—you send a trivial message and get trivia in return. But what if you want instant dirt—instant feedback on your analysis of yesterday's *Melrose Place* or *90210*, for instance? You need to be able to actually talk to someone.

Well, okay, not actually *talk*, but *type* to someone. You type; they type back. You type again; they type back again. It's almost like having a phone conversation, only without the throat clearing, chuckles, and background noise. It's slower, too. Well, I suppose it's a poor imitation of conversation, really, but hey, it has its advantages:

☛ Your boss thinks you are typing a memo; you're actually discussing last night's blind date with your buddy.

☛ It's a lot cheaper to talk to Moscow over the Internet than by phone.

☛ You may be able to contact someone for whom you have an Internet address but no phone number.

☛ The office administrator tracks personal phone calls but wouldn't know what the Internet was if he fell into it.

☛ Large groups of people can put together a conference call online more easily and cheaply than with Ma Bell.

☛ With some systems, you can actually transmit a computer file during a conversation—try that on your cordless phone!

☛ If you're contacting someone in another country, it may be less excruciating to read broken English than listen to it.

What Kind of Talking Do You Want to Do?

The Internet has two basic forms of these *conversation* programs. One type allows two people to *talk* to each other. Even if you've never been on the Internet, you may have used programs that can do this; many networks have programs that let two network users swap *real-time* messages. The Internet has several of these simple programs, the simplest of which is **talk**. You may also run into **ntalk** and **YTalk**, a couple of variations on the theme.

The other form of conversation program is more like a conference call: groups of people chatting together in a giant "conference room." Well, maybe it's more like a party, really, with people in lots of rooms. People walk in and out of the rooms, spending a little time here, a lot of time there, depending on how much time they have to waste or how important the conversation is.

I'd Like a Word with You!

The simplest way to try these systems is with **talk**. At the UNIX shell or an appropriate menu option (some menu systems let you type commands at the menu), type **talk *username*** and press **Enter**. For instance, if I want to talk with jbloe and he's on my host, I simply type **talk jbloe**. If he's not on my host, I have to include his host name. For example, **talk jbloe@apotpeel.com**.

What's joe bloe going to see? He'll see a message like this:

```
Message from TalkDaemon@apotpeel.com at 12:15
            talk: connection requested by pkent@usa.net
            talk: respond with: talk pkent@usa.net
```

All he has to do is respond by typing the **talk** command and my address (as you can see, the message tells him what to type to make the connection). For instance, he would reply by typing **talk pkent@usa.net** and pressing **Enter**.

Like magic, Joe and I connect. Well, maybe not. There are a few pitfalls. Joe has to be logged on, of course, and he can't be running a program that turns off the *paging* that informs him of an incoming **talk** request. Some programs turn off these messages to make sure that they don't mess up the program's output.

Setting up a **talk** session is like dialing a telephone that doesn't ring; the phone's owner has to be waiting to pick up at just the moment you dial. So how are you ever going to make a **talk** connection? Well, you either arrange a time beforehand—if your spouse leaves the house at the same time each morning you could arrange to call your "friend" a few minutes after that each day. Or you could just hang out with people who spend most of their lives on the Internet. (There really are many of them; you just never meet them—they're too busy checking out alt.food.sugar-cereals newsgroup or in a chat session discussing the latest baseball scores.)

Also, if you are trying to set up a **talk** session between hosts, make sure the **talk** programs you are using are compatible—not all are. And you need to be calling a system that allows **talk** sessions. Not all do. There are two main types of **talk** programs, and they can't communicate with each other. (But **YTalk** can talk to either type of **talk**. Talk to your service provider to see what's available, and see the information about **YTalk** later in this chapter.)

But I *Am* Logged On!

Using **talk** to converse with someone else on your host should be easy. However, sometimes talking to someone on another host can be a problem. First, that person may be working on his workstation but you get a message saying he's not logged in. For instance, when I tried connecting to a friend in Dallas, working on a Sun system, that was the case; it wasn't until he opened a "console window" that we were able to connect. This won't happen if you are using a dial-in line, but if you have an Internet connection through a network at your company, school, or government department, you may have to ask your administrator how to make sure you are fully logged on to the Internet.

(Not-So-)Real Life Examples

Another problem is the address—you may find that the e-mail address won't work. If not, you may have to ask your service provider or system administrator which address to use. For instance, here's a sample address:

    fredflintstone@bedrock.com.

Now, this address may work fine for e-mail, but when you try to use **talk**, you may find it's no good. Again, you may get a message saying that fred is not logged on, even though he is. Try to find out if there's more to his address. If he's using a workstation connected to a network, you may find his address is actually

    fredflintstone@techws07.bedrock.com.

He doesn't need the techws07 for his e-mail, but for a **talk** connection, he does.

What if you can connect to fred, but he can't call you? Tell him to try the address in the page message: the message he sees when **talk** "rings" him. For instance, even though I sometimes use the pkent@usa.net e-mail address, when I use **talk**, it appears in the page message as pkent@cns.cscns.com. Anyone trying to connect to me using pkent@usa.net won't get far, but they can connect to me using pkent@cns.cscns.com.

Finally!

If everything goes right, you'll see something like this:

```
[Connection established]
Joe, that you?




_ _ _ _ _ _ _ _ _ _ _ _ _ _ _ _ _ _ _ _ _ _ _ _ _

Certainly is. What's happenin?
```

Now, anything you type appears in the top, anything the other person types is in the bottom. This is a pretty simple, basic connection. When you type a character, it appears on the other person's screen. That means the other person sees anything you type, including typos and rash insults that you decide at the last moment you really don't want to send. Transmission is instantaneous, so the other person sees you type the original text, and sees you delete and replace it.

You can clear the screen using **Ctrl-l** (well, you may be able to clear the screen; on the other hand, you may not. It doesn't always work). That's useful, because as it fills up, you'll find that you have trouble figuring out where you should be reading. You can end the session using **Ctrl-c**.

Stop It!   Tired of co-workers, bosses, network loonies, and ex-spouses trying to get you to join in a **talk** session all the time? Turn it off. Use the **mesg n** command to make sure that if anyone uses the **talk** command on you, you won't be *paged*. Instead, the other person will see a message saying that you are refusing **talk** sessions. When you log off or use the **mesg y** command, the function's turned back on.

Now, before we move on, let's remember the poor old telephone. It really does have its uses, you know. It's chic in certain circles to assume that all the functions of human life can be carried out in cyberspace—even if it is more difficult. People often use **talk** to communicate with a co-worker in an office upstairs, even though they can't type as fast or as smoothly as they can talk. A phone call would be easier, but hey, we've all used the phone for years. It seems to have lost its novelty.

On the other hand, **talk** is a perfect example of the way in which computers can help people with physical disabilities. Instead of buying one of those pricey phones with an LED display and a keyboard, the hard of hearing can set up an Internet account and talk with their relatives all over the world, at rates that beat the phone companies hands down.

Why Talk with talk When You Can Talk with YTalk?

Another system you may have available is **YTalk**. The big difference between **talk** and **YTalk** is that while **talk** allows only two people to communicate, **YTalk** lets several people connect—rather like setting up a conference telephone call. Another great advantage is that while there are a couple of versions of **talk** *daemons*—which cannot talk to each other—**YTalk** can work with either one. So if you have one version of **talk** and your buddy has another, you can use **YTalk** to communicate with him. If you both have **YTalk**, though, there are a few extra features that you can use.

Daemon   A UNIX "process" waiting in the background. That is, a program that is running invisibly, just waiting for something to happen—like a **talk** invitation to arrive from another host. There are two different types of daemons that run **talk** sessions. Oh, and that's pronounced "DEE-mon," not "DAY-mon." This isn't a gothic movie, you know.

YTalk When You Want to Talk

To get **YTalk** up and running, simply type **ytalk** *username username username*. That's right, you can call several users at the same time. For example:

```
ytalk joebloe@apotpeel.com fred@banana.org
suep@colander.com
```

YTalk calls each one, and, as each responds, provides an area on your screen for that person. A dotted line divides each part with that person's username in the middle of the line. Here's what a session looks like if you have two people connected:

```
— — — — — — —= YTalk version 3.0 (2) =— — — — — — —
Sorry to bother you, I was just goofing around with ytalk.
I'd
noticed your name earlier in the listing, so . . .
What do you do? how does one make a living on here?



— — — — — — — — — —= mars@cns =— — — — — — — — —
yes?
is ok
I live on here I think
smile
laugh..I own a karaoke company...days are full of free time
```

talk and YTalk sessions can get confusing enough as it is, what with trying to type quickly and keep up with what the other person is saying. However, trying to keep up with *several* must be quite confusing. Still, there's a limit to how many people can connect; you need three lines of screen space for each one. If you all take turns, you should be able to figure it out.

Now, this may get confusing, but remember that YTalk can communicate with talk. Actually, YTalk can connect to several talk sessions at the same time, but talk can only connect to another talk or one YTalk. So if you're using YTalk and talking to, say, four talks, all they can see is one YTalk, while you see four talks. Each talk would be unaware of the other talks talking to YTalk. Got it?

It's Got a Menu, Too!

YTalk even has a menu. Press the Esc key to display it, then press one of these to carry out an action:

a Adds another user to the session.

d Removes a user from the session.

o   Sets **YTalk** options. You can turn scrolling on and off, so instead of text being displayed at the top when you've filled up the text area, the bottom line scrolls off the bottom (this is really handy, as it make it easier to read). You can turn word wrap on and off; turn on auto-import (which means that if you are connected to A and caller B connects to A, B is also automatically connected to you); turn on auto-invite (meaning that if any user tries to start a session while you are connected already, they will automatically be added to the session without you having to confirm). You can also turn on re-ring, a feature that automatically calls a user every 30 seconds if he doesn't respond. Whew!

u   Displays a user list, which shows who's connected and what type of software they are using.

w   Lets you copy all the text from one of the people in the session into a text file. Sneaky. Kinda like recording a phone conversation, only there are no laws covering it!

q   Quit—ends the session. **Ctrl-c** does the same.

When you're tired of typing, use **Ctrl-c** to end your session, or use the **q** option on the menu.

Okay, I'm Sold! How Do I Get It?

To use **YTalk** (or **talk**, for that matter), it must be loaded on your service provider's UNIX computer. **YTalk**'s actually pretty new, still in development, so your system may not have it. If not, get your service provider to load it. It's superior to **talk** in a number of ways. By the way, **YTalk** works with the UNIX X-11 interface, a UNIX windowing system. If you are using this, take a look at the **YTalk** documentation for more information. (Remember, you can always get documentation on a UNIX program by typing **man** *commandname*.)

Shaddup and Listen! Using Write

There's a neat, one-way communication program called **write**. At the UNIX prompt, simply type **write** *username* and press **Enter**. Then type your message, pressing **Enter** at the end of each line. When you finish the message, press **Ctrl-d** or **Ctrl-c**.

This sends the message to the other person, but you are not really "connected" to the other system in the way **talk** and **YTalk** are. However, if you want to, you can carry on a conversation using this program—each person sends a **write** message in turn. It just requires some discipline. Agree on an "I've finished blabbing now" indicator; the **write** manual pages suggest that you use **-o-** to mean "over." Then you each take turns, writing a few lines and then typing **-o-**, waiting for the other person to write a few lines and finish them with **-o-**, and so on. You can use **-oo-** to mean "over and out"—that's it, the conversation's over.

You can use **write** to send messages to people on other computers across the Internet, in the same way that you used **talk**—for example, **write** *username@hostname*. Unfortunately, you may also run into some of the same problems connecting. And there's another problem. Some workstation users may log on multiple times, or are using several windows in X-windows. **write** doesn't know where to send the message. If so, you'll see a message telling you that he's logged on to more than one place; you should see a list of *tty* (terminal) numbers. You can then append a tty number to the end of the username, as in **write** *username tty#* or **write** *username@hostname tty#*.

Wall—How to Win Friends and Influence People

Here's a neat little UNIX program that will really get you friends. If you want to send a message to everyone connected to your host computer, type **wall** and press **Enter**; then type the message, ending each line with **Enter**. When you're done, press **Ctrl-d** or **Ctrl-c**. The message will be broadcast to everyone logged in. Then sit back and wait for the friendly replies.

When You're Tired of Talking, Try Chatting

YTalk is a talk-type program rather than a chat-type program. However, on a sliding scale, it's somewhere between a simple talk-type program and the chat-type programs. *Chatting*, in Internet parlance, is when you join a group of people in a sort of real-time discussion group. *Talking* was, originally, when *two* people connect and communicate. *YTalking* is somewhere between the two; several people can talk at the same time, but the set-up is really more talk-like than chat-like. **YTalk** is the Internet equivalent of a conference call.

Chat sessions are almost like parties or meetings, when groups of people get together and talk amongst themselves in small groups. If you spend a couple of hours in a chat session, you might spend 20 minutes in one group, 10 in another, 15 talking privately with someone, and so on.

The best-known chat system on the Internet is *IRC—Internet Relay Chat*. It connects dozens of countries and tens of thousands of users. When you log on and pick a channel, you may be talking to users in Istanbul, Adelaide, or London. If you are lucky, you may even both speak the same language.

You can get started by just typing **irc** and pressing **Enter**, or by selecting from a menu if your service provider has added it to the menu system. If you want to use a "nickname" during the session, type **irc *nickname*** and press **Enter**. And away you go. (You can change the nickname *during* a session by typing **/nick *newnickname*.**)

There are IRC *servers*, systems that run the IRC sessions. Unless you specify which one you want to use, you'll be connected to the one specified by your service provider. You can specify a different one, though, by including the server name in the command line, thus: **irc *nickname* server**. There are servers all over the world. You can see a list of the ones connected to the server you are in by typing **/links** and pressing **Enter**.

Once on, you'll probably want to start by seeing a list of all the *channels* that are open, the chat groups. Type **/list** and press **Enter**. Be prepared for a *huge* list, hundreds of different channels. Like this, only much longer:

```
/list
*** #warez6    1
*** #erotica   3        The adult channel for adults
*** #wildness  1
*** #atlantico 1
*** #JOKES     1
*** #realsex   5
*** #SumSum    1        Dun Nei Dun Dou Ngor Sum Tong
*** #growth    2
*** #virus     3
*** #chileno   2
*** #chilimon  1
*** #america   3        girls beauty channel
*** #mas       1        MAS IS WAITING..........
*** #hongkong  1        Welcome to Hong Kong
*** #jaguar    3
*** #antiad&d  1
*** #london    2
*** #Techno    2
*** #Slovenija 1
*** #Beatles   1
*** #Chomsky   1        Noam Chomsky for President!!!
*** #Anarchism 2
*** #Socialism 1        Capitalism sucks.
*** #Wales     2
*** #Klingon   2
*** #veggies   1        Vegetarians of the world - you're
                        great!
*** #BEST      1
*** #Danmark   3        killer mutant bots from outer space
*** #pseudo    1
*** #oulu      9
*** #bored     3        Coolly Radiriferous
*** #Lubnan    1
*** #DOtest    2
*** #WE        1
*** #pusan     2
*** #gayDC     2
*** #kermit    2
*** #BiggerRed 1
*** #Janee     2        Lonely girl that missed her chance for
                        Mr. Right
*** #Bosnia    3
```

If you are looking for evidence that computer networks are a corrupting influence, that they attract people who just want to goof off in the most offensive way possible, that they are a huge drag on the economy as thousands of highly paid programmers and engineers waste time online, what better place to look than IRC? You'll find an immense amount of garbage in IRC. That's not to say you won't find intellectual stimulation and spend a worthwhile hour or two communicating with colleagues about your profession—but you're more likely to talk about aliens, sex, star wars, or stud poker.

Anyway, where was I? Ah, yes, look at the list, and you'll find three pieces of information: the channel name (#Janee, for instance), the number of people in the group, and, perhaps, the channel topic. As you can see, the topic of the #Janee channel is "Lonely girl that missed her chance for Mr. Right." I wonder which major corporation or government department is paying for *this* online time?

Anyway, this list is way too big to make it useful. How about limiting the size a little? Type **/help list** to see the list command options. You can, for instance, list only channels with more than a certain number of people involved—which is handy, because most channels seem pretty moribund. For example, type **/list -min 10** and press **Enter** to see a list of channels with 10 or more members. (For some reason, the more members a group has, the more likely that it has a topic name.) You can also specify a maximum number of members (**/list -max** *number*), only private channels (**/list -private**), only public channels (**/list -public**), only channels with a topic (**/list -topic**), and sort channels by the number of users in each (**/list -users**). Of course, you can mix and match these: **/list -min 10 -topic -users** lists only channels with 10 or more members and with a topic name, and sorts them by the number of users in each.

Let's Get Moving—Joining a Channel

So you've found a channel you want to join. Simply type **/join** *channelname*. For example, to join the channel named #hongkong, type **/join #hongkong**. Then just sit back and watch what goes on—though each time someone joins a channel everyone sees a message giving that person's nickname.

The screen's broken into two parts. The bottom line is where you type. After typing a comment, press **Enter**—nobody sees what you have typed until you press **Enter** (unlike **talk** and **YTalk**, in which every character you type is transmitted). To type a command—we'll look at a few more in a moment—start the line with a forward slash (/).

Above the entry line is a status line, and above the status line is the rest of the screen, where the session appears. Stuff like this:

```
<Kimba> y=e**ipi
<poem> Peppr wwould never ignore You
<zooey> *sigh*
<sierra> imm: just finished dinner.. chilling our for 0.5
hours
<Bob34> howya doin Sarge?
<Peppr> Right Herb...I wouldnt'
<zooey> *sigh*
* Albundy proposes to ZOOEY. Hehehhe
<immigrant> zooey- im in the middle of franney and zooey
right now :)
*** Sulu (~C617331@128.206.2.2) has joined channel #30plus
<Kimba> Peppr's ignoring folk
<Kimba> Peppr's ignofing flok
<mfp> Kimba is back.....yahoo
<mfp> Sulululululululululululul
<Albundy> Sulu!!!!!!!!!!! my love.
<Prism> bye, all.
*** me3 (dagec@abc.abcde.wfull.edu) has joined channel
#30plus
<zooey> immigrant  aren't you that yallie i was talking to
<me3> hi all
<poem> zooey is 29
<Kimba> SULU!!!!
<Peppr> ARGH!!!!
*** mickk has left channel #30plus
<Kimba> mfp!!!!!!!!!!!!!!!!!!!
<Salgak> hmm.... zooey is definitiely 29 and sighs a lot
<Sulu> Albundy!!
<Sarge> Bob: Still having terminal probs... Sent a msg to
help!
```

Well, okay, maybe your channel's more intellectual. Anyway, notice that it gets a little confusing as to who's talking to who (or why, for that matter). People often type a name followed by a colon to indicate that their comments are directed at that person. For instance, the user named Sarge on the last line is talking to Bob. Bob was talking to Sarge about 23 lines earlier.

Do It Yourself—Creating Your Own Channel

If you can't find a channel that quite suits you, create your own. Simply type **/join** *channelname*. Make sure you start the channel name with a **#** sign. Once you are in, you can change the topic name: **/topic** *topic name*.

Who's Who

If you want to know who's on a channel, type **/who** *channelname*. You'll see a list of nicknames, plus each person's real username and hostname. If, while you are watching the conversation, you want to find out about a specific person, use the **/whois** command—**/whois** *nickname*. You'll see the person's username and hostname, the IRC server they are connect to, and how long they've been idle—how long it's been since they sent a message (a lot of IRC users are idle even when they're talking, if you know what I mean!). For instance;

```
/whois peterk
/whois: *** peterk is pkent@cns.cscns.com (Peter Kent)
*** on irc via server irc.colorado.edu (Univ of Colorado
Server (2.8.*))
```

By the way, masquerading by using someone else's nickname is not unknown in IRC, so if you are about to say something sensitive to someone—like propose, or insult them—make sure you use the **/whois** command first. There's also a command called **/whowas**—you can get information about the last person logged on using a particular nickname, even if the person's logged off.

If you want to say something *really* sensitive, use the **/msg** command. This sends a message to a particular user, and nobody else can read it. For instance: **/msg** *nickname message text*. You can also use the **/query** *nickname* command to start a private conversation. All messages sent after this command are private messages, just as if each one was preceded by the /**msg** *nickname* command. When you've finished, just type /**query** and press **Enter**.

Looking for Someone in Particular?

If you are a real IRC junkie, you'll eventually make IRC friends. When you get onto the system, you may want to find a particular person. The /**names** command will display a list of all the channels and all the nicknames of the people in each channel. Of course, this will be a huge list, but you can use your communication program's "save to file" feature and quickly search for the person you want. You can also use the /**lusers** command to get an overview of what's going on:

```
/lusers
*** There are 2301 users and 1725 invisible on 116 servers
*** There are 87 operators online
*** 1 : unknown connection(s)
*** 1276 channels have been formed
*** This server has 454 clients and 4 servers connected
```

Had Enough Yet?

It's hard to imagine, but you'll eventually get tired of this stuff. To get out of the current channel, use the /**part** * or /**leave** * command. Or simply use the /**join** command to join a different group; unless you've used the /**set novice off** command, you can only be in one channel at a time. If you are the last one out of the channel, you'll automatically turn out the lights—the channel will expire. Die. Cease to be. Wither away.

To log out of IRC altogether use the /**quit** or /**bye** or /**exit** or /**signoff** commands. Enough choice for you?

There's Much, Much More

The second version of the IRC program, IRCII, has almost 100 commands. There's no way I'm going to explain them all here, but I'll quickly mention a few useful ones. (Okay, a few of the simple ones, then; some of these get pretty complicated.) If you want more information, use the /**help** command to see a list of commands. While still in the help system, type a command name to get more information. And remember, all commands are preceded by the forward slash.

! Repeats a command from the history list.

admin Displays administrative information about the current IRC server, including e-mail addresses of the people running it. If you include a host name after the command, you'll get information for that specific server.

assign Lets you assign several words to one short word, so when you type that word the entire string is sent. For instance, you can use this command to expand **$intro** to **High, my name is Rumpelstiltskin, what's yours?**

away Lets you mark yourself as away, and provides a message that anyone using the **whois** or **msg** commands will see.

clear Clears text from the screen.

encrypt A way to hold encrypted conversations with a person or channel.

history Displays a list of all the commands you've used, each assigned a number. You can then use the **!** *number* command to repeat an earlier command (such as joining a particular channel).

ignore Lets you ignore various types of messages (all of them, public ones, wallops, notes, and so on) from a particular person.

info Gives you all sorts of information about the people guilty of creating the IRC system.

invite Invites a particular person to join a channel.

join Lets you join a channel. If you type /**join -invite** you'll join the channel to which you were just invited. You can only join one channel at a time unless you use the /**set novice off** command.

kick Channel operators can get rid of people with this command.

kill IRC operators can get people all the way out of the IRC system with this!

lastlog   Redisplays the last few messages on your screen.

leave   Lets you get out of a channel.

me   Sends a "description" of what you are doing: /**me cries in despair!**, for instance. The other users will see ***pkent cries in despair!**

note   This is a tricky one. It lets you, among other things, spy on IRC users to see when they log on and off the system. Great for bosses.

notify   You can use this in a similar way, to tell IRC who you want to keep track of!

set   Lets you set up about three or four gazillion different operating parameters. For example, use the /**set novice off** command so you can join several channels at once. What joy!

time   This one's handy. If you are stuck on the system and lose track of time and space, the /**time** command shows you the first part of the equation, at least.

topic   Lets you change the channel topic, though in some cases, only channel operators can do so.

version   Shows you the version of IRC software being used and the IRC server you are connected to.

wallops   Sends a message to all channel operators at once. This has been disabled on many servers.

If You Really Like This Stuff...

Some people do, you know. If you happen to be one of them and you want to spend half your life in IRC, you should probably find out about the UNIX *.ircrc file*: a file that lets you automatically configure your IRC setup exactly the way you want it each time you get into the system. For more information, type **man irc** at the UNIX shell prompt (not inside IRC itself).

A quick way to create an .ircrc file is to enter IRC, set up everything the way you want it (use the /**set** command), and then use the /**save** command.

The Least You Need to Know

☞ The **talk** command provides two-way typed communications across the world.

☞ **YTalk** is like talk, only better.

☞ **write** lets you quickly send a message to another computer.

☞ **Wall** broadcasts your message to other terminals on your host. Use with care.

☞ Chat systems let huge numbers of people get together and waste time.

☞ IRC (Internet Relay Chat) is the most popular chat system.

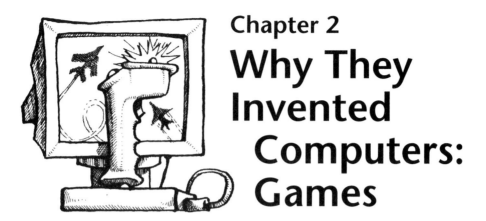

Chapter 2
Why They Invented Computers: Games

In This Chapter

Let's Play in the MUD!

You may have seen the term MUD flung around here and there; it means Multiple User Dimensions (or Multiple User Dungeons, or Multiple User Dialogue, take your pick). It's a type of game in which lots of people get together in a *virtual* environment and play a game.

Well, it's not really so virtual. These are text-based games, so you have to add the real "color" to the environment in your own mind.

Still, MUDs use up many thousands of user and network hours; there's a whole MUD subculture, with different types of MUDs and devotees. Weird stuff like: Tiny and Teeny MUDs (these are *social* in orientation—players chat, meet friends, make jokes, discuss stuff), and LP MUDs, including Diku and AberMUD (role-playing adventure games—players run around killing monsters, solving puzzles, becoming wizards). There are chat MUDs or talkers (perhaps a subset of the Tiny and Teeny MUDS; there's a lot of chatting going on). And there are many others, such as MOOs, UnterMUDs, TinyMUCKs, cools, TinyMUSEs, tiny muck spin-off chat MUDs, oxmuds, and who knows what else.

If Adam Wozniak has tired of maintaining Doran's Mudlist by the time you try to subscribe, use anonymous FTP (File Transfer Protocol) to get to **caisr2.caisr.cwru.edu**. Then change to the **/pub/mud** directory. You should find a file called **mudlist.txt**. Copy this back to your system, and you'll find enough MUD sites to keep you busy well into the next century.

In general, though, each player controls a character, a "computerized persona/avatar/incarnation." This character wanders around, talking with the other players (er, characters), looking for stuff, fighting monsters, solving puzzles, and that kinda thing.

Okay, Where Do We Start?

Let's start off by finding out where these MUDs are. First, try subscribing to Doran's Mudlist. Send e-mail to **awozniak@joule.calpoly.edu**. Put **SUBSCRIBE** in the subject line, nothing in the message itself. This should get you on a subscription list for the latest and greatest MUD list, literally hundreds of different games.

Usually you telnet to a MUD site, or play a MUD game set up by your service provider. But here's a convenient way to find gobs of MUDs. Gopher to **gopher.micro.umn.edu**, then select **Fun & Games**, **Games**, and **MUDs**. You can select from almost 200 MUDs, ranging from ACME Mud to Zork. You might also try a gopher site in Germany, at **solaris.rz.tu-clausthal.de**. Select **Student-Gopher**, **Mud-Servers**. (Most MUDs around the world are played in English. There are a few here in German.) And if you can't get through to these sites, try doing a Veronica search for MUD.

Let's Take a Look

Getting started with MUDs is not something you do in five minutes. You need some serious study time. (After all, you're going to be spending much of your life here, what's an hour or two to learn how to get around?) Use the **help** command to find out a little about the game. You probably need to turn on your communication program's **save to file** feature, go through each command, and then logoff and read the instructions for a while. Unfortunately, most of the MUD instructions assume you know the basics already, so it takes some time to get it all straight.

Real-Life Examples

Let's see a quick example of a game in action. I'm going to gopher to the University of Minnesota site (**gopher.micro.umn.edu**), then select **Fun & Games, Games, MUDs, Links to MUDs via Telnet**, and then **All the MUDs**. A list of 175 MUDs appears. I'm going to try one called **Crossed Swords**. (I had to try a few, because I couldn't connect to the first three or four.) Here's what I see when I get into it (remember, the bold text is what I type):

```
You are in Krasna Square. The two main roads of Praxis
intersect here, where all of Crossed Swords' people gather
in joy and sorrow. The road running north and south is
called Centre Path, while Boc La Road is the name of the
road running east and west. You see a portal here, leading
to the Pregnancy Office. A magnificent watchtower rises
above the square.

There are five obvious exits: portal, east, west, south, and
north.

You notice the following items:
A wooden sign.

The following people are present:
Newbie Arttest the boy
> say hello
You say: hello
> say Arttest, are you there?
You say: Arttest, are you there?
```

I never could get young Arttest to respond to me. He's a *newbie*—a novice. So he probably has even less of an idea than I do.

```
read sign
Welcome new adventurers to our reality! You are in the central
square of the adventuring village of Praxis.  New adventurers
often begin their adventurers beyond the northeast edge of
town.On the way there, it is recommended you stop by the Praxis
library, 3 times east, 1 north, and east again from here. All
adventurers are encouraged to join a class before engaging in
combat.  Use the newbie line to find out information about the
class and other information important to new adventurers.  But,
before doing anything else, use the commands <faq> and <help>.
```

I guess I'd better head out northeast, then. I'll try the instructions to get to the Praxis library—east three times, then north, then east again. I type **e** to go east, **s** to go south, and so on.

```
> e
Boc La Road on the east side of the town is a simple dirt road
leading towards Krasna Square at the centre of Praxis west and
out into the western outskirts west.  The village monastery is
on the north side of the road.

There are three obvious exits: east, west, and north.
```

I travel around like this for awhile. Eventually, I run into Shadowwolf.

```
The following people are present:
Shadowwolf's ghost
> kill shadowwolf
```

Well, I couldn't think of what else to do. I was getting tired of just walking.

```
You attack Shadowwolf's ghost.
You tap Shadowwolf's ghost innocently in the right arm with
your right foot.
hp: 80    sp: 84    mp: 56
```

```
Shadowwolf's ghost taps you innocently in the left foot with
his right foot.
You tap Shadowwolf's ghost innocently in the torso with your
left foot.
Shadowwolf's ghost hits you ineffectively in the torso.
You tap Shadowwolf's ghost innocently in the left leg with your
left hand.
hp: 81    sp: 84    mp: 58
Shadowwolf's ghost taps you innocently in the head with his
left leg.
You headbutt Shadowwolf's ghost furiously.
hp: 80    sp: 84    mp: 58
Shadowwolf's ghost taps you innocently in the torso with his
right arm.
You tickle Shadowwolf's ghost lightly in the left leg with your
left foot.
The ghost says: It's only a flesh wound!!

Shadowwolf's ghost staggers and falls to the ground... dead.
```

That wasn't much of a fight, was it? I'm going to use the **look** command to see where I am again. I could go on (I did, in fact, but my editor cut it out). If you want more, you'll have to join a MUD.

Be Careful Out There!

MUDs can be dangerous. As Kristina Harris—a MUD "Goddess"—wrote in *Newsweek*, MUDs "have been known to drain the lifeblood of hapless players who stumble across them." People get so engrossed in them that they spend many, many hours building their character—only to watch it get killed off by other players. "Users may team up their characters with others in the game, talk to them, attack them—even kill them…. Violent actions may develop into electronic feuds where several users band to-gether to 'kill' a player who has wronged them." People get so wrapped up that some have even threatened lawsuits against players who have killed their characters. It's a good thing guns, knives, and fists don't work in cyberspace, or the risk would be even greater!

Yak, Yak ... Wait, Wrong Chapter!

Okay, we covered chat systems in Chapter 1; now we're going to do a little more chatting—with *talkers*, or *chats*. These systems let people talk to each other within a role-playing game. They are regarded as a form of MUD. Here's a pretty good description from the SomeWhere Else game, which you can get to by telnetting to **atalanta.pcs.cnu.edu 2010**.

```
————— Guidelines for using this talker  —————

This is not a game in the sense that there is a goal, or
winners and losers.You are here to talk to other people and
enjoy yourself.  However so are other people, so if you
start annoying people don't be surprised to find that you
are not wanted here.

Bad language is out.  There is no real line to separate the
acceptable from the unacceptable, and some of the Super
Users are more strict than others, so don't be surprised and
don't bother complaining if you get kicked out for such
words as "damn," just don't use them.

Try to avoid shouting unless necessary, or using CAPITALS
ALL THE TIME.

Multiple characters are frowned upon, if you have more than
one, don't be surprised if you lose them all, and are barred
from the program.  On that note, please make sure you set a
valid e-mail.  They are checked from time to time.  If
information needs to be sent to all users, for example a
change of site, we cannot contact you if your e-mail is not
set.

Above all, please remember that you, and others, are here to
have FUN!
```

Exercise for the Eager and Adventurous

Well, let's jump in and try. Everything you type begins with a command. In other words, the program assumes that when you type, you are typing a command; unlike in IRC, for instance, where you precede commands with / and everything else is message text.

In SomeWhere Else, you have to use a command to send message text. For instance, you can use the **say** command. Like this:

```
say hello
You say 'hello'
->LoveChild smiles at Spang's dejected expression. Nothing
worse than a licked bowl.
Lisa exclaims 'Hi Pete!'
Levi exclaims 'Hello, Pete!'
say I'm new, I guess I'd Prissy hey pete
beFey says 'Hello Pete'
tter Applique says 'hey pete'
just observe for a while.
```

As you can see, the text gets jumbled up a little. In the above example, my typing is in bold, but it's interspersed with incoming text.

I don't have the patience for games like this, so let's listen in for a while. Here's the background: you are "in the grassy courtyard of a great castle. The gatehouse to the north leads into the world outside. The castle keep lies to the south and towers loom from either side. The sun beats down unendingly on the freshly cut lawn. You could explore the castle and its grounds or merely sit down and stay for a chat..."

```
SGT asks 'gumby  hiding over at norms again???'
Prissy WHAT!
Gumby says 'no sgt'
Opium walks to the gatehouse.
Spang shouts 'Someone talk to me'
Phantom lick Spang
Prissy IM HERE
Fey asks 'Hello Spang how are you?'
Opium fills the room with a fragrant smoke that tingles your
nose
```

```
Spang says 'don't lick me again'
Fey says 'It tingles more than the nose Opium Dear...'
Phantom hits Prissy upside the head and says,"DUH!"
Applique says 'well, yeah, but'
LoveChild yanks his nose off, like a muppet.
Fey is referring to Opiums entermsg, nothing else...
Gumby begs for some of that odiferous pleasure from opium
LoveChild sets Opium aflame and inhales deeply.
SGT says 'bri who you with in lts'
Spang whispers something to Prissy
```

If you get on one of these talker thingies and can't figure out how to use it (well, you're not telepathic are you?), try typing **.help**, **/help**, or **help**.

Did you get that? More importantly, did you enjoy it? Obviously some people do; then again, some people enjoy eating cow tongue. It's Monty Pythonish, in a way, but Python was a bit more understandable.

All sorts of commands are available, from the **check** commands, which give you information about your character, to the **room** commands, which let you create and modify a room in the landscape. Use the **/help** command to find more information.

Chess a Minute, Old Chap!

If you'd like to try a little chess, there are a few telnet sites to choose from. These run the Internet Chess Server software that lets you play against people (or computers) all over the world. Try telnetting to these sites:

ics.uoknor.edu 5000 (129.15.10.21 5000)

news.panix.com 5000 (198.7.0.1)

Euro-Server: anemone.daimi.aau.dk 5000 (130.225.18.58 5000)

Aussie-Server: lux.latrobe.edu.au 5000 (131.172.4.3 5000)

(To get a full list of the latest chess servers, use the UNIX **finger** command on these addresses: **chess@chess.uoknor.edu** [US], **tange@daimi.aau.dk** [Europe], **wallez@lune.enst-bretagne.fr** [Europe].)

When you arrive, you may want to use the **open** command. This takes you off the list of people looking for a game. That way you don't have to bother answering people who invite you to play (you can get back into the list of players later by repeating the command).

Now let's see who's in the chess server. Use the **who** command to see a list of players and observers. For more detail, use the **who v** command to see something like this:

```
aics% who v
+— — — — — — — — — — — — — — — — — — — — — — — —+
¦    User      Standard    Blitz   Wild        On for Idle ¦
+— — — — — — — — — — — — — — — — — — — — — — — —+
¦ 14  eronald   1454 [4]    1319    2458            9       ¦
¦ 10  oleg      2350        2299    — — ( 0)        9       ¦
¦  X  franky    — — ( 0)    2295    — — ( 0)       21       ¦
¦  2  gnusurf   1981        2182    1896           23       ¦
¦  2  ragar     2591 ( 1)   2122    1980 ( 5)      22       ¦
¦ 17  Airey     1929 ( 3)   2095    1397 ( 1)       0       ¦
```

This shows each person's information. In the left column is the number of the game they're involved in—if there's no number, they're not in a game. However, if there's an X in this column, the person isn't looking for a game. There's all sorts of other chess-type information, little of which I understand, and none of which makes any sense unless you know a lot about chess. By the way, there are all sorts of different **who** commands, letting you specify exactly what you are looking for. Use the **help who1**. (Who won? No idea!)

If you'd like to watch a game, use the **observe** command. Either use **observe** *gamenumber* or **observe** *playername*. You won't see anything right away; the next time one of the players makes a move, you'll see something like the following figure.

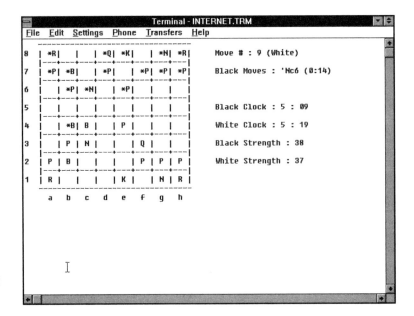

Here's an observation report from a game in progress.

If your idea of fun is watching chess, you can speed things up like this. Use the **history** *playername* command to see a list of the last few games played by the named player. Then type **examine** *number* to see a particular game. You'll see the chess board. Just press **Enter** to see each move in the game.

If you know a little about chess, you can figure this out. R is a *rook*, Q a *queen*, K a *king*, P a *pawn*, and B is the *bishop*. N is a *knight*, because the K's already taken. The letters with the asterisks are the black pieces.

Of course, chess can be rather slow. However, each time someone makes a move, the board updates, and you see a new display. This is ideal for people working for the government or large corporations, 'cos they don't have to pay for online time!

If you'd like to play a game, you can accept someone else's invitation. Simply use the **open** command again to make sure you are available for games, and it won't be long before someone invites you. You can then use the **accept** command. Or you can use the **match** *playername* command to invite someone else. (You can quickly see who's open for a game using the **who o** command.)

Moves on the board are simple; just type the piece and position, thus:

e5   A pawn move or capture to e5

f8=n   Move a pawn to f8 and promote to a knight

d3-e4   A move or capture from d3 to e4

Nh2   Move a knight to h2

and so on.

There are also a variety of commands used to communicate with other players. You can send messages to everyone on the system (**shout**), to a particular player (**tell**), to your opponent (**say**), or to everyone observing the game (**kibitz**).

Read the help files for more information. You'll probably want to use your communication program's capability to save the session in a text file, run all the help files, then logoff and spend an hour or so reading. Check out the help intro files in particular. You'll learn all about registered and unregistered players, rated, unrated, blitz, standard, wild games, and so on.

Go! ...Where?

Telnet to **hellspark.wharton.upenn.edu 6969**, of course, to play the ancient Japanese game of Go. You can log in as a guest to just observe. Then type **observe *number*** and type **Enter**. The *number* is the game number. This server may have lots of games running at a time; when I checked in there were 28 in play. You can see a list of the games by typing **games** and pressing **Enter**. You will see game numbers, player names and ranks, the number of moves into each game, the board size, the handicap, Komi, and byo-yomi. (Don't ask. Did I say I knew anything about Go?)

Anyway, when you take a look at a game, you'll see something like this:

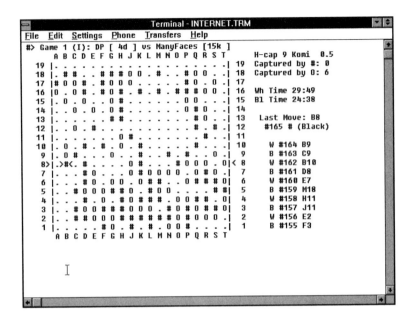

A Go game going on.

That's right, an actual Go board, with 0 against #.

If you want to play, you can use the **who** command. You'll see a list of everyone on the system, and the ones looking for a game are indicated with an !:

All you have to do is type **match** *playername* and press **Enter** to invite a player to a game.

Ah, but we're getting ahead of ourselves. Maybe you should figure out how to play first. Use the **Help** command to see a list of commands, and then the **help** *command* to figure out how to use each one.

Laughter's the Best Medicine

How about a little comedy to brighten your day? It's not exactly a game, but it is good for you. There are dozens of sources of comedy on the net, from newsgroups to gopher sites. You can find enormous joke archives all over the place. Of course, plenty of the humor is offensive, but humor doesn't work if *someone* isn't the butt of the joke.

Try gophering to **wiretap.spies.com**, and then choose **Wiretap Online Library**, **Humor**, **Jokes**. Right now, you'll find four categories, Nerd Humor, Jokes, Everything Else, and Code. You need to be a nerd to understand some of the nerd humor, though I did like this:

```
Unix is a Program Gone Bad
Unix was a program gone bad.  Born into poverty, its par-
ents, the phone company, couldn't afford more than a roll of
teletype paper a year, so Unix never had decent documenta-
tion and its source files had to go without any comments
whatsoever.  Year after year, Papa Bell would humiliate
itself asking for rate increases so that it could feed its
child.  Still, Unix had to go to school with only two and
three letter command names because the phone company just
couldn't afford any better.  At school, the other operating
systems with real command names, and even command comple-
tion, would taunt poor little Unix for not having any job or
terminal management facilities or for having to use its file
system for interprocess communication and locking.
```

There's much, much more to this true story.

The other areas have all sorts of things from Elephant Jokes, to Lawyer Jokes, to an Enormous List of Blonde Jokes:

Plus, of course, Clinton jokes—wouldn't be complete without that, eh?

```
Q: What is the difference between Dan Quayle, Bill Clinton
and Jane Fonda?
A: Jane Fonda went to Vietnam.
```

(There's more to this joke, but I'm not allowed to print it.)

You might also want to try a little British humour (editor, leave that u in there, will you?). You'll find plenty in the **alt.comedy.british newsgroup**. Or by anonymous FTP at **nic.funet.edu** (**/pub/culture/tv+film/series/ MontyPython**) or **ocf.berkeley.edu** (**/pub/Library/Monty_Python**). And if you like to play your own jokes on people, check out the **alt.shenanigans** newsgroup and try anonymous FTP to **elf.tn.cornell.edu** (**/shenanigans**).

A Little Bit of This and a Little Bit of That

You'll find all sorts of stuff all over the place on the Internet. My service provider has set up a special menu with a few local games. Things like **Tell a Fortune**, which actually turns out to be various types of fairly amusing quotes and quips (such as "Do infants have as much fun in infancy as adults have in adultery?"). Then there's **Trivia**, from which you can select one of 13 categories. The program gives you a word, and you have to respond. Here's the game, The Victim-Killer category:

```
      Bobby Kennedy
      sirhan sirhan
      Right!
      J. Caesar
      brutus
      Right!
      Christ
      Pontius Pilate
      Right!
      Pompeii
      Vesuvius
      Right!
      Abel
      cain
      Right!
      Cleopatra
      cleopatra
      What?
      self
      What?
 (I pressed Enter here)
      the asp
```

The last one's a trick question, I believe. There's also a text adventure, a game of solitaire, a robot game (which locks up my system), and more. Look around and you'll find many ways to spend hours—nay, weeks— idling away on the information superhighway. Most service providers and Gopher menu systems have a Games option somewhere. (Is this *really* what Al Gore had in mind?)

The Internet Hunt—an Exercise for the Advanced

I left this one till last because it's a serious game, one that can actually develop your Internet skills. This is a research game run by Rick Gates of the University of California Library. Late each month, he posts 12 questions at various sites around the world. (Other people then copy these questions, so you may find your service provider has them available from a menu option.) You can definitely answer eleven of the questions on the net. The twelfth one may not be solvable; Rick hasn't checked to see if the information is available anywhere.

Unlike most Internet games, though, there are actually prizes for doing well in this one: free books, magazine subscriptions, electronic journal subscriptions, and so on. There are some similarities, though. It may take many hours to play, and your boss won't like you playing on company time.

Now, in case you think this stuff is easy, check out a couple of questions from a recent hunt. You can see them in my WinGopher TextViewer window in the next illustration. (Just thought I'd give you a taste of things to come later in the book.) By the way, you can also play old Internet Hunts; you can find the questions going back to September of 1992. (You'll notice that the questions were much easier in the old days!)

If you can't find the questions locally, try gophering to **gopher.cic.net** (get to directory **1/Hunt**) or **gopher.cni.org** (get to **1/ Coalition FTP Archives/ public/net-guides/i-hunt**). Or try FTPing to **ftp.cic.net** and getting to the **pub/ internet-hunt** directory.

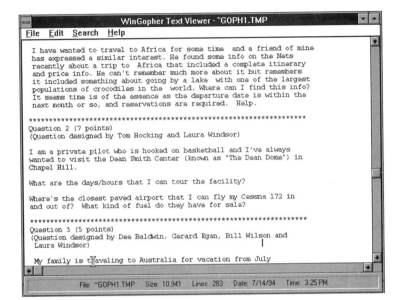

```
WinGopher Text Viewer - ~GOPH1.TMP
File   Edit   Search   Help

I have wanted to travel to Africa for some time  and a friend of mine
has expressed a similar interest. He found some info on the Nets
recently about a trip to  Africa that included a complete itinerary
and price info. He can't remember much more about it but remembers
it included something about going by a lake  with one of the largest
populations of crocodiles in the  world. Where can I find this info?
It seems time is of the essence as the departure date is within the
next month or so, and reservations are required.  Help.

****************************************************************
Question 2 (7 points)
(Question designed by Tom Hocking and Laura Windsor)

I am a private pilot who is hooked on basketball and I've always
wanted to visit the Dean Smith Center (known as "The Dean Dome") in
Chapel Hill.

What are the days/hours that I can tour the facility?

Where's the closest paved airport that I can fly my Cessna 172 in
and out of?  What kind of fuel do they have for sale?

****************************************************************
Question 3 (5 points)
(Question designed by Dee Baldwin, Gerard Egan, Bill Wilson and
 Laura Windsor)

My family is traveling to Australia for vacation from July

File: ~GOPH1.TMP    Size: 10,941    Lines: 283    Date: 7/14/94    Time: 3:25 PM
```

The WinGopher TextViewer, with two questions from a recent Internet Hunt.

The Least You Need to Know

- ☞ MUDs are addictive, if you can figure out how to use them.

- ☞ There are several Chess and Go servers around. It'll take time to figure out how to use them.

- ☞ Comedy abounds on the Internet—though a lot of it is very offensive.

- ☞ Most service providers have a Games option on a menu somewhere.

- ☞ Check out the Internet Hunt for a mind-expanding game that's actually educational.

Chapter 3
The Joy of UNIX

In This Chapter

- ☛ Finding information about Internet connections
- ☛ Working with (and killing) UNIX jobs and processes
- ☛ Closing recalcitrant UNIX programs
- ☛ Using the UNIX history list
- ☛ Using nifty little UNIX utilities

If you've been working on the Internet for a little while now, if the Joy of UNIX is a new experience, you are probably thinking: "Wow, this UNIX stuff is great, I wish I knew more about it!"

And so you shall. In this chapter, we're going to take a look at a few more UNIXy things, like ping, dig, and the history list. All pretty simple, and all a lot of fun. (Nerd fun, but it's still a kind of fun.)

Let's Play Sub! Ping, Ping, Ping

We're going to start with the **ping** command, which is *very* simple. Like the submarine sending out its sonar pings, you can use the UNIX ping to find out "what's out there." Or rather, to find out if what you think is out there is really there, and how far it is (in network terms).

Let's say you have a hostname, but you can't seem to get through to the host; you've tried telnet, FTP, gopher, or whatever, and you just can't get through. Maybe you should try to ping it.

Perhaps, you have an address like this: wuarchive.wustl.edu. At the UNIX shell, simply type **ping wuarchive.wustl.edu** and press **Enter**. In a moment or two, you'll see this:

```
wuarchive.wustl.edu is alive
```

What happened? Well, your **ping** command sent a small message to the named host. The named host then responds with a message of its own. What if you get a different response, though? Look at this ping:

```
CNS> ping warchive.wustl.edu
ping: unknown host warchive.wustl.edu
```

This means that the host isn't responding. Maybe the host itself is down, or the connections to the host, or maybe it's simply not a host. In this case, I mistyped the hostname.

Now, if you'd like to get really geeky, you can use the -s parameter. For instance:

```
CNS> ping -s wuarchive.wustl.edu
PING wuarchive.wustl.edu: 56 data bytes
64 bytes from wuarchive.wustl.edu (128.252.135.4):
icmp_seq=0. time=1378. ms
64 bytes from wuarchive.wustl.edu (128.252.135.4):
icmp_seq=1. time=1439. ms
64 bytes from wuarchive.wustl.edu (128.252.135.4):
icmp_seq=2. time=1707. ms
64 bytes from wuarchive.wustl.edu (128.252.135.4):
icmp_seq=3. time=1492. ms
^C (this is where I pressed Ctrl-c to end the process)
——wuarchive.wustl.edu PING Statistics——
5 packets transmitted, 4 packets received, 20% packet loss
round-trip (ms)  min/avg/max = 1378/1504/1707
```

This sends a request each second, then shows you the performance, and how long it took to get a response. The last couple of lines show you if any packets were lost, and the "round-trip" times, the quickest, slowest, and average time it took for the complete round trip. If the pings are taking longer than usual to get to a host, there's some kind of problem—maybe the network's simply overworked. If the ping program stops displaying a response line, it means that the host isn't sending a response.

If you are trying to impress someone, use this format: **ping -s *hostname packetsize count***. The packetsize is the number of bytes sent in each message (try 64), and the count is the number of messages. For instance, **ping -s wuarchive.wustl.edu 64 5** will send a 64-byte package five times, then stop.

Dig: Ping Gopher?

That's right, *dig*—domain information gopher. Another little utility for checking on hosts, kind of like a ping gopher, I suppose. If your system has dig (it may not have it), you can type **dig *hostname***. Like this:

```
CNS> dig hellspark.wharton.upenn.edu

; <<>> DiG 2.0 <<>> hellspark.wharton.upenn.edu
;; ->>HEADER<<- opcode: QUERY , status: NOERROR, id: 6
;; flags: qr aa rd ra ; Ques: 1, Ans: 1, Auth: 0, Addit: 0
;; QUESTIONS:
;;    hellspark.wharton.upenn.edu, type = A, class = IN

;; ANSWERS:
hellspark.wharton.upenn.edu.  86400      A     165.123.8.103

;; Sent 1 pkts, answer found in time: 127 msec
;; FROM: cns to SERVER: default — 0.0.0.0
;; WHEN: Fri Jul 15 08:46:09 1994
;; MSG SIZE  sent: 45  rcvd: 61
```

This command calls your system's default domain nameserver (a host that keeps a list of other hosts) and asks it about the named host. If you want, you can even name a different domain nameserver (**dig @*nameserver hostname***) to check on that nameserver's records. It asks the nameserver about the host, and the nameserver sends a message back. This shows you that the host exists, and it shows its IP number. The rest of the information won't be of much use to most users, though you can still use the command to impress colleagues with your knowledge.

Look! Up!

There's another handy command for looking around on the Internet, though many systems don't have it. It's the **nslookup** command. You can use it to ask a server for information about the hosts connected to it. You can find IP (Internet Protocol) addresses and the names of the hosts in a particular Internet domain. This is an *interactive* command; you start the program using the nslookup command, then you can type in various other commands to get more information.

You can quickly find out if you have this available. Just type **nslookup** and press **Enter**. If you don't have it, you'll get a message telling you so. If you do, you'll see a > prompt, waiting for you to enter information. You can then type **exit** and press **Enter**, then use the **man nslookup** command to find information on how to use this program.

Who's There? Finger *Everyone*

Want to know who's logged onto your host system right now? You may want to, in case you are looking for someone to talk to with the **talk** or **YTalk** program, or if you are trying to track down your service provider's technical-support staff.

Simply use the **finger** command. You can use this command to find out about a particular person (**finger jobloe@apotpeel.com**, for instance). You can also use it without a username to see who's logged onto your system. For example:

```
CNS> finger
Login     TTY      Idle  Login Time
bones     ttyrf          Jul 15 12:09
burger    ttyq1          Jul 15 11:19
cathy     ttyr2       9  Jul 15 08:30
cathy     ttys0       1  Jul 15 09:18
daisy     ttyr7      34  Jul 15 11:30
ezekiel   ttyqe          Jul 15 12:06
jim       ttyp2          Jul 15 09:32
```

This shows you the usernames of the people logged in, the terminal ID, and how long they've been idle. Daisy hasn't done anything on-line for 34 minutes, even though she's still logged on. You can also see what time these people logged onto the system (and the date—you can get a good idea of who's a real Internet junkie from this). Depending on how the host system is set up, you may get more information: a real name for each username, and perhaps notes that indicate more contact information for each person.

Now you can use this info to contact someone. For instance, **talk bones** will invite bones to a conversation with you using the talk program (see Chapter 1 for more information about talk).

By the way, you can also use the **who** command to get a similar display; you won't usually get as much information, though.

Amnesia Strikes   If you use the **whoami** command, you'll see your username. But hey, you must remember at least *that*. Try **who am i**, though, to see your username, terminal number, and login date and time. Just for fun, you can also use **who is you** to do the same.

Processes: Something's Going On...

Let's talk for a moment about processes. A *process* is a program that is doing something for you. When you log into the system, the shell that starts is a process. If you start another shell, that's a process, too (and, as we'll discuss later, the first shell remains running as a process). When you start a program, such as a text editor, that is a process. In fact, starting some programs actually start more than one process. Lots of things you do in UNIX are run as processes.

Fine. You don't normally need to worry about these processes. However, you may want to remember this stuff in two cases. First, you may want to do something while another thing is doing something. So, wouldn't it be nice if you could leave that process—say, a text editor you are working in—and jump back to the shell prompt and run another process (such as looking at what's in your directory). Well, in some cases, you can do this. You use the **Ctrl-z** command.

Ctrl-z didn't work for you? Some shells won't let you use it, and some programs won't let you use it even if the shell will. Still, read on, because we're getting to the part where we kill something, which may come in handy.

For instance, let's say I'm working in the vi text editor, modifying my .signature file (the file that is sent automatically with my e-mail). I want to take a look at what's in my directory, because I want to modify my .plan file—the one people see when they "finger" me—and I want to make sure I'm making the same change to both.

So I press **Ctrl-z**, and presto, I'm back at the shell prompt. I'll see something like this:

```
[1] + Stopped                 vi .signature
CNS>
```

The first line tells me that I have one stopped job—vi, in which the text file .signature is open. Well, now I can go into .plan, simply by typing

```
CNS> vi .plan
```

The second vi opens, this time with .plan inside it. Oh, I'm forgetful today. Now I realize I need to go and look inside my home directory for something. So, here we go again, **Ctrl-z**. This time, I see this:

```
[2] + Stopped                 vi .plan
```

It's telling me that I have two stopped jobs, and that the one I just stopped is vi, with .plan open inside it. Let's take a quick look at the jobs using—what else—the **jobs** command:

```
CNS> jobs
[2] + Stopped                 vi .plan
[1] - Stopped                 vi .signature
```

The + sign, by the way, means that's the most recently stopped job. There's another way to see what's going on in the "background." You can use the **ps** command (ps for process). Here's what I see when I use it:

```
CNS> ps
PID TT STAT   TIME COMMAND
 1895 p2 T    0:00 vi .signature
```

```
2038 p2 T      0:00 vi .plan
3480 p2 R      0:00 ps
27288 p2 S     0:00 -ksh (ksh)
```

Now I can see four processes—the two "jobs" that I started, plus two more: ps, the ps command itself, and -ksh, the UNIX shell I'm using (korn shell). You can "merge" this stuff by typing **jobs -l**. You'll see the usual jobs stuff and on the left, the process IDs.

Getting Back to Where You Once Belonged

Okay, how do you get back to where you started from? You can use the **fg** command (foreground). Take a look at the jobs list and notice that each job has a number. Just type **fg %*number*** and press **Enter**. For instance, **fg %1** would, in our example, restore vi and the .signature file.

If you would rather use the PID (process ID), you can do that, too. Type **fg *PID*** to start the process substituting a number for *PID*—for instance, **fg 2038** starts vi with the .plan file. Simple.

Process? Job? A *job* is a program you start. A *process* is something going on in the background that you didn't necessarily start. A job may require more than one process. And each shell you run is a process, too.

Killing Whatever Lives

Now and again you are going to run into a problem—somehow you have something running. You don't know what or how, but when you try to logout, the system tells you that you have something running in the background. Some systems will let you go, and close the background processes for you. For example, the first time you press **Ctrl-d** or type **exit**, you see a message saying that you have stopped jobs. If you press **Ctrl-d** or type **exit** again, the system closes the jobs and logs you out. However, other systems won't let you out until you do something about it.

What do you do? Well, you can try the **kill** command. Say you see a message telling you that you have stopped jobs. You can use the **jobs** command to find out what, then use the **kill %*number*** command to kill the job. Sometimes that won't work, though. If you use **kill -9 %*number*,** it should really do the job. That's right; you use an actual 9. Don't ask me why, but it does work. If you want to kill job 3, type **kill -9 %3** and press **Enter**. It's dead. (However, don't use kill -9 unless you are sure what the job is because you may cause serious system problems.)

What if you have some kind of process going on in the background, though, something that doesn't appear in the jobs list? Use the **ps** command. You can then use the **kill** command with the process ID, thus: **kill *number*,** or even **kill -9 *number*.**

Line editors Line editors are like text editors, only you work with just one line of the text at a time. Real people don't use line editors very much anymore, because they're such a pain in the neck. It's sort of like taking panoramic photographs when you suffer from tunnel vision.

How Do I Get Out of Here?

The nice thing about a well-designed graphical user interface is that it provides clues as to how to run a program. You have menus, or buttons, or whatever. A command-line system, such as a basic UNIX shell, provides no clues. You'd better know what you are doing, or else. It's possible to get into UNIX programs and not be sure how to get out. Take a look at **ed**: a basic (very basic) line editor.

```
CNS> ed
```

See that blank line below where I typed **ed**? Think of it as the ed "window" or the ed "document." A blank line. Nice, eh? So, how do you get out of ed? You could try **quit**. Won't do much good. **Ctrl-c** won't help, either. So, if you get into such a situation with this or any other program, what should you do?

Ctrl-c was a good guess. So was **quit**, though in a text or line editor, it's unlikely that a simple word will do it. You can also try these:

q   A quit command.

bye   A logout command.

Ctrl-d   The basic logout command.

Ctrl-   The *quit character*. This stops the process and saves it in a file called the *core*. You can then delete the core.

Ctrl-z   The *stop character*. This should put the program into the background, so you can then use the **kill** command on it.

With ed, **q** will end it. So will **Ctrl-d**. You may find that **Ctrl-z** will work on it, though it may not depending on which shell you are using. And **Ctrl-** won't work on ed.

Each program's different, though. What works on one may not work on another. And what works on one with one shell, may not work on the same program in another shell.

Now What Did You Say ...Yesterday?

Here's a neat one. Some shells have a **history** command. You can use this command to see the last 16 commands you typed. Even if you typed some of those commands yesterday. And if you want to *really* go back, try typing **history 1**. You'll go all the way back to command 1 in the history list, which may be several hundred commands ago, perhaps even several days ago.

You can use this to backtrack and look at what you did to mess your system up, or to recall how you did what you did when you did it a while ago. Or just use it to look back a few lines so you can quickly copy a complicated command you just used. Unfortunately, not all shells have this command. Try it and see.

A Bit of This and a Bit of That

UNIX is full of great, little commands that nobody seems to know about—well, apart from UNIX propeller heads, that is. Some of them are actually useful, in a nerdy sort of way. Just in case you might find these useful, check out the following.

Tail: The End

Have you ever needed to read something way at the bottom of a huge text file? If you use the **cat** command, you have to wait while the entire file shoots by. If you use **more**, you have to hold down the **Spacebar** until you finally get to the end. You can always open it in a text editor, then use the text editor's cursor movement commands to get to the bottom, of course. But here's another way. The **tail** command. Just type **tail** *filename* to see the last few lines of the text file.

As always in UNIX, there's more. Type **tail -*number*l** *filename* to start a certain number of lines from the end. For example, **tail -100l mudlist.txt** displays the last 100 lines of the file called mudlist.txt. You can measure from the beginning of the file, too. **tail +100l mudlist.txt** displays the entire file starting from the 100th line.

Quick, Add This!

Ever sat in front of a thousand-dollar computer and wished you had a five-dollar calculator? System designers have realized that computers should be able to do the simple stuff, so operating systems, such as Windows, come with a built-in calculator. And so does UNIX. Okay, it's not quite as snazzy, but it works. Sort of. Like this:

```
CNS> bc
1+2
3
3/2
1
```

You type the calculation on one line, then press **Enter** to see the result. Oops, the last one doesn't look right: **bc** is obviously rounding the answers. We'll try again. Press **Ctrl-d** (or type **quit**) to close the calculator, then use the -l parameter (which tells it not to round off the results):

```
CNS> bc -l
3/2
1.50000000000000000000
134/5
26.80000000000000000000
(134/5)*(1*15)
```

```
402.00000000000000000000
quit
CNS>
```

That's better. Actually, **bc** will do much, much more. Much, much more than I actually understand about mathematics. So if you want to figure it all out, use the **man bc** command to see the instructions. While you are at it, you might check out **dc**, as well, the Reverse Polish calculator.

When Was That?

Hey, check this out:

```
CNS> cal
     July 1994
  S  M Tu  W Th  F  S
                 1  2
  3  4  5  6  7  8  9
 10 11 12 13 14 15 16
 17 18 19 20 21 22 23
 24 25 26 27 28 29 30
 31
```

Bet you didn't know UNIX could do that, eh? Quicker than Windows, too. Not as pretty, of course, or as "full featured," but a calendar nonetheless. If you want a full year, type **cal** *year* (**cal 32** to get the calendar for the year 32, **cal 1932** for the year 1932). Include the month for a particular month: **cal** *month year*. It's quick, it's elegant, it's UNIX.

While you're at it, what about asking UNIX to remind you of stuff, like your boss's birthday, and such? If your system has the calendar program, you can create a file, called **calendar** in your home directory. Each line contains a date and a note. Then, every midnight, the calendar program automatically looks in the file and sends you e-mail reminding you of the event. Neat, huh? Use **man calendar** to get more information about date formats.

The Least You Need to Know

☞ The **ping** command checks a network connection for you.

☞ The **dig** and **nslookup** commands provide detailed information about connections.

☞ The **finger** and **who** commands show you who's logged onto your host.

☞ You can stop some jobs using **Ctrl-z**. You can return with **fg %***jobnumber*.

☞ The **jobs** command shows a list of jobs you started; **ps** shows a list of processes.

☞ The **kill** command can get rid of jobs and processes you don't want. If kill doesn't work, try **kill -9 %***jobnumber*.

☞ Some UNIX programs are hard to get out of. Try **Ctrl-c, quit, q, bye, Ctrl-d, Ctrl-\, and Ctrl-z.**

☞ The **history** command shows you commands you've used over the last week if you want!

☞ Check out the **tail** (view a text file starting at a particular point), **bc** (a calculator), and **cal** (a calendar) commands.

Chapter 4
New Kid on the Block—Jughead

In This Chapter

- ☛ Where to find Jughead
- ☛ How Jughead differs from Veronica
- ☛ Using Jughead

There's a new kid on the block, and his name is Jughead. You've met Archie already—he searches cyberspace for computer files. You've also met Veronica—she searches gopherspace for whatever you require. Now there's Jughead; he's a buddy of Veronica and searches gopherspace, too, though in a slightly different way.

Jughead searches a particular gopher site, rather than the entire gopherspace. This "narrows" the gopher search so you don't get hundreds of "hits" when looking for something particular.

If you think this is starting to sound like a cartoon, you're right. (Of course, if you're not American, or grew up without a television, you may not realize who Archie, Veronica, and Jughead are. They're all characters from the *Archie* cartoon.)

Still, in the interest of "seriousness," the creators of the last two of these products have turned them into acronyms. Veronica means *Very Easy Rodent-Oriented Net-wide Index to Computerized Archives*. Jughead means *Jonzy's Universal Gopher Hierarchy Excavation And Display*. As for Archie, it's said that he wasn't originally named after a cartoon character, but his name was derived from the word *archive*. Take the *v* out of *archive* and what have you got? *Archie*. And Archie searches file archives, right?

At the time of writing, Jughead is about a year old, so you may not have run into him yet. Rhett Jones, who maintains the University of Utah gopher server, developed Jughead. Mr. Jones' nickname, by the way, is Jonzy (which explains the J in Jughead).

What's New with Jughead?

You already have Veronica, so why would you want Jughead? Well, the two programs are a little different. Veronica searches the wide world of gopherspace—about 10 million items on 5,500 gopher servers. You select which Veronica server to use, but that just determines which index you use, not which gophers are being searched. In theory, there's little difference between servers. Each server is supposed to be searching the same gopher sites (in practice, there are a few differences because the indexes are updated at different times.

Jughead, on the other hand, searches a *particular* gopher server. You are not searching the entire world, just the server that Jughead is running on. Using a different server gives you a different result. If you want to use Jughead to search a gopher server other than the one you are currently on, you can often select another server from a menu.

Veronica Versus Jughead: Battle of the Searches

Both systems now allow Boolean searches (see later in this chapter for more information about that), but Veronica actually has a slightly more capable search "engine" than Jughead.

Although for a while Jughead could manage more complicated searches, Veronica was updated in June of 1994. She leapfrogged over Jughead, and now can do more than he can. Both systems can now use the * wild card and the **and, not,** and **or** Boolean operators. Veronica, though, can also use the **(** and **)** operators in searches.

TECHNO NERD TEACHES...

For more information about Veronica, look for instructions on using Veronica somewhere in your gopher server menus. You'll find that the information about wild cards and Boolean searches that you read in this chapter also applies to Veronica.

Another difference is that you can search Veronica in two ways. You can search for all menu items, so you will get both "directories" (menus leading to other menus) and all the documents within menus. Or you can limit the search to just the directories. With Jughead, though, you don't have these options; you will always see both directories and documents.

Jughead is still in development, so things may change. These Internet programs often take time to evolve, because they are being developed by "volunteers." Perhaps Jughead will leapfrog past Veronica sometime soon.

Which should you use? If you've no idea where what you want is, you may want to start with Veronica. However, if you are looking for something on a particular gopher server—for example, you are looking for information about a particular university's services, or a particular region's hiking trails, you should use Jughead to search the appropriate gopher site.

Meeting Jughead

So where are you going to meet Jughead? The first place to try is, as usual, on your host system. Your service provider or system administrator may have installed Jughead. At the time of writing, though, most haven't.

That leaves you a couple of options. The first is to ask your service provider to install Jughead. That may take some time, though. The second is to go searching for a gopher that already has Jughead installed. Here are a few Jughead servers to get you started.

Hostname	Location
acs6.acs.ucalgary.ca	University of Calgary
gopher.cc.utah.edu	University of Utah
gopher.ic.ac.uk	Imperial College
gopher.unam.mx	Universidad Nacional Autonoma de Mexico
xx.acs.appstate.edu	Appalachian State University

You'll need to gopher to the site before you can use Jughead. For example, to use Jughead at the Appalachian State University, I would go to my UNIX shell, type **gopher xx.acs.appstate.edu** and press **Enter**. Once you get to a gopher server, you may have to dig around a little to find Jughead. Look for a menu option that talks of "searching gopherspace" or something similar.

Using Jughead: An Easy Exercise for the Anxious

If you gopher to **gopher.cc.utah.edu** (the University of Utah, Jughead's "home base") you'll find Jughead close to the surface. Right on the top menu you'll see **12. Search menu titles using jughead/**. Select this option, and you'll see another menu:

```
Internet Gopher Information Client v1.11


           Search menu titles using jughead


 -> 1.  Search University of Utah menus using jughead <?>
    2.  About jughead.
    3.  All Known jughead Servers.
    4.  Search other institutions using jughead/
```

If you select item 3, you'll see a list of the current Jughead servers, and item 2 is a document with an introduction to Jughead. To search, select either 1 or 4. As I mentioned earlier, Jughead searches a particular server.

So the first option searches the menus at the University of Utah. But option 4 lets you select another gopher server to search. Note that this is not the same as when you select a Veronica site.

If you use Veronica, you have to pick a Veronica server. However, when you do so, you are simply selecting which Veronica to use. Regardless of which one you select, they all search pretty much the same place. When you select a server prior to doing a Jughead search, you are selecting *where* you will search.

Okay, let's do a quick Jughead search. I want to find some electronic publications. I'm going to search for **books**. So, I select item **1** (I'm just going to search the University of Utah's gopher menus), and type **book**.

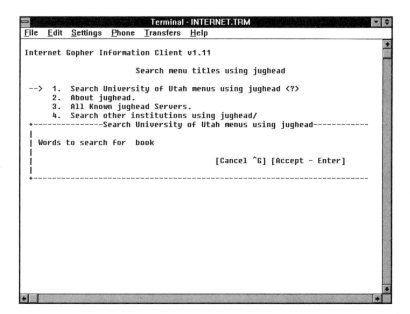

```
                          Terminal - INTERNET.TRM
 File   Edit   Settings   Phone   Transfers   Help

 Internet Gopher Information Client v1.11

                      Search menu titles using jughead

 -->  1.  Search University of Utah menus using jughead <?>
      2.  About jughead.
      3.  All Known jughead Servers.
      4.  Search other institutions using jughead/
 +---------------Search University of Utah menus using jughead-----------
 |
 | Words to search For   book
 |
 |                                   [Cancel ^G] [Accept - Enter]
 |
 +----------------------------------------------------------------------
```

Here's an Internet Gopher client search for "book."

TECHNO NERD TEACHES...

Case doesn't matter. You can enter the search statement in upper- or lowercase, Jughead doesn't care. It regards **BOOK** as the same as **book**.

When I press **Enter**, here's what I see:

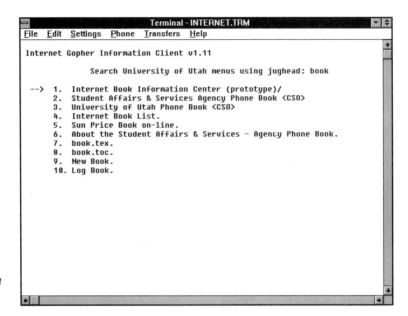

```
┌────────────────────────────────────────────────────────────────┐
│ ▬                   Terminal - INTERNET.TRM                ▼│▲│
│ File  Edit  Settings  Phone  Transfers  Help                   ▲│
│                                                                  │
│ Internet Gopher Information Client v1.11                         │
│                                                                  │
│              Search University of Utah menus using jughead: book │
│                                                                  │
│   --> 1.  Internet Book Information Center (prototype)/          │
│       2.  Student Affairs & Services Agency Phone Book <CSO>     │
│       3.  University of Utah Phone Book <CSO>                    │
│       4.  Internet Book List.                                    │
│       5.  Sun Price Book on-line.                                │
│       6.  About the Student Affairs & Services - Agency Phone Book. │
│       7.  book.tex.                                              │
│       8.  book.toc.                                              │
│       9.  New Book.                                              │
│      10.  Log Book.                                             │
│                                                                  │
│                                                                  │
│                                                                  │
│                                                                  │
│                                                                  │
│                                                                  │
│                                                                  │
│ ◄│                                                          │▼│
└────────────────────────────────────────────────────────────────┘
```

The continuing search for "book."

This doesn't really give me much, and nothing I'm particularly interested in. So, I return to the previous menu (by pressing **u**), and try again. This time, I enter **book or publication**. This is a *Boolean* search: a search in which I can enter more than one thing to search for. The term **book or pub*** actually means "search for the word book or any words beginning with pub."

The **or** is one of the Boolean *operators*. I can use the operators **and, or,** and **not**.

a and b   Searches for a menu item containing the word a *and* the word b.

a or b   Searches for a menu item containing the word a *or* the word b.

a not b   Searches for a menu item containing the word a, but doesn't include it if it also has the word b.

Anyway, when I search for **book or publication**, I get a few more menu options—3 more, actually. How about this, though: **book or publication or publications**. If I search for this, the count goes up to 23.

Wild Cards: Wild Fun

Back in that last example, I could have also used a *wild card* to search. That means I could use a character to take the place of another character. For instance, if I search for **pub***, I am telling Jughead to search for any word beginning with **pub**. The asterisk simply means "some other stuff here."

Jughead only has one wild card right now: the asterisk. You can't use the question mark (?), a common wild card in many other systems. Also, remember these basic rules: you can't *start* a word with the asterisk, and you can't put an asterisk in the middle of a word. All characters after the asterisk are ignored.

I can search for **book or pub*** instead of typing out **book or publication or publications**. However, there are other words starting with pub, so if I searched this way, I would get menu items including the words *public*, *pubs*, *publishers*, and *publishing*. Searching like this would increase my "hit rate" to 128 menu items. Do I want all this extra stuff? Well, the publishers and publishing may be useful, but the public and pubs give me lots of extra stuff I really don't want, like **43. HB0115 Restrictions on Public Nudity**.

More of That Boolean Stuff

Let's take a quick look at the Boolean stuff again. If you enter several words on a line, without one of the Boolean operators between the words (the *and*, *or*, or *not*), Jughead assumes you mean *and*. So, for example, both **book and pub*** and **book pub*** mean exactly the same thing: "find entries that contain both the word book and a word beginning with pub."

You should be aware of a few other things, though. If Jughead sees any special characters (!"#$%&'()+,-./:;<=>?@[\]^_'{|}~) in the search statement, it treats them as if they were spaces, replacing them with the Boolean operator **and**. For instance, if you are searching for **This.file**, Jughead searches for **this and file**. That's not necessarily a problem, though. If I search for **Pubs_by SCERP_Researchers**, I will still find the correct menu item, because Jughead will still search for the words *Pubs*, *by*, *SCERP*, and *Researchers*.

Also, because you are using the words **and**, **or**, and **not** as Boolean operators, you can't actually search for these words. But then again, you'll probably never need to, unless you were doing some really pointless research project on the history and development of the word "and" in modern linguistics. (If you *are*, in fact, a linguistic scholar currently writing your dissertation on this topic, please refrain from sending me nasty letters!)

Special Jughead Commands

Jughead currently has four special commands you can include in a search string:

?all *searchtext*   Tells Jughead to include *all* of the hits it finds. Normally, Jughead limits the hits to 1,024, so if it finds 2,000 matching entries, you won't see 976 of them. Mind you, 1,024 is a lot, more than you are likely to need. For instance, if you search for **?all book or pub***, Jughead will search for the words *book* and *pub**, and, if it finds more than 1,024 matches, it will display them all.

?help [*searchtext*]   Tells Jughead to create a menu option that lets you get to the Jughead help file. You can use the **?help** command by itself, if you want, or do a search at the same time by adding a search word at the end. For instance, **?help book or pub***.

?limit=*n searchtext*   Tells Jughead to limit the number of menu items it gives you. The *n* stands for a limit number, and the *searchtext* stands for your topic. For instance, **?limit=10 book or pub*** will cause Jughead to display only the first 10 items it finds.

?version [*searchtext*]   Gives you the Jughead version number. You'll see this menu option: **1. This version of jughead is 0.9.7.** (or whatever the actual version number is). You can then use the menu option to read the Jughead help file. You can use the **?version** command by itself or do a search at the same time, for example, **?version book or pub***.

You can't combine these commands. You can only use one for each search.

Well, that's pretty much all there is to know about Jughead right now, though maybe it'll develop over the next year or so. In the next version of this book, I'll probably be saying "Jughead is much more capable than Veronica—but take a look at Reggie (the fancy, new Rodent-Style Easy-Going Groper and Internet Excavator).

The Least You Need to Know

☞ Jughead searches a particular gopher server. Veronica searches the entire gopherspace.

☞ Jughead searches for *all* matches, both directories and documents. With Veronica you can choose.

☞ Use the **and, or**, and **not** operators to create specific searches.

☞ Use the * wild card at the end of a truncated word to search for words beginning with those characters.

☞ Use the **?all** *searchtext* command to make sure you see all matches. Jughead has a 1,024 item limit by default.

You say, how much more blank could a page be? and the answer is, none. None more blank.

Chapter 5
Getting the Word Out

In This Chapter

- Distributing information with the **finger** command
- Setting up automatic e-mail responses
- Setting up a simple mailing list
- Setting up sophisticated mailing lists
- Creating your own newsgroup

If you've been goofing around on the Internet for a while, something may have occurred to you: "Hey, I could use this to put *my* information online!" Perhaps your life's work is the study of psychological stress in prairie dogs (all the construction in the Denver area has many prairie dogs suffering from post-traumatic stress syndrome). Maybe you've made a career out of exposing the nefarious deeds of the CIA, or it could be that you want to create an online community dedicated to researching the effects of "The Simpsons" on teenage self-esteem (the cartoon characters, not O.J.'s family).

Well, there are a few simple ways to get into information distribution on the Internet. I'm not going to discuss setting up your own host; that's "beyond the scope of this book." (*Way* beyond, actually!) However, I will show you how to use a few simple techniques to get your story out.

Hand Me That Data, Would You?

If you read *The Complete Idiot's Guide to the Internet,* you probably remember **finger**, a UNIX command that you can use to grab information about a user (Chapter 13). You type **finger** *username@hostname*, press **Enter**, and the program runs off and tries to find out a few basics about the person who uses that Internet address. For example:

```
CNS> finger pkent@usa.net
[usa.net]
Login: pkent              (Peter Kent)
On since Mon Jul 18 14:49 on ttyra

No Plan.
```

As you can see, the **finger** command shows me the person's real name, and when he logged in. You may see other information, too. You may see a note telling you when that person last read his mail.

Well, very nice, but we don't really care about all this right now. What we care about is the Plan. Notice the line, **No Plan**. That means the user hasn't created a **.plan** file. If he had, and if he'd set the *permissions* for that file correctly, you'd see the contents of the .plan file. The **.plan** file is a text file containing… well, whatever details you want people to see when they "finger" you.

Real-Life Example

Details? Like what? Well, all sorts of things. Useful things, of course, like the following figure.

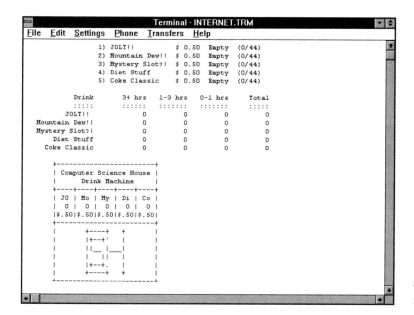

Here's a genuine pop machine online.

Luckily, I now know that there's no point going over to the Rochester Institute of Technology to grab a Jolt, because the machine's run out. I also like this finger posting:

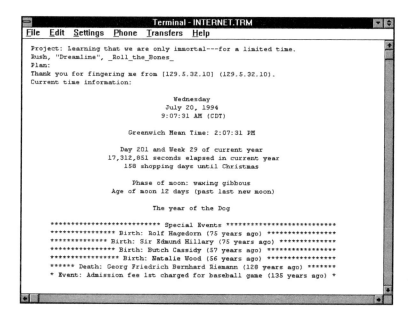

For the clock-watcher in you, get the correct time from this finger posting.

What else might one find with the **finger** command? Weather reports, earthquake reports, lists of Internet resources—anything you think people may want.

An Exercise for the Eager

Try some of these finger addresses. Simply type **finger** followed by the address in the table:

Alabama/Auburn forecast	obs@awis.auburn.edu
	weather@awis.auburn.edu
	aubdaily@awis.auburn.edu
	radar@awis.auburn.edu
Auroral Activity (you know, the world's aura, the aurora)	aurora@xi.uleth.ca
Colorado weather forecast	weather@unidata.ucar.edu
Computer Science FTP Sites	msc@eembox.ncku.edu.tw
Earthquakes, Alaska	quake@fm.gi.alaska.edu
Earthquakes, Central US	quake@slueas.slu.edu
Earthquakes, Nevada	quake@seismo.unr.edu
Earthquakes, North America	quake@gldfs.cr.usgs.gov
Earthquakes, Northern California	quake@andreas.wr.usgs.gov
Earthquakes, Southern California	quake@scec.gps.caltech.edu
Earthquakes, Utah	quake@eqinfo.seis.utah.edu
Earthquakes, Washington and Oregon	quake@geophys.washington.edu
Earthquakes, world-wide	quake@gldfs.cr.usgs.gov
Florida, N.W. beaches, weather forecast	beach@awis.auburn.edu
Indiana weather forecast	weather@indiana.edu

Newsgroup periodic postings, list of	nichol@stavanger.spg.slb.com
Michigan, (S.E.) weather forcast	weather@madlab.sprl.umich.edu
NFL info	nfl@spam.wicat.com nflines@spam.wicat.com
NASA news	nasanews@space.mit.edu
Ohio weather forecast	weather@ysu.edu
Pepsi machine	pepsi@columbia.edu
Soda machine	drink@csh.rit.edu
Solar activity	solar@xi.uleth.ca daily@xi.uleth.ca
Today in History	copi@oddjob.uchicago.edu
Typhoons & hurricanes	forecast@typhoon.atmos.colostate.edu
Washington weather forecast	weather@halcyon.com
Wisconsin precipitation map	precipitation@wisc.edu
Wisconsin radar map	radar@wisc.edu
Wisconsin temperatures map	temperature@wisc.edu
Wisconsin weather forecast	"forecast state@wisc.edu" weather@csd4.csd.uwm.edu
Wisconsin weather summary	summary@wisc.edu climate@wisc.edu cities@wisc.edu
Wisconsin wind map	"weather wind"@wisc.edu

Some of these finger postings are especially useful. For instance, have you been trying to find a list of all the theaters in the world showing *The Rocky Horror Picture Show*? Then **finger nichol@stavanger.spg.slb.com** to receive a huge catalog of places you can find these and other esoteric postings.

I'm Convinced—How Do I Create My .Plan?

Good. Let's set up a .plan file. The .plan file has to be in your home directory. At the UNIX shell, type **ls -a** to see all the files in your home directory. The ones that begin with a period (such as .signature and .newsrc) are hidden files. They are generally used to setup a program in some manner, to make something happen automatically.

You Can't Do Business on the Internet! So they say. Well, you can, if you are discreet. Using the **finger** command can be a simple and fairly unobtrusive way to promote a business. If you have information that people may find useful, you can put it in your .plan file, along with a paragraph or two explaining what your business does.

You need to create a text file and call it .plan. Make sure you are in your home directory before starting. Type **cd** and press **Enter** to make sure you are there. Then open your text editor, create the file, and save it.

Which text editor are you going to use? Well, you may not need to go to the UNIX shell at all. Your service provider or administrator may have set up an editor you can open from a menu. There are plenty of editors around. In *The Complete Idiot's Guide to the Internet* (Chapter 11), I explained how to use **vi**, a miserable little editor that lots of UNIX nerds love. Real people may prefer something like **pico**, though. The pico editor has a menu at the bottom of the screen that shows you the commands. Real UNIX users don't need menus, of course, because they have photographic memories and don't need to be reminded how to use a program. Put anything you want in your file. Whatever information you want to distribute—soccer scores, Congressional votes, the week's Prairie Dog breakdown tally.

Letting Other People See Your .Plan

Once you've created your **.plan** file, you need to make sure other people can view it. First, let's see who can view the file. Type **ls -l .plan** and press **Enter**. You'll see something like:

```
CNS> ls -l .plan
-rw-r-r- 1 pkent      user          35 Jul 18 16:40 .plan
```

The first ten characters on the line show who can do what with the file. Look at the 5th and 8th characters. If you see an **r** in the 5th and 8th positions (as in this example), it means other people can read the file. In some cases, you might see that both positions contain a dash (–). That means, other people won't be able to see your .plan file when they finger you.

If this is the case, you'd better change the character. You'll have to use the **chmod** command. (**chmod** means Change Mode.) Type **chmod ugo+r .plan** or **chmod a+r .plan** and press **Enter**. Then use the **ls -l** command again to make sure it worked.

Before you go to all this trouble, check with your system administrator that people on other hosts will be able to use the **finger** command to get information from your host. Some administrators don't like outsiders using the **finger** command to find out what's happening on their system, so they block it.

Why did it work and what does **chmod ugo+r .plan** mean? Well, **ugo** means "user, group, others," and **+r** means "make it readable." If you want more, read up on the **chmod** command (use the man chmod command to see the command's documentation.) It does work—that's all that matters.

Making People Want to Finger You

Now, any time someone fingers you, they'll also see your .plan file. Who's going to finger you though? Unless you tell people the information is there, they won't know, will they? So, let everyone you think may be interested in on the secret. Tell friends and colleagues, leave messages in the appropriate newsgroups, send messages to the right mailing lists, and send e-mail to people who maintain lists of online resources. Of course, if the information you are putting out is of no interest to anyone, nobody's going to finger you to get it. However, if what you are distributing is of interest, you'll be surprised at how fast the word can spread.

TECHNO NERD TEACHES...

You may want to add information at the bottom of your .plan file explaining how to put data into a text file. If a .plan is very long, it flies across the screen too fast to read. But you can *pipe* the text into a text file like this: **finger** ***username@hostname* >*filename***, where *filename* is the name of the text file. Put instructions explaining this at the end of your .plan file, so people who don't know this can learn about it.

One more thing. Before you put something out on the net, make sure you own it. There used to be a listing of the Billboard Top 10 songs at buckmr@rpi.edu. Now, if you finger that site, all you'll see is a copy of a threatening letter from *Billboard Magazine*'s lawyers! And the Nielson TV ratings at normg@halcyon.halcyon.com have been replaced by a "The posting of the TV ratings is history. Don't ask!" message, perhaps for the same reason.

Auto E-mail—Sending Automatic Responses

By now, you've probably seen a few auto-response messages; you send a message, and the e-mail address automatically sends a response back to you. This is another quick and easy way to get information out, and it's used a lot. I've mentioned this sort of system a number of times; for instance, to see a list of all the LISTSERV discussion groups, send e-mail to listserv@bitnic.educom.edu. In the body of the message, type **list global**.

There are a couple of basic ways to create an auto-response. There's a simple auto-response in which each time a message is received, a message is returned, regardless of the content of the first message. Then there's the system by which the auto-response program looks for particular text, and sends a response according to the text it receives.

Quick and Easy Auto-Response

There's a very quick way to create an auto-response—use the .vacation file. If you read *The Complete Idiot's Guide to the Internet*, you may remember this little utility (Chapter 12). It's intended to let you automatically send a simple message to people telling them that you are away and won't be checking your e-mail for a while. However, there's no reason you can't use it more regularly, to distribute information. Here's how it works.

First, select the vacation program from a menu—if your system administrator has added it to a menu. If not, go to the UNIX shell, type **vacation**, and press **Enter**. You'll see your text editor, like this:

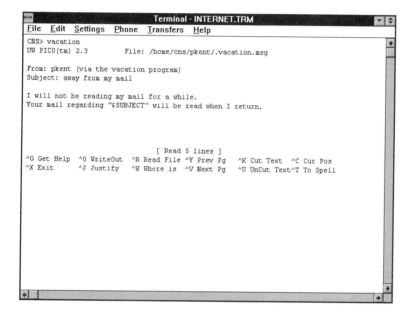

A generic UNIX text editor (PICO), helping you route your vacation mail.

Now, delete the existing text and replace it with the important gems you believe the world is waiting to hear. Using this text editor—pico—I can use the **ctr.-r** to copy a text file into the editor, so if I already have the text somewhere, I don't need to retype it. When you finish, just close the text editor. You'll see something like this:

```
You have a message file in /home/cns/pkent/.vacation.msg.
Would you like to see it? y
From: pkent (autoresponse)
Subject: Albanian Soccer Scores

It's been a hot week in Albanian soccer. Tirana's Captain,
Fred Zog, has
```

```
finally been let out of internment camp. His first game was
a little slow, but
```

It's a good idea to take a quick look at the message, to make sure you entered everything correctly. Then you'll see this:

```
Would you like to edit it? n
To enable the vacation feature a ".forward" file is created.
Would you like to enable the vacation feature? y
Vacation feature ENABLED. Please remember to turn it off
when
you get back from vacation. Bon voyage.
CNS>
```

That's it. Each time you receive a message, your auto-response message goes out, without you doing anything. You can still read your incoming messages and reply later, of course. In the meantime, your highly important information—the latest Australian football results, your literary analysis of the week's soap operas, or the recent history of your company's stock performance—has been sent out to whoever "requested" it.

Be careful with using the .vacation program. If you've subscribed to a mailing list, each time you receive a message from the mailing list the .vacation message is sent to everyone on the list—including you—which will cause the vacation message to go out again… on and on ad nauseum, or at least until someone steps in and kicks you off the mailing list. (Mailing-list-manager programs can automatically stop these "bounces," but not all are set up to do so.)

Of course, as with the finger command, unless people know what you are doing, nobody's going to be sending you e-mail to get the information. It's up to you to get the word out about your "service" so the people who could benefit can find it.

To stop sending out this automatic response, just run the **vacation** command again.

Slow and Complicated Auto-Response

You can take this mail-response thing a bit further. You'll need a special *mail server* program that can examine each incoming message and send out a reply according to what is in the message. You can use such software to manage file archives; users send messages requesting certain files, and the server figures out what they want and sends the files to them.

You can also use the software to maintain mailing lists. In *The Complete Idiot's Guide to the Internet* (Chapter 16), I described how to work with LISTSERV mailing lists. You can send messages to the mailing address that controls the LISTSERV mailing list, and the LISTSERV software checks the message looking for words it recognizes (you must format the message correctly, of course). When it sees words, such as HELP, QUERY, INFO, it sends the appropriate information.

For more information about this software, see the section on mailing-list managers later in this chapter.

Cheap Thrills: Your Very Own Mailing List

Here's another thing you can try: setting up your own mailing list. Again, you can do a quick-and-easy setup or a more complicated one, depending on what you need. If you are going to create a very small mailing list, with changes occurring rarely, you can use the quick and easy method. This may be suitable for a situation in which the mailing list will be used only for a small company, or a club. But if you think your mailing list can become popular with the world at large, you'll have to spend more time setting the list up using a proper mailing-list program.

Quick and Easy Mailing Lists

The quick and easy way to set up a mailing list is *very* quick and easy: use the **.forward** file. This is a file that the UNIX sendmail system—the mail system that does all the work sending messages to and fro across the Internet—looks at when you receive a message. If there's an address in the .forward file, it sends the message onto that address. However, you can put more than just one address in here, so a single message being received can be sent to a list of other addresses.

Simply use a text editor to create a file called **.forward** (the period makes the file a hidden file). Then enter all the addresses you want mail forwarded to, one on each line. Save the file in your home directory (usually the directory that you are "placed in" when you log onto the system). This sends mail on to the other mail addresses, but won't keep a copy on your system. You won't be able to read a copy of the incoming messages. If you also want a copy of each message saved in your system—the one doing the forwarding—then add *username* to the .forward file. For instance, this is what the file may look like:

```
1234.132@compuserve.com
jobloe@apotpeel.com
fred@usa.usa.net
jdoe@apotpeel.com
\pkent
```

The last line (**pkent**) ensures that a copy of the message is saved in the pkent mailbox, the mail system that is doing the forwarding. And that's pretty much it; you've just set up a simple mailing list. If anyone sends a message to your address, that message is sent out to all the other addresses on your list, and you'll be able to read a copy, too.

If you set up a mailing list, you really need two accounts: one for the mailing list and one for the administrator. Call the administrator's account something like **listname-request@hostname**. Then people can send e-mail to that account asking you to add them to the mailing list. There are thousands of these little lists, many of which are private—by-invitation-only. These quick-and-easy mailing lists are suitable for small, private mailing lists, lists that won't require a lot of work to manage because they won't have a huge number of people subscribing and unsubscribing.

Of course, you can also set up a loop using the .forward system. Make sure you are not on a mailing list that is also in your .forward file.

Mail Reflectors: Reflect on This

You can also set up a *mail reflector*: a program specially designed to forward incoming e-mail to a list of other Internet users. Well, okay, *you* can't set it up, but someone with administration privileges can.

Why? Well, think about this for a moment. If you set up e-mail address A with a mail reflector that directs a message to, among other addresses, e-mail address B, and if e-mail address B also has a mail reflector, and one of the addresses on the list is address A... what have you got? An eternal loop, with messages that are sent to A going on to B, and then back to A, and then back to B…. So, to make sure that doesn't happen, a system administrator has to manage a mail reflector system. If you want to set one up, you'll have to talk with your system administrator or service provider.

Mailing List Manager Programs: The Real Thing

If you want to put a bit more effort into it, you can get a mailing-list manager program. These programs let you automatically take "subscriptions" to the list, and respond to requests for information. For instance, send an e-mail message to **majordomo@greatcircle.com**. Don't put anything in the subject or the body of the message. Here's what you'll get back:

```
┌─────────────────────────────────────────────────────────────────┐
│                    Terminal - INTERNET.TRM                        │
├───────────────────────────────────────────────────────────────────┤
│ File  Edit  Settings  Phone  Transfers  Help                      │
├───────────────────────────────────────────────────────────────────┤
│ This is Brent Chapman's "Majordomo" mailing list manager, version 1.63.
│
│ It understands the following commands:
│     subscribe <list> [<address>]
│         Subscribe yourself (or <address> if specified) to the named <list>.
│     unsubscribe <list> [<address>]
│         Unsubscribe yourself (or <address> if specified) from the named  <list>.
│     get <list> <filename>
│         Get a file related to <list>.
│     index <list>
│         Return an index of files you can "get" for <list>.
│     which [<address>]
│         Find out which lists you (or <address> if specified) are on.
│     who <list>
│         Find out who is on the named <list>.
│     info <list>
│         Retrieve the general introductory information for the named <list>.
│     lists
│         Show the lists served by this Majordomo server.
│     help
│         Retrieve this message.
│     end
│         Stop processing commands (useful if your mailer adds a signature).
│ Commands should be sent in the body of an email message to
│ "Majordomo@GreatCircle.COM".
│ Commands in the "Subject:" line NOT processed.
│ If you have any questions or problems, please contact
│ "Majordomo-Owner@GreatCircle.COM".
└───────────────────────────────────────────────────────────────────┘
```

The response from majordomo@ greatcircle.com

This message was returned by a mailing-list manager called Majordomo. The message lists the different commands that users can send to the mailing-list manager. For example, if they send a message with the word **list**, the mailing-list manager returns the names of the mailing lists that it controls. If the message has the word **info *listname***, it will describe the list. And if you want to subscribe to a particular list, you can just send the message **subscribe *listname*** to be automatically added to the list—no need for anyone to intervene and manually add your name to a list, the program does it for them.

Where to Turn for Help...

If you want to go whole hog and set up a real mailing list, check with your system administrator about available programs. If he can't help, you'll have to track one down yourself. You can get a copy of the Majordomo mailing-list manager by anonymous FTP from **ftp.greatcircle.com**, in the **/pub/majordomo** directory.

If you create a mailing list, get the word out by subscribing to the new-list@vm1.nodak.edu mailing list and sending an announcement of your list. Also, announce it in the **news.lists** and **news.announce.newusers** newsgroups.

You can also join a mailing list that gives you lots of information about mailing-list managers. Send a message to **majordomo@greatcircle.com**. In the body of the message (don't worry about the subject line), enter **subscribe list-managers**. That'll get you onto the list. You can then just listen in, or ask for advice about which program you should use.

If you're in a hurry, though, you can check out the archives of earlier list-managers messages. You can find these by FTPing to **ftp.greatcircle.com** and changing to the **/pub/list-managers/archive** directory. You'll find all the messages in files named **list-managers***yymm*, where *yymm* denotes the month and year.

If you hate FTP (it's kinda clunky at the command line, but check out the neat Windows programs for FTP later in this book), you can get the archives by e-mail, using the **get** command. First, send a message to **majordomo@greatcircle.com** and put **index list-managers** in the body. You'll get back a list of the archive files. Then send a message with **get list-managers** *filename* in the body to get an e-mail message containing the text from that file.

Installing your own mailing list is not something you should attempt unless you are comfortable installing software.

> I don't mean running the sort of sissy, rinky-dink Microsoft Windows SETUP "click-here-to-install" programs that everyone's used to working with. I mean a *real* installation procedure. You'll be installing and configuring a UNIX program, with a couple-dozen pages of semi-English UNIX documentation to dig through.
>
> You'll also need help from your service provider to do a few things that you can't do, such as assign group and user IDs. Be aware that this might cost money; you'll end up getting a separate account for each mailing list. You'll have to compile and install UNIX code, set up a configuration file, and so on.
>
> If you hate UNIX, don't try this alone. Find a UNIX nerd to help you, get a case of Jolt and a box of Twinkies, and lock him in the room for a couple of days.

What About LISTSERV?

A LISTSERV mailing list is a particular type of list that uses the LISTSERV software. Setting up a LISTSERV is probably more complicated, requiring more planning and more help from a system administrator. Still, your system administrator may be willing to help you set it up. Some service providers will happily set up a LISTSERV graph for you with just a day's notice. Call and ask.

If you're interested in setting up your own LISTSERV mailing list, you can get some help by sending a message to this address: **listserv@acadvm1.uottawa.ca**. In the body of the message add these lines:

```
info listserv
get basic help
get genintro article1
```

You'll get important information back about the LISTSERV program and how to set up a LISTSERV discussion group.

Also, you can find more information by joining the LSTOWN-L@indycms group—this is a list dedicated to LISTSERV administration topics. Eric Thomas, the man who wrote the LISTSERV program, is a participant in this group. Also, the arachnet@acadvm1.uottawa.ca mailing list offers advice from other LISTSERV administrators.

Make Your Own News

How about starting your own newsgroup? After all, are there really enough newsgroups out there? Yes, I know there are newsgroups about Christi Yamaguchi, S & M, UFO sightings, Shamanism, Rodney King and the LA riots, European satellite TV, and other useful subjects. However, maybe you have your own story to get out, your own idea for a newsgroup that will have people flocking across cyberspace to join you.

Well, there are two ways to create Usenet newsgroups: an official way and an unofficial way. We'll start by doing it right.

The Official Guide to Creating Newsgroups

It's simple, just follow this procedure:

1. Put a message in the news.announce.newgroups newsgroup, and other newsgroups and mailing lists related to the proposed topic. Describe the newsgroup you'd like to start.

2. Spend the next 30 days finding other people who agree with you, and decide how the newsgroup will be run.

3. After 30 days, contact the Usenet Volunteer Votetakers (UVV).

4. Post a call for votes in the news.announce.newgroups newsgroup and the other newsgroups and mailing lists in which you posted the original information. Include explicit instructions for how to cast votes. Votes are cast by e-mail.

5. After about three to four weeks, the UVV counts the votes and posts the vote tally in news.announce.newgroups and the other groups or mailing lists. If you got lots of votes, go on to step 6. If not, sulk, and then go to step 9.

6. Wait five days. If necessary, problems with the vote will be fixed.

7. If you received 100 more YES votes, and at least two thirds of all votes were YES, you're in luck. (Go back and read that again. It really does make sense.)

8. A *newgroup* message is sent out.

9. If you lost, try again in six months, or give up and start your own mailing list. Or... an unofficial newsgroup. That'll show 'em.

If you want to follow this route, you'd better get each step just right, or you'll be sent back to the beginning. Get the documents that explain all the details. These are posted periodically to the news.groups, news.announce.newusers, and news.answers newsgroups. Look for messages with names such as "How to Create a New Usenet Newsgroup" and "Usenet Newsgroup Creation Companion." These are posted every few weeks, but these newsgroups are *very* busy (and quite chaotic), so you may not find the messages when you look. Try again later.

You can also find information in various FTP sites. For instance, try FTPing to **rtfm.mit.edu**. Go to the **pub/usenet-by-group/news.answers/ creating.newsgroups** directory, and get all the text files from this directory.

Also, subscribe to the **group-advice@uunet.uu.net** mailing list. Lots of newsgroup administrators subscribe to this list and should be able to help you. Just send a message to this address, and you should hear back from them eventually. Find as much information as you can before you get started.

Creating The Down-and-Dirty Newsgroup

As you can imagine, some people simply don't have the discipline, the energy, or the time (or, for that matter, the votes) to create a newsgroup the *right* way. So, subversives that they are, they figure they'll do an end run and create a newsgroup by themselves. An *alternative* newsgroup.

If you'd like to try this, check for the **So you want to Create an Alt Newsgroup** message (or something similar) in the **news.groups**, **news.announce.newusers**, and **news.answers newsgroups**. Also, try FTPing to **rtfm.mit.edu**. Go to the **pub/usenet-by- group/news.answers** directory and get the file

alt? The alternative newsgroup names start with *alt*, which means *alternative*. It refers not to alternative subjects, but to an alternative Usenet hierarchy. It has also been suggested that alt stands for Anarchists, Lunatics, and Terrorists.

named **alt-creation-guide**. This guide is also available on the World Wide Web at **http://www.pop.psu.edu/~barr/alt-creation-guide.html**, or you can get it by sending e-mail to **majordomo@pop.psu.edu** with the line **get file alt-creation-guide** in the body of the message. Also, check out the **alt.config newsgroup**, the newsgroup about creating alternative newsgroups.

So, here's an outline of how you set up an alternative newsgroup:

1. Post the idea in the alt.config newsgroup. You don't have to do this, but you'll get good feedback, and news administrators are more likely to start a group if it's been in alt.config first. (see Step 2 and 3).

2. Find a news administrator. Each site has a news administrator—he's the guy who decides whether to carry a newsgroup at the site, and whether to create newsgroups for distribution.

3. Convince said news administrator to let you set up a newsgroup for you. You may be lucky. In many cases, news administrators set up virtually anything that is suggested. (It's quicker and easier than fighting with some crazed zealot about whether it's *really* worth distributing his ideas worldwide.)

4. Your news administrator must send out a **newgroup** message informing the world of your creation. If the administrator also includes a **For your newsgroup file:** line in the message, some news-reader programs will automatically accept the description of the newsgroup. In some cases, though, news administrators have to decide whether or not to take the group.

5. Convince other sites to carry the newsgroup. The third stage is probably the hardest. No site has to accept a newsgroup. There are tens of thousands of newsgroups throughout the world, yet a typical service provider only "subscribes" to 4,000 to 6,000. (America Online subscribes to about 12,000, an unusually high number—see Chapter 20.) So each time a new newsgroup is created and offered worldwide, the world's news administrators have to decide whether to take it or not. (Usually not.) Try drumming up interest for your group in the usual way: e-mail to interested parties, notices in mailing lists and other newsgroups, and so on.

FTP Sites and the WWW

How about setting up your own FTP site? Or your own World Wide Web system? Sound complicated? It really doesn't have to be. See Chapter 16 for information about WFTPD (That's *Windows FTP Daemon*), a program that lets you set up your computer as an FTP site on the Internet (once it's connected via a permanent or dial-in direct connection).

In Chapter 12, you'll learn a little about HTML (HyperText Markup Language) files. These ASCII text files are the foundation of the World Wide Web—and surprisingly easy to create. If you'd like to put your own data onto the World Wide Web, you can create a few HTML pages and put them onto your service provider's system. Talk to your service provider about where to put the documents, and read Chapter 12 for more information.

The Least You Need to Know

- ☞ Text in the .plan file is automatically sent out when someone fingers your account.

- ☞ Text in the .vacation file is automatically sent out when you receive e-mail.

- ☞ You can use the .forward file to set up a simple mailing list.

- ☞ For more a sophisticated mailing list, you need to get a mailing-list management program.

- ☞ Creating a newsgroup can take plenty of time and energy, but you can do it if you are really dedicated.

- ☞ You can set up an alternative-hierarchy newsgroup much more quickly and easily.

You could use this blank page as an
opportunity to express your Inner
Anarchist. You've always wanted
to scrawl some desperate, futile
slogan all over a page in a textbook,
haven't you? Well, go crazy!
"CEASE THE OPPRESSION!"

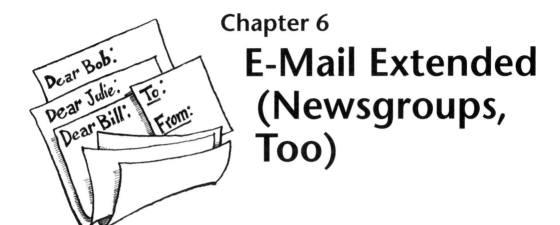

Chapter 6
E-Mail Extended (Newsgroups, Too)

In This Chapter

- ☞ Working with Qwkmail systems
- ☞ Using Pronto, an automated mail system for PC-UNIX connections
- ☞ Using WinNET, an e-mail and newsgroup program

Have you ever used an *offline navigator*? These are programs that let you do online work offline. That is, tasks that you would normally do while connected to an online service, you can carry out *offline*, while you are unconnected.

How can that be? Well, many of the tasks you do while you are online don't really require that you be connected. For instance, in order for you to read a mail message, your software has to read the file off the service provider's hard disk and then you read the message. Do you need to be connected while you are reading? No, of course not. Nothing is happening between your computer and the host while you are reading, except for one thing: the host is keeping track of your online time, so it can charge you for time you didn't need to be online!

An offline navigator, though, lets you automate various procedures, limiting the amount of time you spend online. Perhaps the most-used offline navigators are the ones that work with the CompuServe online system—programs such as NavCIS.

So why shouldn't there be an Internet offline navigator? Well, there probably will be, eventually; though as the Internet is clearly structured very differently from CompuServe, it seems likely that Internet offline navigators will actually be hybrids, part offline navigator and part online navigator.

In the meantime, a couple of Internet functions already have offline navigators: e-mail and newsgroups. Several programs will automatically logon, grab your e-mail and drop off any e-mail messages you have written, then logoff the system. You can then read, reply, and compose offline—while the host's timer is no longer racking up your bill. If you are tired of UNIX mail or Pine, read on.

Reading Stuff with Qwkmail

You can extend your e-mail with an offline navigator without spending much, if anything. Qwkmail is a strange hybrid system that all sorts of people have been writing programs for, so now there are lots of different Qwkmail programs, running on all sorts of different computers, including Windows, DOS, OS/2, Amiga, and Macintosh. These are freeware and low-cost shareware programs.

I say it's a hybrid because these programs are not really single do-it-all programs. First, on the host computer, you use a Qwkmail command to compress your e-mail files into a small "packet," and to transfer the packet back to your computer. Then, after logging off your service provider's computer, you use a Qwkmail reader to open the compressed file and read the contents.

Qwkmail doesn't just work with e-mail. It can also work with newsgroups. That's a real benefit if you are in the habit of saving *everything* you find in the alt.binaries.pictures.erotica newsgroup. In order to use Qwkmail, you'll have to get your service provider to load the uqwk program. Once loaded, you can check out all its options with the **man uqwk** command.

Step 1—Squeezing It

Take a quick look at how to get the packets from the host to your computer. First, check to see if there's a menu option. If your service provider has set up the Qwkmail program, it may also have put the commands on a menu somewhere. If not, perhaps your service provider has setup a Qwkmail script. For instance, my service provider has created two files: sqwk and rqwk. Type **sqwk** to compress the files and send them to your system, or **rqwk** to receive compressed files from your system. For example, at the UNIX shell, I can simply type **sqwk** to see this:

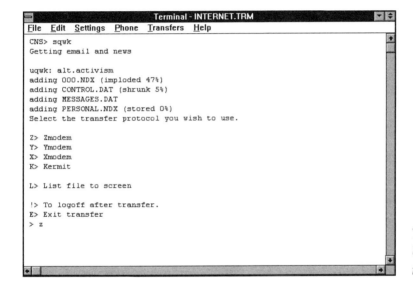

```
                        Terminal - INTERNET.TRM
 File   Edit   Settings   Phone   Transfers   Help
CNS> sqwk
Getting email and news

uqwk: alt.activism
adding OOO.NDX (imploded 47%)
adding CONTROL.DAT (shrunk 5%)
adding MESSAGES.DAT
adding PERSONAL.NDX (stored O%)
Select the transfer protocol you wish to use.

Z> Zmodem
Y> Ymodem
X> Xmodem
K> Kermit

L> List file to screen

!> To logoff after transfer.
E> Exit transfer
> z
```

Typing sqwk at the UNIX shell displays this info.

Qwkmail then transmits the compressed files to your computer. I could have used the ! command, followed by the **z** command, to automatically log off my service provider's computer once the transfer was complete. I selected **Zmodem**, as you can see, because it's quick, and my communication program knows when a transmission is coming in; I don't have to tell it to receive. Of course, you'll want to set up your communication program's download directory so it places the files in a subdirectory of your Qwkmail reader's directory.

Of course your service provider may not have created such a script. In that case, you'll have to use the uqwk command. However, to use the **uqwk** command properly you have to be aware of dozens of different options. Use the **man uqwk** command and spend an hour or two reading.

Step 2—Opening It

Now, you need a Qwkmail reader. There are loads of them around. As usual, check with your service provider. For a list, FTP to **ftp.wustl.edu**, change to the **systems/ibmpc/msdos/offline** directory, and get the **qwkp9406.zip** file (or something similar). This file, updated periodically, contains several text files that tell you everything you ever wanted to know about Qwkmail, including the names of literally dozens of Qwkmail programs and contact information for the programs' authors. You'll also find a few Qwkmail programs in this directory (look for the files with qwk somewhere in the name and read the index file in this directory). You may also use Archie to track down Qwkmail programs. I found dozens listed when I did a search recently.

If something happens to the Qwkmail files you just downloaded, you can resend them using the **rsqwk** command. (The **sqwk** command moves the messages to a backup file, so if you use the normal **sqwk** command you won't get them.)

To go the other way—copying your mail and newsgroup messages from your computer to your service providers—you will use the **rqwk**.

For instance, you may check the Offline Qwkmail program, a DOS program, which is reputed to be pretty good. You simply use the program's menu system to select the .QWK file, and Offline uncompresses the file so you can view the messages. You can see a mail message in the following illustration.

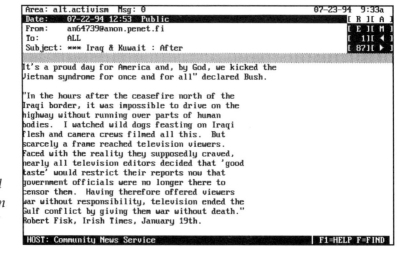

The Offline Qwkmail program lets you open and read your .QWK files.

You can use your mouse in Offline. See the small box in the top right corner? Simply click on one of these commands to do something: click on **M** to see a list of messages, **E** to send a message, **R** to reply, the left-pointing triangle to view the previous message, the right-pointing triangle to view the next, and so on.

Using Qwkmail is pretty easy, but I didn't say *installing* it would be, did I? If your service provider has set it all up with a simple script that you can run, it will be easy. If not, you'd better find someone who knows about UNIX. Or look at the other options later in this chapter.

Step 3—Back Again

Qwkmail programs also enable you to create .QWK files that you can send back to the host system. Offline even has a simple terminal program that will log onto the system and transfer the file, though you may want to use your regular communications program to do this.

On my service provider's system, all I have to do to upload my response file (an .REP file), is to select **Upload Qwkmail** from a menu. Of course, I can also do it from the UNIX shell, like this:

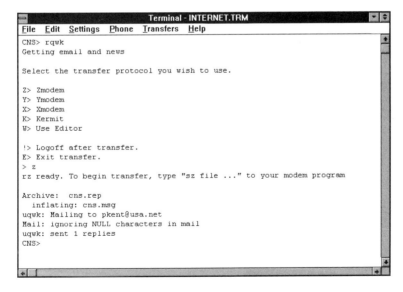

```
                          Terminal - INTERNET.TRM
File  Edit  Settings  Phone  Transfers  Help
CNS> rqwk
Getting email and news

Select the transfer protocol you wish to use.

Z>  Zmodem
Y>  Ymodem
X>  Xmodem
K>  Kermit
W>  Use Editor

!>  Logoff after transfer.
E>  Exit transfer.
>  z
rz ready. To begin transfer, type "sz file ..." to your modem program

Archive:  cns.rep
   inflating: cns.msg
uqwk: Mailing to pkent@usa.net
Mail: ignoring NULL characters in mail
uqwk: sent 1 replies
CNS>
```

Uploading Qwkmail from the UNIX shell.

That's it. The Qwkmail system on my service provider's computer uploads the file, uncompresses it, and sends my mail and newsgroup postings.

Windows User? Try QwkWindows

There are also many Qwkmail programs for Microsoft Windows: WaveRider, UNIQwk, VBReader, and so on. The Windows Qwkmail programs are getting quite snazzy, too. They often have MIDI and .WAV support, so you can play music and digital sound files. Some have MIME support, too. Remember MIME? It's a system that lets you send files attached to your e-mail, without unencoding them first. Plus, you have the usual convenience of Windows programs: tool bars and menus, the ability to cut and paste text, full mouse support, and so on. Another Windows Qwkmail program that has a good reputation is CMPQWK. You can find a copy at the ftp.wustl.edu site I mentioned earlier.

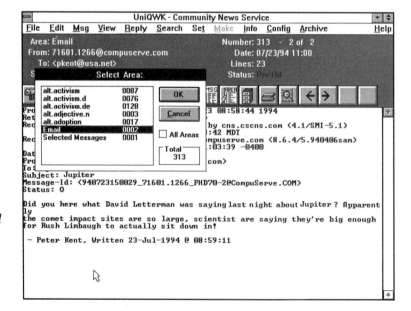

UNIQwk, a Qwkmail reader from Brazil, one of the many readers available for Microsoft Windows.

If you want to work with Qwkmail, talk with your service provider and do a little digging on the net to find a reader you like. There are dozens of these things around; so in the best tradition of the Internet, you can spend many dozens of hours goofing off. You can even pretend you are being productive. After all, once you're set up, you'll be able to save hundreds of hours, at $1.50 or so, of online time. Even if it does take you hundreds of hours, at $15 or $50 an hour trying to get set up.

This Qwkmail stuff's all a little clunky, though. Too many steps for my liking. I prefer to use a program that does it all for me; I select a menu option or click on a button and it logs on, grabs my mail, and comes back. I want a program I can install myself without worrying about having to convince a system administrator to install his portion.

Well, there are a few other methods to get your e-mail system sorted out. Read on.

Do It with Pronto

Pronto is one neat little program with which you can automate your mail if you connect to a UNIX host (like most Internet users). You can install it pretty quickly, too. It took me ten minutes to install and connect to my service provider; the documentation suggests that the first time you connect you do so manually. You go to Pronto's "terminal emulation" window and type **atdt** followed by the telephone number and press **Enter**. (The only problem I ran into here was that when I typed, nothing was displayed on the screen. I had to go to the Dialup Communication Setup dialog box and select Half Duplex; close the box; reopen and reselect Full Duplex; and then close the box, to get my typing to appear properly).

Then you log onto your system, go to the UNIX shell, select **Communication|Update** mail, and Pronto does its stuff. Pronto grabs the mail for you, then asks if you want to log off.

Of course you really need to write a script to do this automatically, and the scripting is fairly simple: it took just another five or ten minutes to create a script file. Remember, though, that the script must take you all the way to the UNIX shell. If you see a menu when you open, you have to write a script that selects the menu option that takes you to the shell.

Here's the script I had to write:

Command	What It Does
DIAL "7582656"	Dials my service provider.
WAITFOR "username:", 30	Waits until it sees **username:** (the 30 means it waits for up to 30 seconds).
USERID	Sends my username. It gets this from the setup information I entered when I first installed Pronto.
WAITFOR "password:", 30	Waits until it sees **password:**.
PASSWORD 1	Sends my password, password number 1 (Pronto will store up to ten passwords, presumably so you can connect to different systems. However, it only stores one username.)
WAITFOR "continue"	Waits until it sees the word **continue**.
TRANSMIT "c^M"	Types **c** and sends a carriage return. (^M means "carriage return," the same as pressing the Enter or Return key.) That's what my service provider's system expects me to do when it displays the **Type "c" followed by <RETURN> to continue** prompt.
WAITFOR "continue..."	Waits for another prompt, **Press <RETURN> to continue**.
TRANSMIT "^M"	Sends a carriage return.
PAUSE 4	Waits for a few seconds, a little more than the time it takes for my service provider's menu system to appear.
TRANSMIT "0^M"	Types **0** and sends a carriage return. 0 is the menu option that takes me to the UNIX shell.
PAUSE 3	Waits for three seconds, enough time to get to the shell.

Then, after the last command in the script, it does its stuff, grabbing my mail. You can then log off your service provider's system and deal with your mail offline. You'll spend less than a minute online, in many cases, then spend the next ten or twenty minutes dealing with your mail *without paying your service provider* for online time.

Scripts Made Simple   This is really a fairly simple script, and the scripting is reasonably well documented. Open the LOGIN.SCR file, and you'll find notes inside the script file explaining what to do. Unlike some script languages, Pronto's is not *case sensitive*. It doesn't care if you enter **Password** or **password**.

Pronto: All the Usual Stuff

Pronto provides all the usual e-mail stuff, in a Windows format. You can compose e-mail, reply to and forward mail, remove mail, and so on. You can create aliases, so you don't have to re-member all those long funky Internet e-mail addresses, and you can copy messages into text files (and text files into messages). You can do all this using fancy little toolbar icons and menu options. Everything you can do in, say, the Pine mail program you can do in Pronto, only more quickly. (See Chapter 27 for information on finding Pronto.)

There's no reason to stop there. Why not add a few extras, such as *folders*, to organize your mail? Of course, some UNIX mail pro-grams use folders, too, but they don't make it as easy as Pronto. Just click on a toolbar icon to move a message into a particular folder. Select the folder you want to view by double-clicking on a name in a list.

What About My UNIX Folders?   If you've been using a UNIX mail program, you've already got a folder or two with messages. You can copy the folders to your hard disk, then use Pronto's **File|Import Folder** com-mand to bring the old messages into Pronto. You can go the other way, too, and export folders.

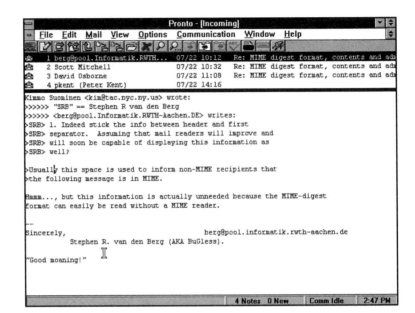

Pronto provides a Windows mail interface for dial-in terminal systems.

There's also a search feature so you can find a particular word inside a message; a spell checker with Replace All and Ignore All commands; plus the ability to add words to the dictionary. You can configure your system so that the folders on the host match exactly the folders on your PC.

WinNet Mail & News

Here's another Windows product that will grab your e-mail and newsgroups: WinNET Mail & News. You can get this program in two ways. You can receive it for free when you subscribe to Computer Witchcraft, Inc.'s service, WinNET. This is an Internet service provider that gives you an e-mail address and access to newsgroups.

Plenty of information is also available about how to use e-mail to do Archie searches for files, and to download files from mail-servers. WinNET also has a "Download request server" on which they store often-used files—for example, photos of the Jupiter comet impacts.

Problem is, this service is a bit pricey, at $8/hour plus 18 cents/minute for using their 800 number, or 12 cents/minute during the evenings and nighttime. Remember, though, you won't necessarily spend too much time online, as WinNET simply grabs your e-mail and newsgroup messages and logs off. (And maybe Computer Witchcraft will be forced to drop prices soon, as Internet connections get cheaper across the board.)

The other way to get WinNET is as shareware; try it for free, then, if you like it, register it ($99). When you register, you receive another version with a few more features. At the time of this writing, you can configure WinNET to work with UUCP (UNIX to UNIX Copy Program) mail systems, but Computer Witchcraft plans to modify it so you can use it with any UNIX host, in a similar way to Pronto.

I can't vouch for connecting WinNET to your UNIX host, of course, though it will probably be similar to the way in which Pronto connects; you'll have to write a script. But installing the system to connect to Computer Witchcraft is very simple.

Here's a handy feature that all navigators, for all systems, really need. You can start writing a message, then drop it into the Draft folder. It won't be sent the next time you log on. You can return and finish it later, then send the completed message. Some UNIX mail programs have this feature, but for some reason, navigators running on PCs generally don't. See Chapter 27 for information on friendly Pronto.

WinNet: Well-Designed Internet Software?

Yes, it is possible. WinNET is probably one of the best-designed Internet program I've seen so far. The big chunky toolbar buttons are great; you can tell what they are for a change. (Why is it that 50% of the buttons on most program toolbars are unintelligible?) These buttons have both a picture and text, so you never wonder what they are for.

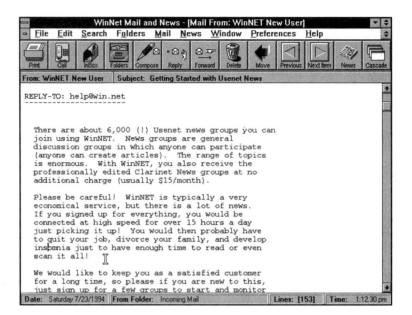

WinNET's user interface—very easy to use.

WinNET provides a feature that few online "navigators" do: the ability to search your messages for a particular word. Not just the message you are viewing, but messages in one or all of your message folders.

Here's another neat feature. When you've read your mail, you can select **Folders|Clear Incoming Mail**. You'll then have two options. If you select **To Old Mail**, all the messages you've read are stored in the Old Mail folder. However, if you select **Assign to folders named after senders**, the program checks who each message is from, and places them in folders named after the person sending the message. If there is no existing folder for a sender, the program creates one.

WinNET Mail & News doesn't use MIME (the system that lets you send binary files across the Internet). It does make uuencoding and uudecoding easy, though. If you receive a message that contains a uuencoded file, simply select a menu option and the program asks you where you want to put the file. Select the directory, and it decodes for you. To encode a file, do the opposite; select a menu option, the program asks which file you want to encode, then it does it for you.

All the Newsgroups That Are Fit to Print

Working with newsgroups is just as easy as working with e-mail (but remember, if you are using the WinNET host, and if you subscribe to lots of newsgroups, your bill can get quite large). To subscribe to a newsgroup, simply enter the group's name into a dialog box, and the next time you log on to grab your e-mail, the program subscribes to that newsgroup. Then, each time you log on in the future, you'll automatically get your newsgroup messages, also.

Newsgroups have a different window from the e-mail. Again, toolbars help you quickly reply to and forward messages; mark messages as seen; send a message to the author's e-mail address; print; and save messages in files.

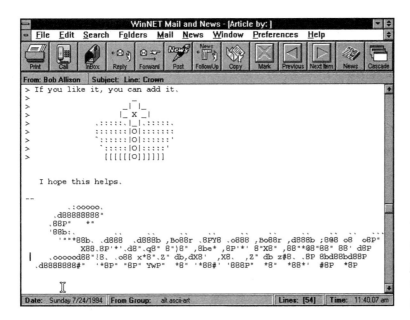

WinNET's Newsgroup window provides easy point-and-click access to your newsgroup messages.

Problems, Problems...

I did run into a few problems with WinNET Mail & News. The first couple of times I tried to get through to WinNET I couldn't. It may have been a line noise problem, but if so, WinNET is more sensitive than my other communications programs. Also, I once found an "unknown" message in the Queue Editor. This is the place where you can see a list of all your outgoing messages. This unknown message was causing problems when I tried to connect, but I couldn't delete it from the queue. In the end, I had to delete the file from the WNMAIL\SPOOL\C directory.

Another time the program spent 30 minutes online, downloading hundreds of messages from three newsgroups. Then, when I opened the News window, it only listed one newsgroup, and only one message in that group. When I reopened the program a couple of hours later, it listed them all. Strange.

It's Nice, But...

Still, I really like WinNET Mail & News. Working with e-mail and newsgroups is really simple with this program. Right now, you can use it with the WinNET service or with UUCP. It won't help you connect to your dial-in terminal account or dial-in direct account, or access your e-mail if you have a direct connection. However, a dial-in terminal version may be available soon.

There's More...

These are not the only products that can automate e-mail and newsgroups for you. I recently stumbled across a shareware program called RFD Mail that will work with dial-in terminal accounts. It works in a similar manner to Pronto. You can use one of the existing scripts, if you work with the appropriate service provider, or write your own script. There's also a product called MKS Internet Anywhere, another UUCP mail product. See Chapter 27 for information about both products.

However, most such mail programs need a direct connection or a dial-in direct connection (such as SLIP). If you have a basic dial-in terminal connection, you're going to have limited choices. Of course, there's always the option of upgrading to dial-in direct, isn't there? It's not as hard or expensive as it was just a few months ago. So read on, and I'll explain what it takes to crack the Internet wide open.

The Least You Need to Know

☛ Qwkmail is fairly simple to use once you have it set up.

☛ You'll probably need your service provider's assistance to set up the host end for Qwkmail.

☛ Dozens of different Qwkmail programs are out there, for just about any platform. Some are free; some are shareware.

☛ Pronto is a commercial Windows product that lets you download your e-mail and work on it offline. It's very easy to install.

☛ WinNET Mail & News is a commercial Windows product that lets you download e-mail and newsgroup messages, and work on them offline.

☛ WinNET Mail & News works with the WinNET online service (which is expensive) or with any UUCP connection. A dial-in terminal version may be available soon.

☛ Check out RFD Mail, a shareware e-mail program for dial-in terminal accounts.

Yeah, this page is blank, but don't worry—you were only charged for the pages with stuff on them.

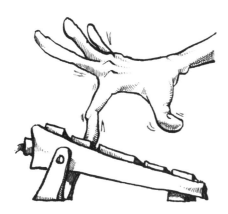

Chapter 7

Turbocharge Your Modem— with a Dial-In Direct Account

In This Chapter

- The four types of Internet accounts
- Picking the type of Internet account you need
- Understanding the benefits (and disadvantages) of dial-in direct accounts
- Why you need WINSOCK.DLL and a dialer
- Using V.fast modems

You have a decision to make. Should you set up a dial-in direct account or not? Don't be fooled into thinking that everyone needs a dial-in direct account. If you have a direct connection to the Internet—one with which you don't need to dial into the system, such as through your company's LAN—you already have something better than dial-in direct, so don't change. Likewise, if you're just an occasional Internet tourist, the simplest dial-in terminal account may suit you just fine. However, if you're a frequent Internet user connecting with a modem, maybe a dial-in direct account is just what you need.

Go Over That Again...

First, let's review the main types of Internet accounts. There are four basic ways to connect to Internet, plus a few variations:

☞ Permanent connections

☞ Dial-in direct connections

☞ Dial-in terminal connections

☞ Mail connections

These are my terms, by the way (though I'm glad to say I've seen them in the press since the publication of *The Complete Idiot's Guide to the Internet*—see Chapter 3 in that book). Why make up my own terminology? Extreme arrogance? Well, maybe, but there really were good reasons. Different service providers use slightly different terms for these accounts, and the standard terminology can get blurred. It gets confusing, but the following definitions should clarify things a little.

Permanent Connections

A *permanent connection* means your computer connects directly to a TCP/IP (Transmission Control Protocol/Internet Protocol) network that is part of the Internet. Actually, the usual case is that your organization has a large computer connected to the network, and you have a terminal connected to that computer. (You may even have a computer that is acting as a terminal; that is, the other computer does all the work, and your computer is simply passing text to and from your screen.) This sort of connection is a *dedicated connection*, a *direct* connection, or a *permanent direct* connection.

Large organizations/universities, groups of schools, and corporations often use such connections. Because they have a *leased line* (a permanent hookup to the Internet), there's no need to make a telephone call to reach the service provider's computer. Rather, the user will simply *log on* to Internet from his terminal.

Dial-in Direct Connections

A *dial-in direct connection* is a *SLIP* (Serial Line Internet Protocol), *CSLIP* (Compressed SLIP), or *PPP* (Point-to-Point Protocol) connection. You may also hear the term XRemote, though you probably won't be offered this variation. These are also TCP/IP connections, like the permanent connection, but are designed for use over telephone lines instead of a dedicated network.

Using this sort of connection, you have to dial across the telephone lines to your service provider's computer, and then log in. Once logged in, your computer acts as if it were a host on the network; you even have a host IP (Internet Protocol) number for your system. When you transfer files across the Internet, you transfer them from the other computer directly back to your computer. You are not using the service provider's system hard disk as a *waystation*.

You may also hear these types of connections referred to as *on-demand direct* connections or as *TCP/IP* connections. And the term *SLIP*, which really refers to just one form of dial-in direct connection, is often used in a generic sense.

Dial-In Terminal Connections

With this type of connection, you have to dial into the service provider's computer. If you don't have a permanent connection, and you didn't specifically ask for a dial-in direct connection when you signed up, you probably have a dial-in terminal connection. This sort of connection is a *dial-up* connection, which seems ambiguous, because you have to dial to get a dial-in direct connection, too. Some service providers call this an *interactive* service, which seems only slightly less ambiguous. I call it a *dial-in terminal connection* because you have to dial the call to your service provider; once connected, your computer will act as a terminal.

Unlike a permanent or dial-in direct connection, your computer doesn't appear as a host on the network. It is simply a terminal of the service provider's computer. All the programs you run will run on the service provider's computer. That means you can transfer files across the Internet to and from your *service provider's* computer, not to and from yours. You'll have to use a separate procedure, such as xmodem or zmodem, to move files between your computer and that of the service provider.

Mail Connections

The Internet has several different mail connections. However, I don't regard these as true *Internet* accounts, so I haven't covered them in this book. If your account lets you send and receive e-mail and newsgroups but nothing else, it's a *mail connection*. It may be a *UUCP*, *e-mail*, or *messaging* account. (Most on-line services these days have an Internet e-mail connection; CompuServe, America Online, Prodigy, MCI, Genie, and so on can all send e-mail across the Internet.)

So What's the Problem?

The main problem we're going to deal with in this chapter relates to dial-in terminal accounts. When you dial into a service provider's system and connect, your computer becomes a terminal of that computer. In most cases, you'll use a generic communications program to connect—something such as Windows Terminal, HyperACCESS, CrossTalk, or whatever. By *generic*, I don't mean the software is bad in any way. For instance, HyperACCESS, which I use, is an excellent program. It's generic in the sense that you can use it to connect to any standard bulletin board or on-line system.

In other words, you are not using specialized software to connect to a dial-in terminal account. (At least not in most cases; later in the book, we'll get to The Pipeline, which uses a dial-in terminal connection, although it also has special Windows software designed to connect to it.)

So, here's the problem. Each service provider sets his system up differently. No one communications program can be configured so that it will work with all service providers' systems. So you're at the mercy of the service provider's setup.

Because most service providers are not in the business of creating software, they usually don't create fancy graphical user interfaces for their clients. (The Pipeline, founded by best-selling author James Gleick, is an exception. As you'll see when you install the software at the back of this book, The Pipeline has its own neat, easy-to-use interface.)

Here's another problem. A dial-in terminal account is just that; it makes your computer a terminal of another computer connected to the Internet.

All "transactions" that occur while you are online are between the host computer—your service provider's computer—and some other computer somewhere out there in cyberspace. When you use a communications program on your system to do something on the Internet, what you are really doing is using the communications program to make the host computer do something on the Internet.

That's not really what you want, though. After all, if you're sitting at home with a couple thousand dollars' of computer equipment on your desk, you really want your *computer* connected to the Internet.

Real-Life Example

Say you want to grab a piece of clip art you've heard is somewhere on the Internet. You connect to your service provider and use some tool to go to the site and grab the file. Perhaps you are using FTP, or maybe a gopher. You find the file, and then transfer it back to your service provider's computer. Remember, your computer is simply telling the host to do something: you are telling it to grab a file, so it does. And it places it on its hard disk. Then you have to use zmodem or xmodem to transfer the file from the host back to your system.

Wouldn't it be nice if you could connect directly to the Internet, without using the host as a waystation?

So What's the Solution?

You *can* have a direct connection to the Internet—with a dial-in direct connection. There are two main benefits to dial-in direct connections.

First Big Benefit: Lotsa Software

Lots of fancy Windows software is available for the Internet, most of it written for permanent connections. Software that runs on a permanent connection will also run on a dial-in direct connection, because both types of connections use software the same way. So if you don't have a Windows permanent connection, getting a dial-in direct connection opens up a totally new world of Internet tools—many of which are far better than the basic UNIX tools you are probably used to.

What can this software do for you? Well, for starters, it's easier to use than most UNIX software because it provides *cues*: buttons, toolbars, menus, and so on. It often provides features that are sometimes awkward to use with UNIX programs, such as the ability to view a text file at an FTP site. It also provides features that UNIX programs generally don't have, such as the ability to log on, grab your e-mail, and log off, all in a few minutes.

Second Big Benefit: Direct Connection

Once you are online with your dial-in direct connection, your computer acts like an Internet host, not a UNIX terminal. You work directly with FTP sites. Files from the FTP site are transferred directly back from the FTP site to your hard disk, with no need to use zmodem or xmodem to transfer them from the service provider's system.

There are a couple more advantages. First, a dial-in direct connection allows multiple sessions. That is, you can be doing more than one thing at a time. You may have an FTP session running in one window, downloading files from a computer somewhere across the world, and at the same time be using a Windows gopher client to dig around in gopherspace. You don't have to wait for the download to stop before you do something else.

And TCP/IP connections handle downloads better than normal Windows telecommunications software. Windows doesn't multitask too well (I'm talking about Windows 3.1 and 3.11 here; Windows 4.0/Chicago should be better), and has real problems dealing with communications. If you're downloading a file while working in another Windows application that tries to read or write something large from or to your hard disk, you may find your download is disrupted. (Did you follow that? I make a habit of not touching my keyboard while downloading something large.) However, Windows TCP/IP connections are much more stable. You can work in other applications, and in most cases, you'll find that your connection and downloads are not broken.

Where to Start?

If you want to connect all the fancy software we're going to discuss later in this book, you have a couple of options. You can either install it on the computer you use to connect right now (if you have a permanent connection), or you can go out and buy a dial-in direct connection.

However, even if you have a permanent connection, *can* you install all this software on your system now? That depends on what sort of system you have.

Requirement 1: A Computer

First, you need a computer connected to the system you log into—not just a terminal. If you are sitting at a VT100 terminal, for instance, connected to a large UNIX machine, no dice. You are at the mercy of your system administrator. All you can use is what your system administrator installs on the host for you. Why? Because a "dumb" terminal, such as the VT100, doesn't do any computing. It simply sends information from you to the host, and back again. All the programs are being run on the host, not in the terminal.

Requirement 2: The *Right* Computer

Okay, so you have a computer connected, not just a "dumb" terminal. But do you have the *right* computer? Well, there's Internet software available for just about any computer these days. However, there's a lot more made for IBM PC-compatibles running DOS or Windows than for any other type of computer. Why? Because there are so many of them.

Yes, you'll see programs for UNIX. You'll also find Macintosh software, but not much; it's a sad fact that although Macs are well represented in the art and music world, they are not so well-represented in the areas that have historically made the most use of the Internet: academia and companies running large UNIX machines. You'll also find software for the Amiga and, for all I know, the abacus. But fewer choices.

To cut a long story short, the rest of this book covers software for the IBM PC-compatible running DOS and Windows—specifically Windows 3.1. Mainly, I cover Windows because more Windows software is written than DOS software. (The market is demanding Windows software, and in many ways, it's easier to write than DOS software.)

So you don't like windows? Okay, so some people don't. I sorta do, maybe, on my good days. The theory is great, but in practice it has some shortcomings—which I hope Microsoft will fix by the next version of Windows, currently code-named *Chicago*. However, like it or not, comparatively little DOS software is being written or sold.

So there you go. If you have a permanent connection, you need a computer running Windows to make full use of the rest of this book.

Requirement 3: The Connection

If you are running an IBM PC-compatible on a network with a permanent connection to the Internet, there's one more step. Do you already have Windows installed and running on the network and able to use the network's Internet (TCP/IP) connection? If not, you're going to need some help, probably. I'm not going to get into how to install a Windows network connection in detail. (I'll mention a few points of interest a little later, but I'm not going to take you through it step by step.) Why? Because there are too many different networks and network programs.

So, if you don't have Windows connected to your network yet, you'll probably have to get the system administrator to do it for you.

The Dial-In Direct Connection

In order to run Microsoft Windows on the Internet, you need special software. You need a TCP/IP *driver*, and you need a *dialer* that will dial out using the TCP/IP driver.

You are probably familiar with print drivers; in order to send data from, say, a word processor to a printer, you need a print driver. It used to be, in the old days, that when you bought a program, you installed print drivers along with the program. You handle things differently in Windows, though. You install print drivers when you load Windows itself, and perhaps install updated print drivers later. Any Windows program can then use the Windows drivers to print. This saves software developers a lot of trouble. As long as their programs can send data to Windows' printing system, they don't have to worry about how each print driver handles the data; that's up to the guys who design the print driver.

It's much the same for TCP/IP connections, the type of connection you must make to get running on the Internet. You have to install a Windows TCP/IP driver. Then any Windows program that's set up to run on TCP/IP should be able to work with the TCP/IP driver to send data across the TCP/IP connection.

The Windows TCP/IP driver is the WINSOCK.DLL. It's not really a *true* driver; there are differences in the way print drivers and WINSOCK interface with Windows programs. However, the principle is the same. If you want to print, you need to load a print driver first. If you want to connect to the Internet, you have to install WINSOCK.DLL first. Many Windows programs can use a print driver, as can WINSOCK.DLL.

Right now there are a few of these TCP/IP drivers around. You can:

DLLs (dynamic link libraries) Look in your WINDOWS\SYSTEM directory and you'll see dozens. A DLL is a file that contains special program code that other programs can use; a program can go to the "library" and "borrow" the code. The WINSOCK.DLL contains special utilities that let Windows programs communicate using the TCP/IP protocols.

☞ Install a shareware or public domain TCP/IP driver.

☞ Install a commercial TCP/IP driver; these often come with Internet programs. For instance, NetManage's Internet Chameleon software has the necessary TCP/IP driver.

☞ If you have Windows 3.1, you can download drivers from various Microsoft libraries. You'll find it in the MSNET forum library on CompuServe (library 15) and on the Microsoft FTP site, (**ftp.microsoft.com**). Look for a file named TCPIP32.EXE.

☞ If you have Windows 4.0 (or 95, or Chicago, or whatever they end up calling it), you will already have the TCP/IP drivers built in.

Wait—Where's the Dialer?

You don't necessarily need a dialer. If you are connecting a Windows machine to a permanent connection, you don't need a dialer because you don't have to dial anywhere. However, if you are installing a dial-in direct connection, you do, of course. So where's the dialer?

Some versions of WINSOCK.DLL come with a dialer. The Trumpet Winsock, the most popular shareware WINSOCK.DLL, comes with a program called TCPMAN, which has a dialer. Internet Chameleon, a commercial system we'll look at later in this book, comes with an application called Custom, which contains a dialer. WinGopher has a built in dialer. And so on.

So what about the four options I mentioned a moment ago?

- ☞ **Shareware or public domain**   The one you'll probably use in Trumpet Winsock (that's the one I'll help you install in Chapter 10). It has a built-in dialer. No problem.

- ☞ **Commercial software**   Commercial programs generally come with the dialer you need.

- ☞ **Windows for Workgroups 3.11**   The WINSOCK.DLL for Windows 3.11 is, at the time of writing, a beta program, with no SLIP/PPP support. You can use it to connect directly to a network, but it won't dial into a dial-in direct connection.

- ☞ **Chicago (or whatever they plan to call it)**   The next version of Windows is supposed to have a built-in dialer. If you are reading this book after the release of Windows 4.0/Chicago, run out and buy a copy. You'll have the WINSOCK and dialer already there, so you don't have to worry about finding another.

It's Getting Easier

When I wrote *The Complete Idiot's Guide to the Internet* late in 1993, I said that you could get a SLIP account for as little as $100 to connect, and $15 a month (though most service providers charge more). Change that to $35 to connect, and a monthly minimum of $10. The Internet "business" is changing very quickly, and one of the most significant changes is that dial-in direct accounts are getting *much* cheaper.

Dial-in direct accounts are also getting much easier to set up. As recently as March of 1994, *Boardwatch* magazine described Internet TCP/IP software as "uninstallable by humanoids." With the exception, that is, of NetManage Inc.'s Chameleon that it described as the best of the lot—but still "barely installable." (To be fair to NetManage, their new Internet Chameleon is much easier to install than their earlier product, especially if you read my guidelines in Chapter 17.)

As you'll see in later chapters, though, getting a SLIP account up and running is not impossible. It's certainly not as easy as installing your average Windows program, but with a couple hours of careful work, you should be able gather the information you need, install the program, and get it into action.

Is It Really Worth the Effort?

Is it worth the effort to acquire special software? It depends. If you like working at the UNIX shell, if you never make typing mistakes, if you think graphical user interfaces are a curse from the devil, designed to make your work slower and more complicated, if you can "use typed commands to do anything that can be done in Windows, and faster too," then stick with the command line.

However, Internet disappoints many people. They've read all the hype about the Internet, tried to use it, and found that, as columnist Mike Royko put it, you need "the time, the patience, and the inclination to become a computer nerd." Why can't the Internet be as easy to use as a CompuServe navigator?

The answer is, it can; you just need the good software. If this is the way you feel about the Internet, you need to install all this neat software designed for TCP/IP connections—whether a permanent or dial-in direct connection.

So What's the Catch?

Catch? Well, yes, there is a catch.

On the surface, being connected directly to the Internet seems a nice idea—files coming out of cyberspace directly onto your hard disk. The catch, though, is that if you use a dial-in direct account, files are going to transfer across the Internet much more slowly than with a dial-in terminal account. Why? Well, remember, if you are using a dial-in terminal ac-count, the host computer is doing the work for you. It transfers the file from the FTP site, for example, back to the service provider's computer. And the service provider's computer can transfer files across the net much, much faster than you can.

For example, transferring a 230 KB file from the net to your system at 14,400 baud could take two and one half minutes or so. From your service providers system, the same transfer might take just five or six *seconds*. (That's at about 51 KB/second, compared to about 1400 bytes/second through your modem.)

Once it's on your service provider's system, you may want to transfer it back to *your* system. But using zmodem, for instance, may take only two minutes, so the total time is still less than the time it takes to transfer using the dial-in direct's TCP/IP link. And anyway, do you really need all the files you transfer back on your hard disk? Couldn't you just read index files straight off your service provider's system, using the UNIX **cat**, **more**, or **tail** commands? Working with a dial-in direct account may mean you spend more time online than you need to.

Maybe it's not such a problem. For example, consider an FTP session. With a dial-in terminal account, I have to connect to the FTP site, usually by typing the hostname (though it would be possible with some communications programs to create toolbar buttons that would type the hostname for me). I have to dig my way through the directories, searching for the one I need. I have to use the **get** command to transfer the file. I have to close the FTP session, then use the **sz** command to transfer the file using zmodem. Yes, the actual transfer time may be less, but I'll spend more time setting up each operation.

With a good Windows FTP program, I can create a library of FTP sites, and then select a site from a drop-down list box and click on a button. The program then logs onto the site for me and goes to the directory I defined. Then I just double-click on the file I want, and it's transferred all the way back to my computer. Simple, and therefore fast.

You can already buy V.fast modems,but the manufacturers are guessing at the standdard. If you buy one, make sure it can be upgraded when the committees publish the final standard.

V.fast = Very Fast!

By the time you read this, the speed problem may be no more—if you buy a V.fast modem, that is. At the time of this writing, the international telecommunication committees are trying to figure out a V.fast standard: the manner in which a new generation of ultra-high speed modems will operate. Service providers are standing by, waiting to make the decision about installing V.fast modems until after the standards have been established.

Right now, the fastest modems that most service providers use are 14,400 bps. The new V.fast modems will generally run at 28,800 bps. (And new modem technology may bring us speeds up to 115,200 bps soon!) What's more, they handle "line noise" much better. You know, the crummy phone lines that crackle and pop. This line noise slows down transmissions, because each time one of the modems gets confused, part of the transmission has to be redone. V.fast will solve the line noise problem, requiring fewer retransmissions. With a V.fast modem connection, the 2 minute 30 second transmission I mentioned earlier would come down to 1 minute and 15 seconds, perhaps as low as 20 seconds (with modem advances coming soon); an incredible increase that will really make your Windows Internet software fly.

Don't Run Off!   Before you run out and buy a dial-in direct account, do two things. First, read the chapters on the NetCruiser (Chapter 18) and America Online (Chaper 20) programs. It's very easy to install and use these, but they only work with NETCOM or American Online; you can't install them on just any service provider's system. (The first is a dial-in direct system, the second a dial-in terminal system.)

Second, install and use the software we've included with this book. It provides a "Pink SLIP" connection—a sort of hybrid SLIP/terminal connection—to the Internet through The Pipeline. It takes you 30 minutes or less to install and run the system, and it doesn't require a dial-in direct account.

Bottom Line: What Do You Need?

If you are going to get a dial-in direct account, here are a few things you need:

Modem   A fast modem, 14,400 bits per second at a minimum. Consider 9,600 bps as the *bare minimum*, the "buy-food-or-buy-another-modem" speed. Anything less than that would be intolerable.

Windows   Get the latest version of Windows. (Remember, the rest of the software in this book is, in the main, Windows software.) If Microsoft releases Windows 4.0/Chicago/Whatever by the time you read this, upgrade. Not only will you get a system with built-in WINSOCK.DLL and a dialer, but you'll get a more stable system that has resolved many of the Windows 3.1 memory problems.

Software   You need a variety of different programs to let you connect to the Internet and carry out typical Internet tasks. See Part II for information about shareware, public domain, and freeware programs. See Part III for information about commercially distributed programs.

The Least You Need to Know

- ☞ If you have a permanent connection with Windows connected to the Internet, you can install the fancy Windows program and get started right away.

- ☞ If you have a dial-in terminal account, you need a dial-in direct account to use all the fancy stuff

- ☞ You can get a dial-in direct account for as little as $35

- ☞ Dial-in direct accounts running on Windows need the WINSOCK.DLL file and a dialer. The shareware Trumpet Winsock has both. The new version of Windows (4.0/Chicago) will have both, also. And you can buy commercial software that comes with both.

- ☞ Dial-in direct accounts have slower transfer times between Internet sites than you are used to on your dial-in terminal account, but you don't need to do *two* transfers. Files go straight onto your hard disk.

- ☞ The time you lose in transmissions may be more than made up for by the time saved by the fancy software we're going to look at.

Chapter 8

Homework Time! Gathering the Information

In This Chapter

- 👉 Collecting information for dial-in direct
- 👉 Testing your dial-in direct account
- 👉 Gathering information for the login script

So you've decided to go ahead and try TCP/IP. In the long run, you'll probably be pleased. In the short run, however, you may wonder if you made a stupid decision. Syndicated columnist Mike Royko believes that the experts running the Internet want to create a world of computer nerds, so that "their daughters might find suitably nerdy husbands." The programmers who write Internet software seem to have conspired against real users. The software is often hard to use and the documentation atrocious—that goes for both public domain and many commercial products.

You *can* avoid problems—and maybe even the stigma of nerdhood—with careful planning. If you want to connect your computer to a dial-in direct TCP/IP connection, you must get your facts right. You'll need to know all sorts of tricky little numbers and names, so this chapter is all about what they are and where to get them. In later chapters, I'll explain how to use that information.

Call Your Service Provider

Okay, e-mail them, I don't care. Whatever's easiest. (There's a bias against calling people in much of Internet-land, but there are times when you just can't beat the phone.) Whatever you do, you must somehow gather the information discussed in this chapter. If you find that your service provider is not very helpful, consider finding another provider before attempting to connect your dial-in direct account. You can write the data as you collect it in the table at the end of this chapter. But first, take a look at the information you're going to need.

Basic Connection Information

First, let's find the information about the connection you are going to make, and how it connects at the service provider's end.

What's the telephone number?   Critical information, this. No number; no connection.

What type of connection is this? (SLIP, CSLIP, PPP)   There are several different kinds of TCP/IP dial-in direct connections. Make sure you know exactly which type your service provider is using, as you'll have to let your TCP/IP software know. Some service providers may let you use any of these. For instance, when I log in, I can use SLIP, CSLIP, or PPP. CSLIP may be slightly faster than SLIP, though perhaps not much. CSLIP simply compresses the *header* information, information sent by your programs telling the service provider what each batch of data is and what to do with it. PPP is supposed to be much faster and more reliable. But if your modem has error-correction capability, you may find little difference. (Some engineers claim PPP has little effect, except for improving communications on noisy lines.) Note that if you want to use Trumpet Winsock, the shareware WINSOCK.DLL, you'll need SLIP or CSLIP; the current version won't work with PPP.

TECHNO NERD TEACHES...

SLIP, CSLIP, and PPP That's Serial Line Interface Protocol, Compressed Serial Line Interface Protocol, and Point to Point Protocol. These are all types of TCP/IP (Transmission Control Protocol/Internet Protocol) connections that can run over the phone line. Less than one Internet user in a thousand can tell you what these acronyms mean, so feel free to forget them.

What is your username or account name? This is the name you use to login to the service provider's system. You usually take this from your name. For instance, at one service provider, I had a login of pkent, at another peterk. In most cases, though, you'll be able to tell the service provider what name you want to use (assuming nobody else is already using it). Your service provider may give you two account names, one for the dial-in direct account, and one for another, associated, account (often called a *shell account*). You can dial into the shell account with an ordinary dial-in terminal connection. This is handy, because you can then dial in and check your e-mail even if you're having trouble with your SLIP software, or if you are calling from a machine without the fancy software, such as a laptop. Some service providers may make you pay extra for the shell account. Other service providers will simply give you one account name and password, and the ability to login with both a dial-in direct and a dial-in terminal connection (not simultaneously, of course).

What is your password? You may get to choose your password, or the service provider may give you one. Either way, change it when you log in. Again, you may have *two* passwords, one for your dial-in direct account, and one for your shell account. Make sure you have the right one. Typically, passwords are eight characters or more, and are case sensitive—thus *324iel4* is not the same as 324IEL4. And different service providers may have different rules about how to create passwords; some won't allow real words.

What is the TCP/IP startup command?   When you first make your connection to the host computer, it probably doesn't know if you are going to be using a dial-in direct or dial-in terminal connection. It may give you the option of making either kind of connection. At some point during the login session, you have to tell the host computer that you want to change to a TCP/IP dial-in direct mode. Generally, you have to type *slip* or *ppp* or something similar, then press **Enter**. (To use CSLIP, you'll probably still type **slip**. Your service provider's computer will figure out if you are using SLIP or CSLIP when it receives data from you.) Check with your service provider what you must type.

When do you use the startup command?   You also need to know at which prompt you use the startup command, though this is usually pretty straightforward. You enter your username and password, and then the system displays a prompt asking you what you want to do. (You'll see an example later in this chapter.) This is the point at which you must enter the command. However, if you don't have a ready-made login script, you need to know this information so you can write your own. (I'll discuss scripts later in this chapter.)

What is your Internet Protocol (IP) address?   Once connected to the Internet, your computer will act as a host, so it needs a host address. This is a four-part number, each part separated by periods. For example, my IP address is 199.190.133.121.

What is your hostname?   Once connected to the Internet, you'll also need a hostname. This is normally the same as your login name. If your login name is jbloe, you will use jbloe as your hostname also.

What is your domain name?   You also need to know the domain name of the service provider's system. This is the part that appears after the @ sign in your e-mail address. For example, if your e-mail address is jbloe@cscns.com, the domain name is cscns.com. Many service providers will let you create your own domain name, in which case you should enter it here (sometimes there's a small charge, sometimes they'll do this for free). Having your own domain name can be handy—once you have one, you can change service providers and take the domain name with you. You will have to register the name to the new provider when you do so, and there may be a charge for that. Changing service providers doesn't mean you have to change your e-mail address. (If you didn't get your own domain name when you first signed up for the dial-in direct account, you may still be able to do so. Check with your service provider.)

What is the domain name server (DNS) address?   This DNS address is the address of the host computer that your service provider uses to figure out network addresses. If you send e-mail, the Internet has to figure out where to send it. It does this by contacting a DNS (domain name server) and asking it for information. Your service provider should give you at least one DNS address, but maybe several. Again, this is a four-part number (the DNS I'm using is 192.156.196.1).

What's the Subnet Mask?   Your service provider may give you a subnet mask number, but he probably won't. This is simply one of those strange network-thingy numbers that only network nerds understand, so don't worry too much about it.

What is the gateway address?   Your service provider may have a gateway address, the address through which they actually connect directly to the Internet. Then again, they may not. This is *not* the mail gateway, by the way—we'll look at that later.

More Connection Stuff

There's more. We already have the information you need to get your account up and running, but once connected, you may need more information to carry out certain operations. Ask your service provider for these items (you may find the addresses are all the same, perhaps even all the same as the name server address):

What is the Mail POP (Post Office Protocol) server name or address?   You use this server to get your mail from your service provider. Although, while connected, your computer will become a "host" on the Internet, while it's not connected your mail is being stored somewhere, in the POP server. When you connect, your mail program can then grab your messages from the server. There are different POP versions—most systems run POP3 these days. You should get the address and the port number.

What is the SMTP (Simple Mail Transfer Protocol) server name?   You can use SMTP to send and receive mail. You'll probably use SMTP to send mail; you can't use it to receive mail. An SMTP mail program can receive mail directly. That is, the mail doesn't need to go through the POP server. If you are not connected when mail arrives, the service provider's system will probably store the mail and try to resend it every 15 minutes or so. When you reconnect, the mail will go into your

SMTP mail program. The advantage of this is that you can set up your own e-mail accounts, using your domain name. For instance, you can have separate accounts for each person in your company, or each member of your family, your dog, or whatever. Not all programs do this, however, so you may or may not need this address. You might as well get it anyway. Get the address and port number.

What is the mail gateway name or address?   A mail gateway receives your mail on its way out. That is, when you write and send a message, the first place it goes to is the mail gateway. The gateway takes a look at the address and then sends the message on.

What is your Internet mailbox username?   You need a username to login to your mailbox. This is usually the same as your account username.

What is your Internet mailbox password?   You also need a password for your mailbox. Again, this is usually the same as your account password.

What is the NNTP (Network News Transfer Protocol) news server name or address?   You can use NNTP to transfer newsgroup messages and to store local newsgroups. You need this address to connect your newsgroup program so it can find the newsgroup messages. Get the address and the port number.

What is the gopher host name or address?   If you want to connect your gopher client up to your service provider's gopher server, you need the host name or address. Also, make sure you get the port number.

Is it a Gopher+ server?   Gopher+ is a new gophering standard, in which gopher servers can provide more information about items in a gopher list. In most cases, you won't need to tell your gopher client program whether a server is a gopher+ server or not, but in some cases you may.

What is the World Wide Web home-page URL?   URL means Universal Resource Locator, and it's a sort of WWW address. If you want to connect to your service provider's "home page" on the web, you'll need the URL. It will look something like this: **http://usa.net/ HomePage.html**. You learn more about URLs in Chapter 12.

Your Modem

You also need information about your modem and its connection to the service provider's system. Here's what you need:

COM port   You must know the communications port that you connect your modem to. It's probably COM1 or COM2. If you are not sure, check your computer's documentation.

Baud Rate   The baud rate is a measurement of how quickly a modem transfers data. It's *almost* synonymous with bits per second (bps), though not quite—and I have no intention of getting into the argument of whether or not they are the same thing. Just be aware that you'll see both terms used to describe the same thing, the data-transmission speed. At the time of writing, 14,400 baud is about the fastest connection available from most Internet service providers. Some may soon go with faster modems. You *don't* want a *slower* modem for this type of connection. You'll be transferring data directly back to your computer, and you need all the speed you can get.

Telephone number   You already have the phone number you must dial to connect to the service provider. You also need to know any other numbers you need to dial to get through, such as **9** to get an outside line and ***70** to turn off call waiting. With most modems you can also use commas (,) to add a short pause between these numbers. For example, *70,,555-4567.

Here's a quick way to find out which com port your modem uses. Open **Windows Terminal**. Select the **Settings|Communications** command. Click on COM1 and then on OK. If a message says that you have the wrong port, try again with **COM2**. Continue until you find a COM port that doesn't give you the error message. Then select the **Settings|Phone Number** command and enter a number to dial. Close the dialog box, and select the **Phone|Dial** command. If the modem dials, you have the right port. If not, go back and try another port.

Many communications programs, including some TCP/IP programs, don't show a 14,400 option. If not, you can select the next higher speed, such as 19,200.

Initialization string   A modem initialization string is a command, made up of several characters, sent to the modem to tell it what to do.

Modem Type or initialization string   For now, you probably just need to know the modem type. Some communications programs will give you options, such as Hayes, Telebit, and MultiTech. If yours isn't one of these, you'll select Hayes, as it's the industry standard that most modems try to emulate these days. However, modem initialization strings are a constant source of problems. If you have trouble with your modem not connecting, you may have to enter a custom initialization string. You can find the information from your modem's user manual, and, I hope, your service provider will be able to help.

Hardware Handshake   Ask your service provider whether your modem should use hardware handshaking. *Handshaking* is the means by which two computers tell each other when they are able and unable to accept further data, and there are two ways to do this: software handshaking and hardware handshaking. You are unlikely to be using software handshaking, but may be using hardware handshaking.

Parity   What parity setting should your modem use. This is probably set to None.

Stop bits   What stop-bits setting should your modem use. This is probably set to 1.

Data bits   What data-bits settings should your modem use. This is probably set to 8.

Communications port speed   Some TCP/IP software requires that you enter the speed of the communications port. Not the speed of the modem, but the speed at which the data is transferred from your computer through the COM port. You may not run into such a program; we're not going to look at one in this book (though earlier versions of some of the programs we will look at used to ask for this information). If you do, though, you may be able to find the port speed using a computer diagnostics program. (Windows comes with Microsoft Diagnostics. Close Windows, change to the WINDOWS directory, type **MSD**, and press **Enter**.)

These diagnostics programs are not always good at showing the port speed (MSD is kind of flaky). The program should show the UART chip type, though, if it's an 8250, it will be slow. If it's a 16450, it should be much faster. If it's a 16550, it may be 19,00 bits per second or as much as 57,600 bps. Try entering 19,200 into any program that asks for this speed; it will probably be correct. Then experiment to find the highest speed you can use.

An Exercise for the Eager: Testing the Login

It's a good idea to test logging into your system using an ordinary telecommunications program, such as Windows Terminal, CrossTalk, or HyperACCESS. You can dial into the number given you by your service provider and try to use the dial-in direct logon procedure. You won't be able to get all the way, because these communications programs are not TCP/IP programs, but you will be able to check that you have the correct username, password, and startup command.

Record the session; virtually all such programs these days let you record every word that passes over the lines during the session. In Windows Terminal, you'll use the **Transfers|Receive Text File** command to select a file in which Terminal can store the session.

Here's a sample session I recorded when testing my connection to Colorado Springs' Internet Express:

```
ATDT758-2656
CONNECT 14400/ARQ/V32/LAPM/V42BIS

====> Connected 10:41am Wednesday, June 22, 1994
Checking authorization, Please wait...
CHECK OUT THE NEW BBS MENU SYSTEM & TELECONFERENCE:
     Select Z from the top menu (in Power Tools)
     Communicating with fellow users has never
     been easier.

Welcome to the CNS Network
      If you are a new user, please login in as
                   userid    "new"
                   password  "newuser"

Username: pkent
Password:
```

(I entered my password, but it's not "echoed" back, so it doesn't appear)

```
Permission granted

                Community News Service (CNS,Inc.)
                       in affiliation with
                      ==TELEPHONE EXPRESS==
                     If you need assistance,
                 please call CNS at 719-592-1240


Type "c" followed by <RETURN> to continue slip


Switching to SLIP.
Annex address is 165.212.9.10.  Your address is
199.190.133.121.
_E4φ@-_b¥φ
                ç*y*xφÜ#Ä#_
```

(this is where I hung up, ending the session)

```
NO CARRIER
```

From this session, we can see that the service provider's system is asking for a **Username:** and **Password:**. I entered both, and both worked. There's the line, **Type "c" followed by <RETURN> to continue**. I'd type c if I wanted to access my dial-in terminal account, but to get to my SLIP account, I have to type **slip** and press **Enter** to get into SLIP mode. The service provider's system then tells me my IP address. Check this number against your IP number, and make sure they are the same. In this case, the address was not the same as the one given to me by the service provider. If you find such a problem, call the service provider and ask why you are getting a different number.

Once in slip mode, I just see garbage—that's okay, I've gotten as far as I need, so now I can disconnect using the telecommunications program's hang-up command. This test has helped me make sure the account was set up correctly (after I got the mismatched numbers problem cleared up, that is), but it gave me something else—the information I need to write a login script.

Creating a Login Script

Many programs require a login script for you to connect to your service provider's system. That is, you write a short text file telling the program what the host system will do, and what the program should tell the host.

If you are lucky, your service provider has already written a script for the program you plan to use. For instance, if you are using Internet Chameleon, you'll find that there are already setups—including the scripts—created for ANS, NetCom, PSI, Alternet, Cerfnet, and, currently, four other services. If you want to use Trumpet Winsock, you may find your service provider has already created a setup that you can download from them using a dial-in terminal account.

However, you may have to create your own login script. So testing the connection using a telecommunications program not only ensures you are using the correct username and password, but it also provides information you can use when writing a login script: the sequence of events that occur when connecting to your dial-in direct account.

If your service provider doesn't have the script and configuration files you need, why not "donate" them once you've created them and are sure they work. The service provider could put them in his library and let others use them. (But if you put your password in the script, remember to remove it!)

I'm not going to look at script writing here, because it varies depending on the type of software you are using. You'll look at scripts elsewhere in the book, though—when you look at Internet Chameleon (Chapter 17) and Trumpet Winsock (Chapter 10).

Your Info Here

Gathering the info you need for a TCP/IP account is a messy business, as you've just spent the last 10 pages discovering. I've included the following table to help you compile all the information you need. Later, when you are setting up your TCP/IP software, you can refer back to this table to find the data you need.

TECHNO NERD TEACHES...

You will probably find that your service provider gives you incomplete information, and when you ask for more details treats you like an idiot (slipping into "techno-babyspeak"). That's the nature of technical support people (I've spoken with hundreds). Don't be intimidated. The more information you have, the smoother things will go.

Essential Account Information	Write Your Info Here
Telephone number to call	
Type of connection (SLIP, CSLIP, PPP)	
Username (e.g. pkent)	
Password	
"Shell account" Username (e.g. pwkent)?	
"Shell account" Password?	
Startup command (e.g. slip)	
System prompt at which you enter the startup command	
Internet Protocol (IP) address (e.g. 199.190.133.121)	
Hostname (e.g. pkent)	
Domain name (e.g. cscns.com or kent.com)	
Domain name server (DNS) addresses (e.g. 192.156.196.1)	

More Stuff	Write Your Info Here
Subnet mask (e.g. 255.255.255.254)	
Gateway address (e.g. 192.156.196.1)	
Mail POP server name or address and port number	
SMTP server name or address and port number	
Mail Gateway name or address	
Mailbox username	
Mailbox password	
NNTP news server name or address and port number	
Gopher address and port number	
Gopher+ (yes or no)	
WWW home page (e.g. http://usa.net/HomePage.html)	

Modem Information	Write Your Info Here
COM port (e.g. COM1)	
Baud rate (e.g. 14,400)	
Modem type/initialization string (e.g. Hayes)	
Telephone number prefix (e.g. 9,*7)	
Hardware handshake (yes or no)	
Parity	
Stop bits	

Modem Information	Write Your Info Here
Data bits	
Communications port speed (e.g. 19,200 bps)	

The Least You Need to Know

☞ Make sure you get all the information in this chapter's table before trying to setup a dial-in direct account.

☞ Test the login procedure using Windows Terminal or another telecommunications program. Make sure you have the right username, password, IP address, and TCP/IP startup command, and know where to enter the command.

☞ Record the login procedure in case you need to use the information later to write a login script for your TCP/IP program.

Part II
The Freebie/Almost Freebie Route

You have a problem. You want to run your PC—running Windows or even plain old DOS—on a dial-in direct or permanent connection. You want the benefit of all that neat software you've heard about, but you don't have money to burn.

Don't worry; it doesn't have to be expensive. In this part of the book, I show you how you can set up a low-cost Internet system using shareware, freeware, and public domain software.

Lots of great software is freely available on the Internet. In many cases, it's much better than the commercial equivalents. So cast your fears aside, step out of the 1970s, and join me in the 1990s.

Chapter 9
DOS Does It, Too—UMSLIP and Other DOS Programs

In This Chapter

> ☞ Installing UMSLIP, a DOS SLIP program
>
> ☞ Writing a UMSLIP script
>
> ☞ Installing PC Gopher II
>
> ☞ Installing NCSA FTP and NCSA Telnet
>
> ☞ Installing Trumpet (a newsreader)
>
> ☞ Installing Minuet, a multi-task application

In the interest of fairness, I should say that there *is* a lot of DOS software for the Internet. Most of this book covers Windows software, but you can also set up a perfectly good dial-in direct account using DOS software. This chapter shows you how.

One Last Attempt to Convert You to Windows

Before we start, let me make one shameless attempt to convince you that Windows is the way to go. Sit through this quietly, and I won't bring it up again (maybe). Here are a few reasons to skip this chapter and move on up to Windows:

I'm the first to admit that Windows can be a real pain, especially if you load lots of different applications and peripherals. It crashes a lot and has memory problems. I put up with it, though, because when it does work, it makes life much easier than DOS ever could. And maybe Windows 4.0 will fix most of the problems.

☞ Windows programs are easier to use than DOS programs.

☞ The user interface is visually attractive, which I believe helps make Windows easier to use.

☞ Windows programmers often take more care in designing the user interface. Having worked with literally hundreds of DOS and Windows programs, I've concluded that DOS programmers are sloppier about user-interface design than Windows programmers. I think this is because Microsoft has worked to create standards in user-interface design, and programmers try to follow them.

☞ Windows programs are usually handled in much the same way in almost all Windows programs; once you've used a few, you can quickly find your way around a new one.

☞ Because of the aforementioned points, most people with PCs want Windows software. Very few companies are now writing new DOS programs, and many are letting their old ones die, moving to Windows. Why? Because people don't want DOS programs.

The last point is the most important: Most people with computers capable of running Windows properly *don't want DOS programs*. If they did, someone would write them. That's why I'm sticking mainly to Windows programs in this book.

Okay, no more DOS-bashing for the moment. Assuming you're still waiting patiently with your DOS machine, let's get down to business.

UM- What?

A well-known DOS alternative lets you connect a DOS machine to a dial-in direct account: UMSLIP (that's "U-M-SLIP"). Once you've set up the connection using UMSLIP, you can add other DOS programs to your system. There are many around.

There is a problem, though. The UMSLIP documentation is confusing. The system is designed for use at the University of Minnesota; if you attend that hallowed institution, installing and running UMSLIP will be very easy. However, if you need to connect to a SLIP account somewhere else, you have to write a script, and the documentation doesn't provide a series of step-by-step instructions to do that. But I do.

As with all the programs discussed in this book, you should always check with your service provider to see if they have configuration files or a login script for the program you want to use. If they do, you'll save much time and grief; writing scripts and config files is not for the computer neophyte.

UM- Slip!

UMSLIP stands for University of Minnesota SLIP, because that's where it comes from. UMSLIP is shareware; there's no charge for using it if you work or study at the U of M. If you don't, it costs $50. See chapter 27 for information on getting the program.

Once you have the compressed archive file containing all the required UMSLIP files, place it in a directory called UMSLIP, or whatever. Extract the files from the ZIP file in which they came. If the file has a .ZIP extension, you'll need PKUNZIP to extract them. If it's an .EXE file, you can just run the program by typing its name and pressing **Enter** at the DOS prompt.

You should see these files:

PHONE.EXE   A dialer that dials up your service provider and makes the SLIP connection.

PHONE.HLP   PHONE.EXE's online help file.

You can find PKUNZIP at almost all FTP sites, and almost certainly on your service provider's system. Ask where it is. To use it, place PKUNZIP in the same directory as the file you want to "unzip." At the DOS prompt, type **pkunzip** *filename* and press **Enter**. See the text files that come with PKUNZIP for more information.

README.TXT   A very simple text file that explains how to set up the PHONE.EXE program.

SLIP.BAT   A batch file used for starting the PHONE.EXE program. This file lets you run PHONE.EXE and start another DOS dial-in direct program at the same time.

TERMIN.COM   A program used to remove UMSLIP.COM from memory.

UMSLIP.COM   A *packet driver*; a program that makes your computer's serial port look like a network connection.

UMSLIP.TXT   A text file with information about UMSLIP.COM.

You also need the PHONE.DOC file: the full instructions for this program. This may be in the same archive file with all the others, or it may be in the same FTP directory.

Once you extract the files from the compressed archive, add the UMSLIP directory to your PATH statement in your AUTOEXEC.BAT file. Using a text editor program (for instance, EDIT, which comes with DOS 5.0 and above), add the name of the directory in which you placed the UMSLIP files to the PATH line. For example, if you see something like

   PATH C:\DOS;C:\WORD;C:\WINDOWS

then add the UMSLIP directory to the end. You need a semicolon between each directory name. It should look something like this when you finish:

   PATH C:\DOS;C:\WORD;C:\WINDOWS;C:\UMSLIP

An Exercise for the Adventurous: Writing an UMSLIP Script

Unless you happen to be a University of Minnesota student or faculty member, or unless your service provider has a prewritten UMSLIP script for your use, you have to write a script. There's no way around it, so quit whining.

Let's get started. I assume that you are at the DOS prompt, in the directory where you placed UMSLIP. First, you need to create a script file. To do this, type **umslip** and press **Enter**. This loads the UMSLIP program into memory so the Phone program can work.

Next, type **phone write** and press **Enter**. This creates two files: PHONE.CFG and PHONE.CMD. The second of these, PHONE.CMD, is a script file that you can edit. In fact, that's the next step: open the PHONE.CMD program in a text editor. If you have a recent version of DOS (5.0 or above), you can type **edit phone.cmd** to put the file into the DOS Editor.

Theory Break: What Are We Doing Here?

Before we go on, let me explain what this script we're creating actually does.

There are two main areas in this PHONE.CMD script that you now see on your screen (assuming you completed the steps I just listed): the modems and the hosts. The modems section contains different scripts for different modems. Later, when we enter configuration data into PHONE.EXE, you will select the type of modem that you have. That tells the program which of the modem scripts to run. Unless you're a real techno-weenie who wants to fool with it, or unless you have a really odd modem, you can leave the modem scripts alone, and move onto the host scripts.

Look through the file until you see a modem name that matches the modem you use. For instance, you'll see *Modem.ADI.Dial*, *Modem.US-Robotics-Sport.Dial*, and so on. If you can find your modem, that's the one you will select later. If you can't find it, you have two options: either create another modem script for your modem using the same format as the others or select *Modem.Hayes.Dial*. If you want to create your own script, you'd better understand what you are doing; you may just want to select the *Modem.Hayes.Dial* script and hope for the best. (Most modems are Hayes-compatible.)

The host login script tells the program what to expect from the service provider's system, and what information it has to send. You'll find the host area at the bottom of the file. It's the part we want to modify.

...And Now Back to Our Script-Making

Look for a section that starts with **#Procedure Host.UofM.Login**. This is the login used for the University of Minnesota. It's the sample that you'll use to create the login for your own service provider.

In theory, the best way would be to copy the entire UofM host login script, paste it at the end of the file, then modify the pasted copy for your own system. Then start modifying (your copy, not the original) by changing the following lines:

```
#Procedure Host.UofM.Login
EndProcedure   Host.UofM.Login
Procedure Host.UofM.LogOut
EndProcedure   Host.UofM.LogOut
```

to something like this:

```
#Procedure Host.yourhostname.Login
EndProcedure   Host.yourhostname.Login
Procedure Host.yourhostname.LogOut
EndProcedure   Host.yourhostname.LogOut
```

However, I found this didn't work on the system I played with. The *only* way I could get the system to dial using my script was to modify the UofM script, leaving the UofM name in place; I didn't put my hostname in there. (It doesn't matter much; you simply use this information to tell the program which script to run.) You can try it both ways, if you want; maybe my version had a bug that later versions will fix.

Editing the Host Login Script: Down to the Nitty-Gritty

Let's take a look at the script I created (by modifying the UofM script). I referred to the test session I ran in Chapter 8 to find the necessary system prompts and responses.

```
Procedure          Host.UofM.Login
TimeOut 60         'The server is not responding.'
Expect    'Username:'
Message            'Sending your user name and password.'
```

```
 Send '%u<'
 Expect    'ssword:'
Private
 Send '%p<'
Message          'Username and password sent'
Reject    'Access denied'   'Your user name or password was
not accepted.'
TimeOut 8     'SLIP server did not respond to your validation
request.'
Expect     'continue '
TimeOut 10     'SLIP server did not respond to SLIP command.'
 Send 'slip<'
 Expect 'Your address'
#Grab MYIP
 Message 'Login to SLIP server successful.'
EndProcedure   Host.UofM.Login


Procedure Host.UofM.LogOut
EndProcedure   Host.UofM.LogOut
```

Let's look at it piece by piece. First, remember that by the time the program gets here, it has already run the modem script; the system has already connected to the service provider's system.

```
Procedure         Host.UofM.Login
```

This is simply the script name. I didn't bother to change it to my own service provider's name, remember, because the bug in my version means that the program only works with the Host. UofM Login script.

```
TimeOut 60        'The server is not responding.'
```

This means that if the system waits for 60 seconds and doesn't get a response from the service provider's system, it displays the message **The server not responding**.

```
Expect    'Username:'
```

This line tells the program to expect to see the word **Username:**. Look back at my test session in Chapter 8, and you'll see that this is the text my service provider's system prompts me with.

```
Message          'Sending your user name and password.'
```

Yep, another "this is what's happening" message. The script throws this message up on the screen to reassure you that your user name and password are being sent.

```
Send '%u<'
```

This tells the program to send my username (%u) followed by a carriage return (<). The **%u** command means "grab my username from the configuration file." We'll look at that in a moment.

```
Expect   'ssword:'
```

Now we are waiting for the **password:** prompt.

```
Private
```

This command means "display ##### when you send the next line, so anyone looking at the screen can't see the text." I don't really know why it's here. One might think it was to stop the password being displayed, but the password isn't displayed even if this command is not here.

```
Send '%p<'
```

Now we are sending the password (%p) and a carriage return. Again, the **%p** means "send the password I entered into the configuration."

```
Message          'Username and password sent'
```

Another info message.

```
Reject   'Access denied'   'Your user name or password was
not accepted.'
```

If for some reason your service provider rejects you, you'll see this message.

```
TimeOut 8    'SLIP server did not respond to your validation
request.'
```

We're now giving the service provider eight seconds to send the next Expect text. If it doesn't, we'll see the above message.

```
Expect    'continue '
```

This is what we are looking for. Look at my session in Chapter 8 to see why; the line at which I send the **slip** command ends with the word *continue*. Yours may vary.

```
TimeOut 10     'SLIP server did not respond to SLIP command.'
```

We're now giving the service provider's system 10 seconds to respond to the next line that we are going to send.

```
Send 'slip<'
```

This is the **slip** command we have to send, followed by a carriage return (<).

```
Expect 'Your address'
```

We're telling the program to look for the words **Your address**. (See my test session.)

```
#Grab MYIP
```

This is, apparently, a command that tells the program to grab my IP address when the service provider's system sends it. However, the command is undocumented, so I'm not using it. You can tell I'm not using it because of the # sign at the beginning of the line, which means "skip this line."

```
Message 'Login to SLIP server successful.'
```

Another info message.

```
EndProcedure    Host.UofM.Login
```

This line tells the program that the host has finished.

```
Procedure Host.UofM.LogOut
EndProcedure   Host.UofM.LogOut
```

The sample script has QUIET ON and QUIET OFF commands. I took these out, because I like to see what's going on during login. These commands tell the program not to display anything being sent by the service provider's system between the ON and OFF commands.

These two lines are for the logout script. When you hang up, the program does simply that—sends a hang up command to the modem. If you have to use certain commands first, to inform the service provider's system that you are logging out, you can put them between these lines. You may not (probably won't?) have to mess with this.

There are many more options for the scripts. Read mine; try to put yours together in a similar way, and if you need to do more, read the scripts section in the PHONE.DOC file. When you finish the script, save it, and close the text editor.

Logging On with UMSLIP—The Rest Is Easy

The next step to logging on with UMSLIP is very simple. Follow this procedure:

1. At the DOS prompt, type **slip setup** and press **Enter**. The PHONE screen appears.

2. Press **F4** or select **Setup|Modem** to see the Modem Settings dialog box.

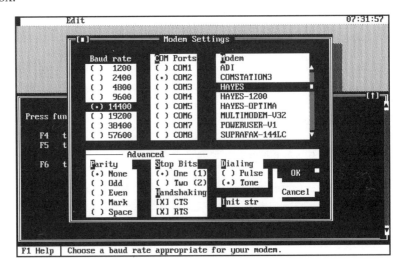

The Modem Settings dialog box is where you tell your modem how to connect to your service provider.

3. Make any changes needed to the following settings:

   Baud rate   Enter the baud rate you will use to connect.

   COM Ports   Select the COM port you are using.

   Modem   Remember the modem scripts in the PHONE.CMD file? You can see each one listed here. Select the one you want to use. If you are not sure, use HAYES.

CTS, RTS   CTS is Clear To Send; RTS is Request To Send. Both are forms of *hardware handshaking*, a method that modems use to synchronize their transmissions correctly, so they don't lose data.

   Parity   Select the parity you will use. You'll probably use None. Check the table in Chapter 8.

   Stop Bits   Select the Stop Bits you will use. You'll probably use 1. Check the table in Chapter 8.

   Handshaking   Check with your service provider on this. You may want to turn handshaking off (make sure there is no check mark in the check boxes). If you have a data-compression modem (most are, these days), you'll probably need to turn on both options.

   Dialing   Select the type of dialing your phone system uses (probably Tone). If your telephone makes a beep sound when you dial, it's Tone; if it makes a click-click-click sound it's a pulse telephone (though the line still may be a tone line). Select tone unless you are sure it's pulse. (If it doesn't work, you can always come back.)

   Init String   You can probably leave this empty. It's sent just before the modem dials, and can be used to set up the modem in some way. But most of that is done by the modem scripts, so you can ignore this.

4. Click on **OK** when you're finished.

5. Now press **F5** or select **Setup|SLIP** to see the Slip Setup dialog box, with a list of the available host scripts. Or not. If there's only one host script in PHONE.CMD, it doesn't bother displaying the list—why bother, after all? So, if you are dialing into the University of Minnesota, or if you modified the UofM script rather than creating a new one, you won't see the list.

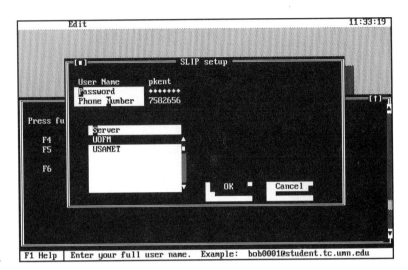

Enter your login information into the SLIP setup dialog box.

6. Enter the pertinent information in the SLIP setup dialog box:

   User Name   Enter the username you use to log in to your service provider's system.

   Password   Type your password very carefully; you won't see it on the screen as you type.

   Phone Number   Enter the phone number you need to dial. Remember to include any extras: 800 numbers, a number to get an outside line (9, for instance), and a number to turn off call waiting (usually *70).

   Server   Select the host script you want to use. Remember though, this wouldn't work when I tried it. If I try to use my USANET script, PHONE just locks up. But if I select the UOFM script, it works.

7. Click on **OK** when you finish.

But Does UMSLIP Work?

Well, let's find out. First, click on the window's maximize arrow (the little up arrow in the top right corner of the Transaction Log window). Then select **Actions|Dial**. Your script begins running, and you see the messages you entered into the script as it runs. These messages are very handy, because if anything goes wrong, you see how far you got in the script. Then you can return to the script and figure out what you did wrong.

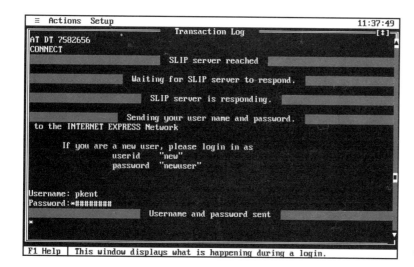

Testing your connection.

When you finally connect, you know that the system works. You can now leave this setup area. Select **Actions|Exit**.

The manner in which we just dialed into your service provider is not the way you'll usually do it. Normally, you will go to the DOS prompt and type **slip dial**. This runs the SLIP.BAT file, which can do various things according to the word you enter after **slip**: Typing **dial** makes it run the UMSLIP program, which loads the packet drivers, then runs the PHONE program, making it dial your service provider.

Here's the procedure:

1. At the DOS prompt, type **slip dial** and press **Enter**. The same screen you worked in when you set up and tested UMSLIP appears. Your system will log on to the service provider's system. The screen then closes, and you're back at the DOS prompt.

2. Start your other DOS dial-in direct programs (yes, you'll get to that in a minute).

3. When you have closed your dial-in direct programs and want to close the connection to your service provider, at the DOS prompt type **slip quit**. The UMSLIP screen appears again, hangs up your modem, then closes. You end up at the DOS prompt again.

Easy, eh?

There's one thing left: what software are you going to use with UMSLIP, in step 2?

Other DOS Software: Now What Do I Do?

There's a lot of DOS software around. You can find a great little program called Minuet, which we'll look at in a moment. It's well worth checking out, because it's a multiple-purpose tool: e-mail, FTP, newsreader, finger, Telnet, and more.

You should also check out the SLIPDISK.ZIP file that you can find in various places: it contains a DOS gopher, a Telnet program, and an e-mail system. (It also comes with another dialer you can experiment with.) See Chapter 27 for more information about finding programs.

PC Gopher II

I'm not going to tell you that *all* DOS programs are going to be simple to set up. However, PC Gopher II—a gopher client from the U of M (do they do any teaching over there?)—is very easy. (See Chapter 27 for information on where to find the program.) Here's all you do:

Confused about step 2? Use the **MD** command to make a directory, the **COPY** command to copy, and the **CD** command to change to the directory. See your DOS manual or online help for more help.

1. Start UMSLIP, in the manner just described.

2. Make a directory for the PC Gopher files, and copy them into it. Then change to that directory and type **Gopher**. The program will start and try to connect to a gopher server.

3. Select **Options|Configure**.

4. Now, look back at the table you filled in Chapter 8. Enter all the information into the appropriate blanks on-screen.

5. Click on the **OK** button to close the Network Configuration box.

6. Select **File|New Gopher** to connect to the gopher server.

7. Use the gopher in the same way you use the basic UNIX gopher you are used to, except you can double-click to move around instead of using the Enter key.

TECHNO NERD TEACHES...

There are two settings in the Options box we haven't discussed. **Allow Telnet Sessions** (which means, if selected, that you can run a Telnet session from the Gopher—if you have a Telnet application, of course) and **New Gopher on Startup**, which means that PC Gopher will try to connect to the gopher server you just entered automatically when you start the system. If you didn't set this, you'll have to use the **File|New Gopher** command (Alt-G).

It doesn't have many features, but it's quick and easy. Notice the **File|Open Bookmark List** option. If you want to save a gopher menu, use that menu option to open the Bookmark List, click on the Add button, type a name, and click on **OK** to save the menu option for future reference.

```
 ≡  File  Window  Options                        210304    16:19:18
 ┌──────────────────────── PC Gopher II ──────────────────────────┐
 <F> .message
 <F> .notar
 <D> 4dos
 <F> DIRLIST.TXT
 <┌─[■]──────────────────── DIRLIST.TXT ────────────────────[↑]─┐
 <│SimTel Software Repository /SimTel/msdos directories as of July 23, 1994
 <│
 <│4dos            4DOS command processor and utilities
 <│ada             ADA programming language-related files
 <│ai              Artificial intelligence-related utilities
 <│animate         Animation players and utilities
 <│archiver        Archiving programs (ARC, ARJ, LZH, UC2, etc.)
 <│arcutil         Utilities for handling archived files
 <│asm_mag         Assembly Language 'Magazine'
 <│asmutil         Assembly language source code, libraries & utilities
 │astrnomy        Astronomy-related programs and utilities
 │at              Utilities for PC AT+ machines
 │autocad         AutoCad and AutoLisp utilities
 │awk             MS-DOS versions of Unix awk programming language
 │bakernws        Baker's PC press releases
 └◄■─────────────────────────────────────────────────────────►┘
F10 Menus  Alt-X Exit  Alt-G New Gopher  Alt-F3 Close
```

Gophering made simple.

This is a nice, simple little gopher. However, if you really want a neat gopher, you'll have to check out the Windows versions later in this book. Hey, I told you DOS is lagging behind Windows, didn't I?

NCSA Telnet & FTP

Here's another simple one: a program that lets you run both Telnet and FTP sessions (see Chapter 27 for details on finding it). You place the files in a directory, start UMSLIP, then type **telbin** at the DOS prompt, and press **Enter**. The program starts. You press **Alt-A** to start a connection, and then dial in the Telnet address. Fairly simple, but it may take a little while to remember the commands and figure out what everything does (there's no documentation, at least not in the version I found).

Is it easier than using Telnet from the UNIX shell? No, not much. You can say the same for NCSA FTP. It's easy to start (just type **ftpbin** once you've got UMSLIP running), but once it's running, it's no better than UNIX FTP. It is pretty much a DOS version of UNIX FTP. (At the **ftp>** prompt, type **help** to see all the commands.)

Trumpet: You Need the News

You really need a good newsreader, so you can while away the hours in the world's newsgroups. Try Trumpet, for instance (it comes in the SLIPDISK.ZIP file). Again, once you have UMSLIP setup, Trumpet is easy to install.

This time, don't start UMSLIP yet. Go to the Trumpet directory, type **news** and press **Enter**. When you get to the main screen, select **Special|Setup**. Then enter the information you gathered in Chapter 8. Click on **OK**, then select **Quit**, start UMSLIP, and then restart Trumpet. The program should automatically connect and display a list of news groups.

Trumpet looks in the TRUMPET.INI file for a list of newsgroups that you have subscribed to. To see the full list from your service provider, press the **Ins** key, and Trumpet will grab the full list; it'll probably take a while. Then you can subscribe to the ones you want.

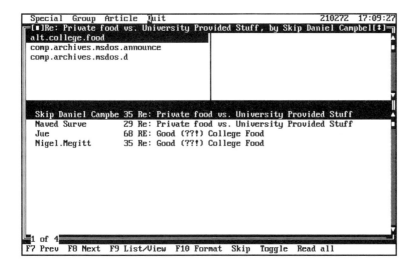

```
 Special  Group  Article  Quit                        210272  17:09:27
┌[■]Re: Private food vs. University Provided Stuff, by Skip Daniel Campbel[‡]┐
 alt.college.food
 comp.archives.msdos.announce
 comp.archives.msdos.d




 Skip Daniel Campbe 35 Re: Private food vs. University Provided Stuff
 Naved Surve        29 Re: Private food vs. University Provided Stuff
 Jue                68 RE: Good (??!) College Food
 Nigel.Megitt       35 Re: Good (??!) College Food




■1 of  4
 F7 Prev  F8 Next  F9 List/View  F10 Format  Skip  Toggle  Read all
```

Trumpet, a nice, little newsreader, easy to install and easy to use.

Minuet: You *Must* Try This One

You really should check out Minuet, yet *another* goodie from the U of M. This one's easy to install, but better still, you are actually installing *ten* different applications: an e-mail program, a news reader, a gopher, a simple Telnet program, a nice FTP program that displays directories at the FTP site in a "tree" format, Webster, Ping, a couple of different calculators, a calendar, and an "IP Finder." (Check Chapter 27 for information on finding Minuet.) By the way, this isn't simply named after a 17th century dance. It's an acronym, in the best tradition of the Internet. It means, *Minnesota Internet User's Essential Tools.*

Minuetting Step By Step

Alright, let's take this slowly. The first thing you do is place Minuet in a directory and start UMSLIP. Then, at the DOS prompt and in the minuet directory, type **minuet** and **press Enter**.

Once you are into the program, select **Setup|Network**. In the dialog box that appears, enter your computer's IP address, a Net Mask (if your service provider gave you one), and the Gateway and Nameserver addresses. There's lots of other complicated network stuff in here, but you probably don't need to mess with it unless your service provider tells you to do so. Click on the **Test** button, wait a few seconds, and you'll see a box telling you if the system passed or not, and, if it did, how well the connections performed. Once you have the Network stuff running correctly, you can move on.

If there's no Close, OK, or Cancel button, click on the little box in the top left corner of the box.

Next step. Select **Setup|Servers**. In the dialog box that appears, enter the address for your host's Mail (Minuet needs a POP2 or POP3 server), News (NNTP), Gopher, Finger, and Webster. You can enter the actual IP number or the host name. (See Chapter 8 for this information.) You may have to change the port numbers shown for some of these—again, check the table in Chapter 8.

When you have all the numbers in, click on the **Test** button, and Minuet will test each connection. When it's finished, it shows a dialog box displaying the results; if a particular component passed, that component should work correctly. If it didn't... it won't.

One more major step: select **Setup|User**. Enter all the information. The E-Mail Address entry may be your username—all the stuff to the left of the @ sign, or your full e-mail address. Make sure you enter your password correctly; type very carefully, because you won't see it in the box. The rest of the info is optional, though you may as well enter it: the e-mail address you want to appear in the Respond To line of your messages, your full name, and the subdirectory on your hard disk that you want Minuet to place your e-mail into.

Using Minuet: No Problem

That wasn't too hard, and you can easily use the program. You can select the major programs (e-mail, newsgroups, Gopher, Telnet, and FTP) from the Windows menu. The others are hidden. See the three horizontal lines in the top left corner, to the left of the File menu? Click on that and you'll see the other programs. There are three Finger utilities. The Global Address Book and Finger options open exactly the same thing, a Finger utility (one of the developers told me that there were two menu entries simply because most people don't know what Finger means, but they understand what an Address Book is). The U of M Address Book is a Finger program that just searches the U of M.

What else will you find on this menu? The IP Finder: type in a hostname and press **Enter**, and you'll get the IP address for that host. There are two calculators: one simple calculator and one that converts between different bases (decimal, binary, octal, and hexadecimal). There's a ping program: type a hostname or IP address and the program "pings" it for you. There's Webster, a very simple calendar, and an ASCII table—click on a character and you'll see its number in the table.

Now, there's currently no "paper" documentation for Minuet—or files that you can print out—but the online help is good. And if you look around at all the menu options and at the status bar (which shows some commands), you can usually figure out what you need to do. It's an easy application to learn and use.

SPEAK LIKE A GEEK

Webster A little application that lets you check a word's spelling, look up its definition, and use a thesaurus. It connects to a Webster "server," a site somewhere with a Webster's Dictionary just sitting waiting for your request. Unfortunately, I couldn't get it to work. If you want to try, though, you can connect to cs.indiana.edu 2627 or chem.ucsd.edu. These are Telnet sites, too, so you can use Webster directly.

Check out all the other Setup menu options. For example, you can automatically check for mail each time you start the program, add a signature to each message, include the original message in your reply, and so on.

```
 ≡  File  Edit  FTP  Window  Setup  Help                    21:30:55
┌─[■]──────────────── FTP - File Transfer Protocol ════════════[↕]─┐
│ ftp.msstate.edu                                                ▲ │
│   ┌...                                                            │
│   └┬pub...                                                        │
│    └┬pc...                                                        │
│     ├net...                                                       │
│     ├pkz204g.exe - 202.5 k - May 13 14:44                         │
│     └windows...                                                   │
│                                                                ▮  │
│                                                                ▼  │
├──────────────────────────────────────────────────────────────────┤
│The response 'pkent@192.156.196.1' is not valid                 ▲ │
│Next time please use your e-mail address as your password       ▮ │
│       for example: joe@199.190.133.121                           │
│             Welcome to the Mississippi State University archive.  │
│             Local time is Fri Jul 29 22:30:26 1994               │
│All transfers are logged with your host name and email address.   │
│If you don't like this policy, disconnect now.                    │
│If your FTP client crashes or hangs shortly after login, try      │
│using a dash (-) as the first character of your password.  This ▼ │
└═ FTP Idle ═══════════════════════════════════════════════════════┘
 F1 Help  F3 Fetch File      F4 Send File       F6 Delete File
```

Minuet comes with a decent FTP utility.

The Least You Need to Know

☞ The DOS dial-in direct software is not as good as the Windows programs.

☞ Installing UMSLIP, a SLIP program, can be tricky, but once installed, it's usually easy to install other dial-in direct programs.

☞ PC Gopher II is a good DOS gopher client and very easy to install.

☞ You should check out Minuet, a simple multi-task application; there's FTP, Telnet, Mail, News, Finger, Gopher, and more.

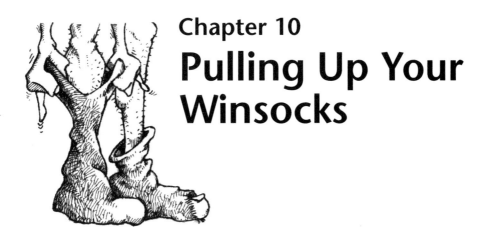

Chapter 10
Pulling Up Your Winsocks

In This Chapter

- ☞ Deciding which WINSOCK.DLL to use
- ☞ Installing Trumpet Winsock for a dial-in direct connection
- ☞ Writing a Trumpet Winsock login script
- ☞ Setting Trumpet Winsock options

I'll warn you now—this chapter's the toughest in this book. Once you're past this point, installing that really neat Windows software is going to be a snap. So grab a bottle of aspirin and a pot of coffee, take a deep breath, and read on. If you've read Chapter 7, you know that you need to install a file called WINSOCK.DLL in order to run Windows on the Internet. WINSOCK.DLL is a *dynamic link library*, a system from which programs can "borrow" when they want to carry out some common task.

WINSOCK.DLL provides a way for Windows programs to communicate across a TCP/IP link. That makes it much easier for software writers to create new Internet programs. Instead of writing a program that contains the necessary tools to transmit data over a TCP/IP link, all a programmer needs to do is write a program that can talk to WINSOCK.DLL. For example, the programmer who created WS_FTP, an excellent FTP program for Windows, just needs to concentrate on the FTP features. (See Chapter 11 for information about this program.) He doesn't really care about transmitting information directly to and from the Internet; he just cares about sending it to and from WINSOCK.DLL, and WINSOCK.DLL takes care of the rest.

That means a lot of Windows software can't talk directly to the net. They have to have WINSOCK.DLL first. And although various programmers have created a WINSOCK.DLL, there's a set of standards—the *Windows Sockets* standards—that define what the file should do. A program that can work with one version of WINSOCK.DLL should be able to work with any of them.

Decisions, Decisions—Which Do I Use?

Which to use? Easy question:

- ☛ If you are using a commercial Internet package, such as Internet Chameleon or WinGopher, use the WINSOCK.DLL that came with the product.

- ☛ If you have the new version of Microsoft Windows (unreleased at the date of writing; it's currently known as Windows 4.0 or Chicago, but might have a completely different name when released), use the WINSOCK.DLL that comes with Windows. This version should also come with a dialer, so you can use it for permanent or dial-in direct connections. (It may actually be a .VBX file rather than a .DLL, but the principle is the same; just follow the instructions for installing the TCP/IP stack.)

- ☛ If you have Windows for Workgroups 3.11 and are setting up a permanent (not dial-in direct) connection, get hold of the latest TCP/IP software. See Chapter 27 for more information on finding the software.

- ☛ If you want to install shareware, freeware, or public domain Windows software, use the Trumpet Winsock. See Chapter 27 for information on where to find this.

General Winsock Installation Wisdom

First, before you do anything, *talk to your service provider*. Some service providers have already set up the necessary files—just download the files, make a few small changes, and away you go. If your service provider has done this, you can save a lot of time by grabbing those files. However, you may (probably) find that your service provider's documentation is still rather vague. Try to get Winsock up and running, but if you have problems, come back to this chapter and see if I can help.

If your service provider doesn't have a Winsock setup available for users, ask yourself this: "If I try to go it alone, will I get any help from the service provider?" This is not something that's easy to do on your own. One service provider told me, "We'll connect the SLIP account on our end, but if you have problems with your SLIP software, that's your problem. We can't help."

Maybe I'm making this all sound too complicated. You might get your connection running in a few minutes and wonder what I'm talking about. I hope this chapter will help you avoid the problems I've run into!

They then went ahead and made several mistakes in setting up my account, making it impossible for me to connect the SLIP account. If you want to connect a SLIP or PPP account, you must have a cooperative service provider. If you think you can rely on your service provider to help, go ahead and find the compressed file containing all the Trumpet Winsock bits and pieces (see Chapter 27). At the time of writing, the most recent "release" version was version 1.0A (though there's a beta version 1.0.B.10).

Assuming You Chose Trumpet Winsock...

The rest of this chapter concerns installing Trumpet Winsock, the most popular WINSOCK.DLL widely available on the Internet. This is a shareware product; the registration fee is $20. You can use this program to connect in either of two ways: to a dial-in direct account using SLIP or CSLIP, or to a network with an Ethernet *packet driver* already installed and a permanent connection to the Internet.

If you are planning to install on a network, you'll have to look elsewhere for help. There are many different configurations, and how you install Trumpet Winsock will depend on how you are running your network. If you are the network's system administrator, you'll probably be able to figure it out from the Trumpet Winsock documentation relatively

Packet driver A packet driver is a program that sends "packets" of data out through your network card and across the network. Ethernet is a common form of Local Area Network.

easily. If you are not, talk with the administrator and find out if he can help. An ordinary user shouldn't be messing with this sort of thing, anyway. If you know nothing about network software, don't touch it.

Okay, so, if you want to install Trumpet Winsock for use with a dial-in direct account, follow the steps below. If you don't, skip to Chapter 11.

Let's run through installing Trumpet Winsock step by step.

1. Start by creating a directory from which you will run Winsock. Call this something like **C:\WINSOCK** or **C:\TRUMPET**.

2. Copy the Winsock files to the directory. You'll probably have these files:

   BUGS.LST A text file containing information about Winsock versions and bugs.

   BYE.CMD A text file containing the commands sent to your modem to end a session.

   DISCLAIM.TXT A text file containing a disclaimer and copyright notice.

   HOSTS A sample text file containing a list of host names. Some TCP/IP programs may refer to this list, but most don't, so you can forget about it for now.

   INSTALL.DOC A text file containing the Winsock user manual.

   INSTALL.TXT A Word for Windows file containing the Winsock user manual.

   LOGIN.CMD A text file containing the commands sent to your modem to begin a session.

   PROTOCOL A text file containing a list of Internet protocols. Not used for dial-in direct connections.

   README.MSG A short text file providing the software author's e-mail address.

SERVICES   A text file containing a list of Internet services. Not used for dial-in direct connections.

TCPMAN.EXE   The program that you run to set up and use the WINSOCK.DLL program.

WINSOCK.DLL   The Windows dynamic link library that is the "guts" of TCP/IP driver.

Later, after running setup, you'll find a **TRUMPWSK.INI** file in this directory. This is a text file containing the initialization information used when starting a Winsock session. It's created the first time you enter setup information.

3. Use Windows Notepad or Windows Sysedit to change the PATH statement in your AUTOEXEC.BAT file to include the name of the directory you put the Winsock files into. For example, if you put them in **C:\TRUMPET**, make sure the path statement contains **C:\TRUMPET** (such as, PATH C:\DOS;C:\WINDOWS;C:\TRUMPET). (You can find the AUTOEXEC.BAT file in your root directory.)

4. Reboot your computer and then restart Windows.

5. Start the **TCPMAN.EXE** program. You can create an icon, if you want, and start the program by double-clicking on the icon. Or select **Run** from the Program Manager or File Manager **File** menu, then type **TCPMAN** and click on **OK**. The program will start. (If it doesn't, you didn't put the path information into AUTOEXEC.BAT correctly.) The Trumpet Winsock Network Configuration dialog box should appear (see the following figure).

I'm going to assume you understand a few basics, such as how to create directories and copy files, and how to edit an AUTOEXEC.BAT file. If you don't, you may find Winsock a little more of a problem than you imagine. Pick up *The Complete Idiot's Guide to DOS* for a quick education on the subject.

The next time you start Winsock, this dialog box won't appear. You can open it later by selecting the **File|Setup** option from within Trumpet Winsock.

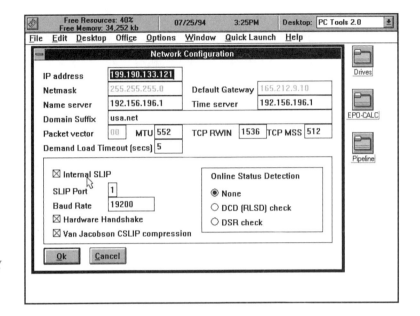

The Trumpet Winsock Network Configuration dialog box, after you have entered all the data.

6. Go find the data you collected in Chapter 8. You're going to need this data to set up Trumpet Winsock.

7. Click on the **Internal SLIP** check box. This disables certain options you don't need, and enables others that you do need. (If you were connecting to a network with a permanent connection, you would leave the Internal SLIP check box cleared.)

8. Type your Internet Protocol address into the **IP address** text box. This is the address by which your computer will be identified on the Internet once connected. (In some rare cases, you may have to type **bootp** instead of a number. Only do so if instructed by your service provider.)

9. Now enter your service provider's domain nameserver IP address into the **Name server** text box. If you have more than one nameserver IP address, you can enter them one after the other, leaving a single space between each one.

10. The **Time server** option is, at the time of writing, unused, though future versions may use it. If so, your service provider will give you the time server address.

11. Enter the domain name given to you by your service provider. For instance, if you connect to Internet Express, and your e-mail

address is jbloe@usa.net, you'll type **usa.net** in the **Domain Suffix** text box. You may be given several domain names to put in here; separate them within spaces.

12. **TCP MSS** means *Transmission Control Protocol Maximum Segment Size*, some kind of network thing (measured in bytes) you don't need to worry about too much. If you are using a SLIP account, enter 512; if you are using a CSLIP account, use 254. If your service provider suggests certain values for this and the next two items, use those instead.

13. **TCP RWIN** means *Transmission Control Protocol Receive Window*, another esoteric network term. Make this value about three to four times the TCP MSS value; say, 1536 for SLIP and 765 for CSLIP.

14. **MTU** is the *Maximum Transmission Unit*. (Yes, another one.) This is usually the TCP MSS value plus 40; 552 for SLIP and 294 for CSLIP.

15. The **Demand Load Timeout** is the number of seconds that the Trumpet Winsock program remains loaded after an application has finished with it. You can leave this set to 5 seconds.

16. Enter the port number of your COM port that your modem connects to in the **SLIP port** text box. Enter **1** for COM1, **2** for COM2, and so on.

17. In the **Baud Rate** text box, enter the modem speed you want to use. If you have a 14,400 bps modem, try entering 19,200.

18. If your service provider's system supports a *hardware handshake*, also known as *hardware flow control* (a method for two modems to keep synchronized during transmissions), check the **Hardware Handshake** check box. Also, if your modem does not use hardware handshake as the default, you need to turn it on in the login script. See your modem's documentation for information for the correct command.

19. If you have a CSLIP connection, check the **Van Jacobsen CSLIP Compression** check box.

20. If your modem can use DCD (Data Carrier Detect) or DSR (Data Set Ready), click on the appropriate **Online Status** option button. These are methods that modems use to tell a program their online status. You may need to turn on the feature if it is not the

modem's default. In the script, you would have to use the modem command for turning it on. (Generally, AT&C1 for DCD and AT&S1 for DSR.)

21. Click on the **OK** button. You'll see a message telling you to restart Trumpet Winsock.

22. Click on the **OK** button in the message box, then select **File|Exit** to close Trumpet Winsock.

23. Reopen **Trumpet Winsock**.

Whew! You made it. But no, the TCP/IP hell week isn't over yet. It's time to set up your log in script. Read on.

Script Writing 101

It's time to write (or, at least edit) the script that Trumpet Winsock will follow when connecting. First, go find the sample login session you created in Chapter 8. Then select **Dialler|Edit Scripts** in Trumpet Winsock. A typical File Open dialog box appears. Double-click on the **login.cmd** file, and the login script appears in a Notepad window. Here's the script you'll see:

```
# initialize modem
#
output atz\13
input 10 OK\n
#
# set modem to indicate DCD
#
output at&c1
input 10 OK\n
#
# send phone number
#
output atdt242284\13
#
# my other number
#
#output atdt241644\13
#
```

```
# now we are connected.
#
input 30 CONNECT
#
#  wait till it's safe to send because some modem's hang up
#  if you transmit during the connection phase
#
wait 30 dcd
#
# now prod the terminal server
#
output \13
#
#  wait for the username prompt
#
input 30 username:
username Enter your username
output \u\13
#
# and the password
#
input 30 password:
password Enter your password
output \p\13
#
# we are now logged in
#
input 30 >
#
# see who on for informational reasons.
#
output who\13
input 30 >
#
# jump into slip mode
#
output slip\13
#
# wait for the address string
#
```

```
input 30 Your address is
#
# parse address
#
address 30
input 30 \n
#
# we are now connected, logged in and in slip mode.
#
display \n
display Connected.  Your IP address is \i.\n
#
#  ping a well known host locally...  our slip server won't
work
#  for a while
#
exec pingw 131.217.10.1
#
# now we are finished.
```

All the lines that begin with # are simply comment lines; they don't do anything. Let's break the script down, piece by piece.

output atz\13   First, at the top, you have the initial message sent to the modem. The line means "send the ATZ command." This command resets the modem, clearing out any settings that it may have picked up from an earlier communications session. (/13 means "send a carriage return, the same as pressing **Enter** or **Return.**)

input 10 OK\n   This means "wait 10 seconds to see if the modem sends the OK signal back." OK means that it's ready to receive more commands.

output at&c1   This is a message being sent to the modem; at&c1 turns on the Data Carrier Detect feature of your modem, if available. DCD sends a signal to the program when connecting to or disconnecting from another modem. In some cases, you may have to modify this line, if your modem can't seem to connect to the service provider's. If so, talk with the service provider's technical support about what you should use.

input 10 OK\n   Again, the script waits for up to ten seconds for the modem to respond.

output atdt242284\13   This line sends the telephone number to the modem; the modem dials the number. Replace the number (after the

t and before the **\)** with the number you need to dial to connect to your service provider. If you need to add a number to get an outside line, precede the phone number with that number and a comma or two for a pause, for example, **9,,5551212**. If you are dialing long distance, include all the necessary numbers (such as **18005551212**). If you have call waiting on the line you are using, use the correct code to turn it off, along with a comma or two to create a pause (usually *70 as in **9,,*70,,5551212**).

 # my other number and **#output atdt241644\13**   This is a sample script, and below where you change your telephone number is space for an additional number, in case the first is busy. If you have two numbers, place the second number in this space. Remember to remove the # sign from the start of the line.

input 30 CONNECT   The script now waits up to 30 seconds for the message from the modem informing the program that it has connected to the other modem. That message is, for most modems, CONNECT, so it's unlikely that you will have to change this line.

wait 30 dcd   This tells the script to wait for 30 seconds, to make sure you fully connect before continuing. When you've established a connection for the first time you may want to experiment with this number, to reduce it and speed up your connection time. The **dcd** at the end of the line means "wait for a Data Carrier Detect single from the modem." You can remove this if you want.

output \13   This is a sample script, and the way in which your service provider's system works will probably differ from this sample system. In this sample, after connecting, a user has to press **Enter** to send a carriage return to get the host's "attention." This line sends the carriage return. Your system may not require this.

input 30 username: This line tells the script to wait for up to 30 seconds for the **username** prompt. Your system may not have such a prompt, though. The prompt may be **login:**, for example. If so, replace the word **username** with **login:**.

Make sure you enter the text that is being waited for exactly like it appears on the screen. If your service provider's system displays the word *username*, don't enter **Username** or **USERNAME**. The case of each letter must be correct. If there's a colon at the end of the word, include that. Make sure you don't add any spaces after the word.

username Enter your username   This line tells Trumpet Winsock to display a dialog box at this point. The dialog box will say "Enter your username." (You can change that to login, if you want.) You will have to type your name and then press **Enter**. If you would rather have the script enter your username automatically for you, remove this line.

output \u\13   This tells the script to send the username you typed into the dialog box. If you removed the previous line, though, you should replace the **\u** with your username, leaving a space between **output** and your username. For example, **output pkent\13**.

input 30 password: This time we're waiting for the password. Same warning applies; make sure you get the case of the prompt correct (Password or password or PASSWORD). Include a colon if necessary; don't add extra spaces.

You wouldn't want to break the first rule of security—*Don't write down your password!*—would you?

password Enter your password   Again, this tells the program to display a dialog box into which you can type your password. If you don't want to type it—if you want to automatically send your password—remove this line.

output \p\13   This tells the script to send the password you just typed in. If you deleted the previous line, you must use your actual password, replacing the **\p**. For example, **output *password*\13**.

input 30 >   This tells the program to wait for the > prompt. There's a good chance that your system won't display a > prompt. (In a moment, I'll show you what my script does after the password.)

output who\13   This line sends the word **who**, to run the UNIX **who** command (which shows you who is logged on).

input 30 >   Again, we're waiting for the > prompt.

output slip\13   Now we send the word **slip**, the command that puts the system into slip mode.

input 30 Your address is   We're waiting here for the words **Your address is**. That's the line where the service provider tells you your IP address.

address 30   This means "take a look at the IP address that's about to be sent, and store the address."

input 30 \n This says, "wait for the IP address."

display \n This says, "display a carriage return and line feed on the screen." That is, move all the previous text up a line.

display Connected. Your IP address is \i.\n This says "display the words **Connected. Your IP address is**," followed by the IP address that has just been stored, followed by a carriage return and line feed. The term **\i** is the IP address that has been stored. **\n** is a carriage return and line feed.

exec pingw 131.217.10.1 This executes the **pingw** program, which automatically pings another site for verification that you are up and running. You should remove this, it's really not essential.

My Sample Script

I modified the script we just looked at so it would work on my system. Here's what I ended up with. You can compare it with my sample login session I showed you in Chapter 8.

```
output ATZ&H1\13
input 10 OK\n
output atdt7582656\13
input 45 CONNECT
input 30 sername:
output kent\13
input 30 ssword:
output not.my-real-password\13
input 30 continue
output slip\13
input 30 Your address is
address 30
input 30 \n
display \n
display Connected.  Your IP address is \i.\n
```

This is similar to the sample script we just looked at. Notice these differences, though:

output ATZ&H1\13 I changed this line and used the commands advised by my service provider. This tells my modem to use hardware flow control.

input 30 sername: Notice that I have **sername** instead of **username**. This is common practice in the writing of such scripts, just in case the case of the word is changed (from Username to username or vice versa).

output kent\13 Notice that I'm not using the dialog box to ask for my username, I'm entering it automatically.

input 30 ssword: Again, I've knocked off the first letter (okay, the first two, so I didn't upset anyone) of the prompt the program is looking for.

output not.my-real-password\13 Okay, so I'm breaking a security rule by putting my password in here instead of making Trumpet Winsock prompt me for it. I live in a concrete bunker with one door and no windows and I never leave home, so I figure I'm safe.

input 30 continue As you can see from my session in Chapter 8, my service provider's system will prompt me to "Type "c" followed by <RETURN> to continue." Instead, I have to type **slip** and continue to get into slip mode.

Now, Let's See If It Works...

Save your login script. Then select **Dialler|Login** and the script begins. You can follow through, and if you run into any problems, you can figure out more or less where in the script the problem lies. If you reach the **Script completed SLIP ENABLED** lines, you've succeeded. You are logged in with your SLIP account running (see the following figure). However, if your script just hangs up, you'll need to log out. First, press **Esc**. Then select **Dialler|Bye**. This runs the BYE.CMD script, which tells your modem to hang up. (You may have to try several times to close the script.)

Go examine your script and see where it hung. If you can't find anything obvious, check all your Trumpet Winsock configuration settings, too. Try a different baud rate, perhaps. Make sure you entered the correct IP addresses. Check the script for spelling errors.

If you still can't get it working, talk with your service provider. Maybe you need a particular modem setup. You may need to change the Packet Vectors in the Network Configuration dialog box. You may need to use the **bootp** command somewhere in the script. Your service provider should be able to tell you exactly how to set up your script and configuration. If you register the program, you can contact the program's publisher for technical support.

```
[=]                         Trumpet Winsock                        [▼][↕]
 File   Edit   Info   Trace   Dialler   Help
Executing script e:\slip\Winsock\login.cmd.   Type <esc> to abort
SLIP DISABLED
ATZ&H1
OK
atdt7582656
CONNECT 14400/ARQ

Checking authorization. Please wait...

Welcome to the INTERNET EXPRESS Network

        If you are a new user, please login in as
                userid    "new"
                password  "newuser"


Username: pkent
Password:

Permission granted
[2J
[5;1H                        Community News Service (CNS,Inc.)
[7;1H                               in affiliation with
[8;1H                              ==TELEPHONE EXPRESS==
[13;1H                            If you need assistance,
[14;1H                          please call CNS at 719-592-1240
[19;1H                   Type "c" followed by <RETURN> to continue slip

Switching to SLIP.
Annex address is 165.212.9.10.   Your address is 199.190.133.121.

Connected.   Your IP address is 199.190.133.121.

Script completed
SLIP ENABLED
```

Logging into my SLIP account with Trumpet Winsock.

Getting Out of Cyberspace

To close Trumpet Winsock, first make sure you close all your other TCP/IP programs: your FTP program, your e-mail program, and so on. Then use this method to close:

☞ Use the **Dialler|Bye** command to run the BYE.CMD script, which hangs up the modem.

If you have the **Automatic login and logout on demand** option set (see later in this chapter) you can also use these options:

☞ Double-click on Trumpet Winsock's **Control** menu.

☞ Press **Alt-F4**.

☞ Select **File|Exit**.

If you have any TCP/IP programs running, you'll see a warning message. Also, you'll find

If you don't have the **Automatic login and logout on demand** option set, and you close the window without using **Dialler|Bye** first, Trumpet Winsock will close but will not hangup the connection. Your Internet TCP/IP programs won't be able to run without Trumpet Winsock, even though you are connected to the service provider. Reopen Trumpet Winsock, press **Esc** a couple of times, select **Dialler|Bye**, and then close the window.

that in some circumstances Trumpet Winsock can't close. You'll have to press **Esc** first, then use one of the above methods to close.

Some More Details Before We Leave

There are a few more things to know about Trumpet Winsock. Let's look at some of the other menu options.

Edit|Copy   Highlight text in the Trumpet Winsock window, and then select this option to copy it to the Clipboard. This can be very useful when using the Trace menu commands, if you understand what the text means.

Edit|Clear   Clears all the text from the window.

Info   This isn't in the current Trumpet Winsock documentation. It gives you some sort of strange network stuff. See Trace.

Trace|all sorts of weird stuff   This has a variety of options that you can use to diagnose network connection problems. If you understand what all the terms on the menu mean, you'll know how to use them. If you don't, leave them alone—they can crash the system in some cases.

Dialler|Bye   Runs the BYE.CMD script, which hangs up the modem.

Dialler|Other   You can create other types of scripts that run from this option. For instance, if you have two SLIP accounts, you could run one with the **Dialler|Login** menu option and the other from **Dialler|Other**.

Dialler|Options   This is handy. Select **Automatic login on startup only** to run the LOGIN.CMD script each time you start the Trumpet Winsock application. Select **Automatic login and logout on demand** to automatically run the script when you start the application, and to close Trumpet Winsock automatically after the **SLIP inactivity timeout (minutes)** value. For instance, let's say this value is 5. That means that if you go for five minutes without a TCP/IP program running, Trumpet Winsock will close automatically. It does not mean that if you have a TCP/IP program open and don't use it for five minutes Trumpet Winsock will close, only if there are no such programs open. Also, when you have **Automatic login and logout on demand** selected, closing the Trumpet Winsock window will automatically run the BYE.CMD script, hanging up the phone. (If you want to use this feature but not the inactivity timeout, put **0** in the **SLIP inactivity timeout** text box.)

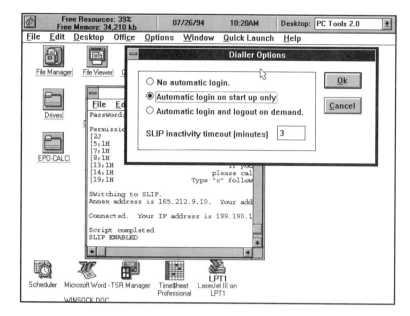

The Dialler Options dialog box lets you automatically start and close Trumpet Winsock.

Dialler|Manual Login   Lets you log into your SLIP account manually, by typing commands into the window. Press **Esc** to end this mode.

Help|About   Displays the Trumpet Winsock version number.

Be Ethical—Register the Program!

Trumpet Winsock can open up a totally new Internet world, letting you bring the 1990s to a system still stuck in the 1970s. If you use Trumpet Winsock for 30 days or more, please register it. You receive a registration number that will remove the UNREGISTERED VERSION signs that appear here and there. You'll also get technical support, and Trumpet Software International says that it will give registered users preference for requests for bug fixes and enhancements.

Working on the Internet with a dial-in terminal account is like writing a book with a typewriter. Working on the Internet once you've got Trumpet Winsock installed is like writing a book with a word processor. Pay the registration fee. (See the end of the INSTALL.TXT or INSTALL.DOC file that came with Trumpet Winsock.)

Where Next?

Once you have your Trumpet Winsock up and running, all you have to do is run your dial-in direct programs: programs that will let you run FTP sessions, work with e-mail and newsgroups, ping other hosts, run Telnet sessions, dig around in gopherspace, fool around in the World Wide Web, and so on. But which programs? On to the next chapters, kemo-sabe.

The Least You Need to Know

- ☞ Don't be intimidated. Installing Trumpet Winsock can be relatively easy if you follow these instructions.

- ☞ You need a login script to automate your connection to your service provider. It's reasonably easy to create one.

- ☞ This program is shareware; remember to register it (it only costs $20).

- ☞ Once Trumpet Winsock is up and running, you can easily install your other Windows Internet software.

Chapter 11
FTP's Finally Fun!

In This Chapter

- ☞ Using WS_FTP, a Windows FTP program
- ☞ Using WS_Archie, a Windows Archie tool
- ☞ Getting files automatically when you find them with WS_Archie
- ☞ Setting up your system as an FTP site, with WFTPD

What's the clunkiest Internet tool? Assuming you're no UNIX lover, assuming you don't think the UNIX shell is the ultimate in programming beauty, which Internet tool do you hate the most? It has to be FTP. Everyone uses e-mail; gopher and WWW are quite straightforward; Telnet is no big deal. However, FTP is just plain clumsy.

It doesn't have to be that way; there are some neat FTP programs for Windows. Imagine being able to see the contents of the FTP site's directories in a list box and the contents of your computer's directories in another. Imagine being able to quickly view the FTP site's index files in Notepad or Windows Write, being able to transfer several files by simply clicking on them and then clicking on a transfer button, and then being able to see what percentage of the file has transferred. Better still, how about integrating Archie and FTP. Search for a file with Archie, then run FTP from within the Archie program to retrieve a file you've found.

As usual, check with Chapter 27 for information on finding this stuff.

If you are planning to build a suite of Windows Internet programs, the very *first* one you should get is an FTP program. Once you have a good FTP program up and running, you'll find getting all the other bits and pieces you need much easier.

There are a few FTP programs around, and they're free or very cheap, too:

- ☛ **WS_FTP**   A great little FTP program.

- ☛ **WS_Archie**   This program lets you use Archie to find the file you want, and then launch WS_FTP to get it.

- ☛ **WinFTP**   Another version of WS_FTP, with a few extra features.

- ☛ **WFTPD**   A program that lets you set up your system as an FTP site, so you can allow other people to access your files.

Remember, you have to install your dial-in direct connection before you can install these programs. But once you have some sort of WINSOCK.DLL up and running (see Chapter 10), installing these FTP programs is very simple.

WS_FTP

Compared to WS_FTP, UNIX FTP is like eating soup with a fork. Not particularly satisfying. WS_FTP is what FTP should be. You have all the commands at your fingertips, and a library of FTP sites to select from—no more mistyping FTP hostnames.

Installing is simple. Just place the files in a directory and create a Program Manager icon. (To do that, drag the WS_FTP.EXE file from File Manager into a program group.) Start your Internet connection and double-click on the icon. The first thing you see is a dialog box asking you for your e-mail address. You can use this when logging on to FTP sites; to start an anonymous FTP session you normally enter your e-mail address instead of a password.

Next, you see the Session Profile dialog box. You can select an FTP site from the list (it comes with about 20 already configured). Or click on **New**, type an FTP site's information in, and then click on the **Save** button. It's all pretty straightforward and well documented; just click on the **Help** button to get information about each field.

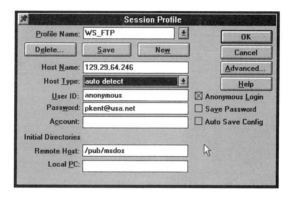

WS_FTP's Session Profile dialog box stores your FTP site information.

When you click on the **OK** button, WS_FTP tries to connect to the FTP site. Once connected, you'll see the FTP site's directories on the right, and the directories on your computer's hard disk on the left.

You can move around in the directories by double-clicking, or by using the **ChgDir** button. This is really handy, because if you know where you want to go, it's a lot quicker to type it in and go directly than to go through each directory in the path to get there. The two buttons you'll use most are the **View** and <— buttons. Let's say you find an index file you want to read. Just click on it, and click on the View button on the right side of the window; it's placed into Notepad so you can read it. And when you find the files you want, hold **Ctrl** and click on each one, then click on the <— button to transfer them to your hard disk.

Some of the buttons you probably won't use much, at least not on the FTP site. You can create a new directory and delete a directory (**ChgDir** and **RmDir**); if you are using an anonymous login, you won't be able to do this on the FTP site. You can also rename and delete files, and even automatically transfer a file and load it into the program the file's extension is associated with in Windows (use the **Exec** button).

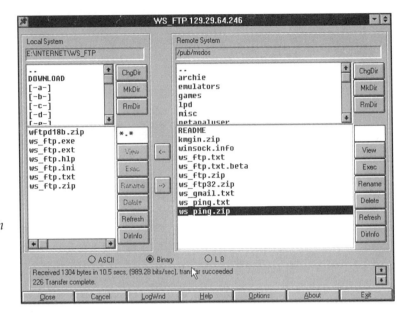

Transferring files with WS_FTP is simple. Click on the file and click on the arrow button.

Sometimes, WS_FTP is unable to figure out what type of host it's connecting to. It can usually do it, but now and then you'll notice strange stuff, such as no directories appearing in the directories list, and file dates appearing instead of file names, or partial file names appearing. When you try to transfer one of these strange files to your system, you'll get a message saying that it doesn't exist.

The online help is very good, and there's a lot more I haven't covered. So read it. Also, try pressing the right mouse button in the window to see a pop-up menu with various options.

This is easy to fix. First, click on the **LogWnd** button to see the session log. You'll see a log showing the entire FTP session from the command-line point of view. Go back to the start and see if you can find the type of host mentioned; usually an FTP site will identify its type.

Then click on the **Options** button, and click on the **Session Options** button in the dialog box that appears. Select the host type in the drop-down list box. If you can't see the host listed, try using the UNIX (default) option.

WinFTP

There's a variation on WS_FTP you may want to check out, WinFTP. John Junod, who wrote WS_FTP, distributed the source code so other people could fool around with it. One of the results is WinFTP. It's very similar to WS_FTP, though it has a few extras, such as the ability to ping the host. However, I prefer WS_FTP because when you maximize the window, the file and directory lists get bigger, showing more information. On the version of WinFTP that I checked out, the list box sizes were fixed (small).

WS_Archie

It's all very well being able to run out and grab files from all over the world, but what if you know the file you want, but not where it is? You need Archie, right? And if FTP is the clunkiest application on the Internet, Archie can't be far behind.

This is why you need WS_Archie. Not only does WS_Archie automate Archie searches, it also automates getting the files you want, by interacting with WS_FTP, ordering it to go and get the file you select.

Get the files, place them in a directory, create a Program Manager icon, start your Internet connection, and then double-click on the WS_Archie icon. When the program opens, select **Options|User Preferences**. In the dialog box that appears, you should select the Default Archie Server, the Archie server you want to use in most cases. This should be an Archie server that is close to you. On the other hand, the ones close to you are probably always busy, and you may want to try one in a country without too much Internet traffic, such as Albania or Arkansas.

You should also select the type of search you'll normally want to use, probably **Substring**. (You learned all about these in Chapter 20 of *The Complete Idiot's Guide to the Internet*. If you've forgotten, press **F1** to see more information. The WS_Archie Help file gives some good information about Regex searches, by the way, if you've been wondering what that's all about.) No need to change the **User ID** field in this dialog box.

Click on **OK**, and then select **Options|FTP Setup**. In this dialog box, you need to enter the path to WS_FTP, so Archie can automatically launch WS_FTP and grab a file for you. (Don't remove the **%h:%d/%f** at the end of the **Command** line, as these tell WS_Archie to send the information WS_FTP is going to need.) Also, change the **Directory** to show the directory you want WS_FTP to download the information to. Now close this dialog box, and you're ready to search.

The first time you search, you'll have to select the Archie server you want to use. (The next time you open the program, it will automatically show the one you selected in the User Preferences dialog box.) Type the text you want to search for, then click on **Search** and off it goes. Remember, though, that Archie searches are often very slow, and it sometimes appears as if nothing is happening; the program is simply waiting (read the help file for an explanation of what the status bar messages mean).

When Archie finally responds, you'll see something like the following screen. If you've found what you need, click on the file, select **File|Retrieve**, and Archie launches WS_FTP, which downloads the file and then closes. Fantastic. That's how the Internet *should* work!

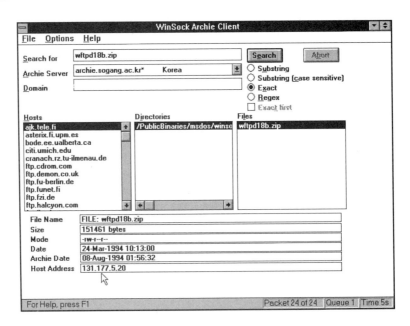

Archie meets Windows.

Pssst! Wanna See Some Files?
—Your Own FTP Site

Have you ever thought about setting up your own computer as an FTP site? Okay, maybe you don't want to have everyone and his dog logging in and downloading your Quicken or MS Money files, reading your unfinished novel, or grabbing your phonebook database. You don't have to allow anonymous FTP. However, it might be handy to let colleagues get in and share files, drop off files for you, and grab files that they need. (And if you do want to allow anonymous FTP, you can restrict which directories are accessible.) What you need is WFTPD (that's short for *Windows FTP Daemon*, if you hadn't guessed).

This program comes with very little documentation, but then it doesn't seem to need much. It costs $15 to register the program; you receive a version of the program with more features when you do so. If you want to set up an FTP site, $15 doesn't sound like a lot; and anyway, if you set up the system with the unregistered version, everyone logging into your system will see the following message:

Daemon A UNIX term (pronounced "DEE-mon") for a program that sits around in the background waiting to carry out some kind of service.

```
This copy of WFTPD is NOT REGISTERED

This means that the institution, company or individual that
you are connected to is a cheap skinflint who couldn't find
$15 in his/her back pocket.

The author of this program encourages you to mercilessly
tease the person running this program until he/she pays up.
```

Setting up the system is simple. A security dialog box lets you enter the names and passwords of people you want to allow into your system. You can also restrict each person to a particular directory and its subdirectories, or let them go wherever they want. And this dialog box also lets you set up an *anonymous* account, if you want to allow *anonymous FTP* sessions.

You can also write your own greeting: the text that people see when they log into your system (assuming you have the registered version, that is; there's no way to remove the skinflint message from the unregistered version!).

Finally, there's a menu called **Logging**, a sort of options menu. Selecting the items in this menu turns them on. You can turn on logins, allowing people access to your computer, and tell the program to create a log file. In that log file, you can store lists of all the files copied from or to your system each time a user logs in, and all the commands used by each user, so you can see exactly what they did while on your machine. You may not want to risk letting Internet *crackers* (see the Glossary) onto your machine, so give this some thought before jumping in!

That's it, there's nothing more to do than wait for people to log in. This little program makes setting up an FTP site quite simple. Don't be cheap; don't be embarrassed; pay him his $15.

The Least You Need to Know

- ☛ WS_FTP is a great, little FTP program that actually makes FTP *easy*.

- ☛ WinFTP is a modified WS_FTP, with a few more features.

- ☛ WS_Archie integrates with WS_FTP. Find a file using Archie, and then automatically launch WS_FTP to grab it.

- ☛ WFTPD makes setting up your own FTP site very easy.

Chapter 12
Magical Mosaic

In This Chapter

- ☛ Deciding what you need to run Mosaic
- ☛ Installing Win32s
- ☛ Installing Mosaic
- ☛ Using Mosaic
- ☛ Changing menus and the home page
- ☛ Creating your own home page

If you've spent any time at all cruising the Internet, you've probably heard of Mosaic. It's the king of Internet graphical interfaces—to hear people talk, it's almost as if there were no other programs in existence! Even people who have never touched the Internet seem to have heard of Mosaic, though they often don't really know what it does.

So what *does* it do?

Mosaic is a World Wide Web viewer. Remember the Web? It's the Internet's *hypermedia* system, a massive hypertext system that crosses the world. It's like having a huge book that's spread out across the contents. Open page 1 and you are in, say, a database about music in Vienna. Move to a referenced page, and perhaps you are in a history database in London. Move from there to another reference, and perhaps you've just opened a page in Dallas.

For information on finding this and other programs, see Chapter 27.

You are not just viewing text. You'll see many color pictures, and you'll run into sound and video, too. You can use a variety of other Internet tools from the Web: Telnet, FTP, Archie, and so on.

Mosaic's purpose is to help you use this vast system of cross-references efficiently. Mosaic is "published" by NCSA, the National Center for Supercomputing Applications. The program's free for most of us, but if you want to use it for commercial purposes, you need to contact NCSA for licensing information.

Which Flavor?

You have three basic choices when choosing a flavor of Mosaic:

Alpha software (no relation to Alpha Books) is not always stable and contains bugs. However, it has all the available features, so it can be neat to use, if you don't mind occasional problems. If you want to use the Alpha versions, make sure you are always using the latest, so you have all the latest bug fixes.

Version 1.0   This is a "released" version. It should be stable, but doesn't have all the features of the latest software.

Version 2.0alphax   At the time of writing, the latest version was 2.0alpha6, with 2.0alpha7 due in a few weeks. This product is a 32-bit version. The NCSA designed it to run on Windows NT or the soon-to-be-released Windows (4.0 or something). You *can* run it on Windows 3.1, Windows for Workgroups 3.1 or 3.11, but only if you install extra software, called Win32s (I'll explain how).

Version 2.0alpha2   If you want to run Mosaic 2.0 on Windows 3.1 or Windows for Workgroups 3.1 or 3.11, and you don't want to mess with Win32s, you can stick with Version 2.0alpha2. It will run on these 16-bit programs with no problem. Of course, this earlier version won't have all the features of the later one, and may be less stable.

In this book, I'm going to be looking at Mosaic 2.0alpha6. Versions will vary, so some of what you read here may not apply directly. The basics will be the same, though.

What Will It Take?

To install Mosaic, you need several things:

The right computer   You can't run Mosaic on a 286. You need at least a 386SX with 4MB of RAM but the faster your computer and the more memory, the better. Run out and buy a 486-66 with 16 MB, or better still, a Pentium or 486-100. You have the cash lying around, don't you?

Mosaic can also run on DEC computers running Windows NT, and there are also versions for other systems: UNIX's X-Windows and the Macintosh. However, we're sticking to MS Windows versions here.

WINSOCK   Before installing Mosaic, you must have some version of WINSOCK installed. If you've already installed Trumpet Winsock (Chapter 10), if you have installed a commercial version of WINSOCK that came with another program that you bought, such as Internet Chameleon (Chapter 17) or WinGopher Complete (Chapter 21), or if you have installed the new Windows WINSOCK (Windows 4.0/Chicago/What-ever-it's-called-when-released), then you're ready to install Mosaic.

You need a "Winsocks Winsock 1.1-compliant" version of WINSOCK.DLL. That's simply a set of standards that describes what WINSOCK.DLL should be able to do. Trumpet Winsock is 1.1-compliant, as are most of the other WINSOCK.DLLs you are likely to run into.

Win32s   The latest Mosaic is a 32-bit program. That means it will run in Windows NT, but if you want to run it in Windows 3.1 or Windows for Workgroups, which are 16-bit operating systems, you'll need Win32s. (You must have version 1.1.5a of Win32s.) You'll learn more about Win32s in the next few pages.

A 256-Color VGA board   Okay, you don't *have* to have a 256-color board, but it's nice because many of the images on the Web are 256-color images.

Mosaic's installation files   Of course, you need the program itself and its associated files. For information on finding these, see Chapter 27.

Win32s—and a Free Game, Too!

Windows operating systems come in two basic flavors: 16-bit systems (Windows 3.1 and Windows for Workgroups) and 32-bit systems (Windows NT and the as-yet-unreleased new version of Windows). You can't run 32-bit programs on a 16-bit system *unless* those programs have been designed to run with Win32s. Win32s "fools" the program into thinking it's running on a 32-bit system (or does it fool the operating system into thinking it's a 16-bit program?).

So, do you need Win32s? You do if:

- You are using Windows 3.1.

- You are using Windows for Workgroups 3.1 or 3.11.

You don't if:

- You are using Windows NT.

- You are using Windows 4.0/Chicago/Whatever-they-call-it-when-they-finally-release-it.

- You have successfully installed another 32-bit program on your 16-bit operating system. If it's running, it means someone has installed Win32s on your system. However, the version of Win32s you need for Mosaic is 1.1.5a or later, so if you have an earlier version installed, you'll have to upgrade.

If you need Win32s, go to Chapter 27 to find out where to get it. Follow the procedure in the documentation file that comes with it. It's very simple to install. As for that free game, Win32s comes with FreeCell, a neat card game originally released with Windows NT. Try running the card game before you start Mosaic. If the card game works, Win32s was installed correctly.

Win32 Problems? Well, Maybe Not *Quite* So Simple

A few of you may run into problems with Win32s. If you have a LaserMaster printer, you may find that your system is unable to extract the WINSPOOL.DR_ file from the ZIP file. This is because LaserMaster has a print driver called WINSPOOL. The same way DOS won't let you create a file called LPT1, because it conflicts with a printer port, Windows won't let you create a file that conflicts with one of its printer ports.

To get around the problem, do this.

1.   Open your SYSTEM.INI file.

2.   Find these lines:

```
device=LMHAROLD.386 ;WinPrint
device=LMCAP.386 ;WinPrint
device=LMMI.386 ;WinPrint
```

3.   Place a semi-colon in front of each line (;device-LMHAROLD.386, for instance).

4.   Close Windows, reopen Windows, extract the ZIP file, and run the installation program.

5.   Return to the SYSTEM.INI file and remove the semi-colons. You should now be able to run Mosaic and use your LaserMaster Printer.

If you run into any other problems, take a look at the Microsoft Knowledge Base document titled *INF: Troubleshooting Win32s 1.1 Installation Problems*. See Chapter 27 for information on finding this document.

Getting Rid of Win32s

If you decide you want to remove Win32s, do this:

1.   Open your SYSTEM.INI file.

2.   Go to the [386enh] section.

3.   Remove this line:

```
device=windows\system\win32s\w32s.386
```

4. Close and save SYSTEM.INI.

5. Remove the WINDOWS\SYSTEM\WIN32S directory and its contents.

6. Remove the WIN32S.INI, WIN32S16.DLL, and W32SYS.DLL files in the WINDOWS\SYSTEM directory.

7. Close Windows and reopen.

Install Mosaic? It's Easy, Really

Many Internet users seem to think that installing Mosaic is tough. It's not; it's *very* easy. The complicated part of setting up Mosaic is setting up the TCP/IP connection in Windows. Once you've installed Trumpet Winsock or some other version of the WINSOCK.DLL, installed Win32s (if necessary), and found the Mosaic files and put them on your hard disk, it takes five minutes or so to install Mosaic (assuming you follow my directions). Don't believe me? Watch this:

1. Copy the MOSAIC.INI file to your WINDOWS directory.

2. Open the MOSAIC.INI file in Notepad.

3. Change the first line.

   ```
   E-mail="Put_Your_Email_Address@here"
   ```

   Replace the Put Your Email Address@here with your e-mail address. For example:

   ```
   E-mail="pkent@usa.net"
   ```

4. Search for this line:

   ```
   Directory="c:\ncsa\annotate"
   ```

   This is the directory in which Mosaic saves your annotations, notes that are related to a particular WWW document—perhaps on the other side of the world. For instance, put this in:

   ```
   Directory="e:\internet\mosaic\annotate"
   ```

5. Save and close the .INI file.

6. Go to File Manager and create the ANNOTATE directory.

7. Go to Program Manager and create an icon for the program (using the **File|New** option). See your Windows documentation if you don't know how to do this.

That's it. I told you it'd be easy, didn't I?

Can't Wait to Try Mosaic?

Before you open Mosaic, make your connection to the Internet. Then, double-click on the **Mosaic** icon. And Mosaic will start. If you are using V2.0alpha6, Mosaic will automatically connect to your *home page* (more about this in a moment). If you have an earlier version, it won't. Try selecting one of the entries from the Starting Points menu.

If you are used to the WWW browser from your crummy old UNIX shell, Mosaic will amaze you. Color, movement, pictures—it's closer to a multimedia application than the text WWW browser you are used to. That's because it *is* a multimedia app. It's what's sometimes called *hypermedia*, a hypertext document with a lot more than just text, such as sound, pictures, and video.

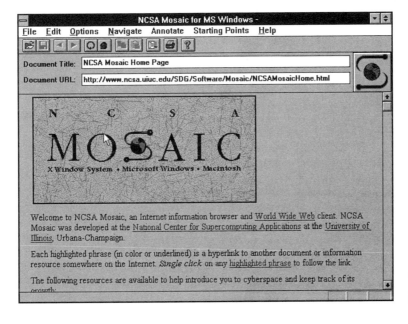

The NCSA Mosaic Home Page.

Now that you've had a quick look, I want to back off and cover a few basics. (If you want to close Mosaic while you read, use **File|Exit**. Remember to close your connection to save money.)

Theory Break: A WWW Primer

At first glance, Mosaic can be a little confusing. What are all these strange names? What, for example, is

```
http://www.ncsa.uiuc.edu/SDG/Software/WinMosaic/Docs/
WMosTOC.html.
```

Well, let's start at the basic WWW component: the HTML document. This is the address of the *NCSA Mosaic for Microsoft Windows User's Guide* contents document. (If you have V2.0alpha6, you can see this page using **Help|Online Documentation**.) It tells your program, a WWW *browser*, where to look to find that document. The address is that of a WWW *server*: a location containing hypertext documents that your browser can read.

This address is a URL, *Uniform Resource Locator*. Every component in the WWW must have a URL, so other documents can reach the component. The component uses the URL to identify the document (or sound, or video, or picture, or smell, or whatever else you can put into a computer file). You'll see later in this chapter how you can enter these URL addresses into a WWW document, so that when you click on a hypertext link, the required information transfers to your computer.

So what's HTML? It means HyperText Markup Language. (A *markup language* is a system that codes a simple text document (ASCII) in such a way that different programs on different computers can read it.) Because the markup language doesn't define exactly how the document will look, programs can display it differently from each other.

For example, a markup-language document will define a piece of text as the title, another piece of text as a heading1, another as heading2, some text as the body text, and so on. Then, when that file is read into a program, the program defines what it will look like: what text format and paragraph format to use for each piece of text.

So let's look at that address again:

```
http://www.ncsa.uiuc.edu/SDG/Software/WinMosaic/Docs/
WMosTOC.html
```

Right at the end of the line you can see *WMosTOC.html*. This is the name of the file containing the document. The file is a simple text document using the HTML's markup language. (We're going to look at an example of an HTML document later.) Preceding the document name, you can see the hostname and directory.

Have you ever used a Windows Help file or another form of hypertext? When you click on a *link* or *hotspot*, something happens. It may take you to another document, page, or topic, or display something, or play a sound, or whatever. Well, in Mosaic when you click on one of these links (the underlined text or a picture), you transfer information from another document, the document referenced by the URL. That might be text, graphics, or sounds.

Back to Mosaic: Let's Play

Now let's go back and fool around. Start Mosaic again. Then spend some time reading the first screen that appears. This is the NCSA Mosaic home page. It's a good place to start, but you probably won't want to keep it as your home page. I'll show you how to change it later.

Now, notice the links (known as *anchors* in WWW-speak). Most colored text is a link. The text is, by default, blue, and it's underlined. Clicking on the text gets another document (or some other kind of data).

As you move around on the Web, you'll notice lots of pictures, too. Some are simply decoration, but some are anchors; because the anchors have a blue outline around them. You may even run across *sensitive* pictures, in particular, *sensitive maps*. Not only can you click on these pictures to get something, what you get depends on the part of the picture you click on. For instance, if you click on **Glasgow** in the picture of Great Britain shown here, you'll see information about that city.

SPEAK LIKE A GEEK

Home page   The home page is the one you want to see when you first start Mosaic and that you will see when you select **Navigate|Home** or click on the **Home** toolbar icon (the little house).

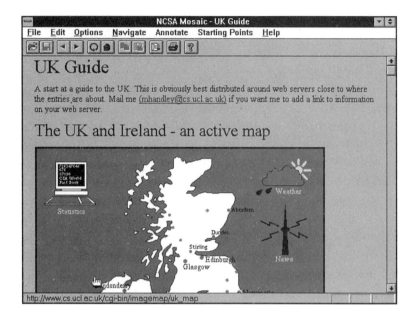

Sensitive maps are all over the place on the Web.

You should check out the **Starting Points|World Wide Web Info** menu. This leads you to several useful documents, including directories of Web resources. Use the **Starting Points Document** and the **NCSA Mosaic Demo Document**, both on the **Starting Points** menu. If, in your travels, you find a document you think you'd like to return to, select **Navigate|Add Current to Hotlist**. It will save on one of your menus; I'll explain that in detail a little later in this chapter.

You've just clicked on an anchor, and Mosaic has started transferring something. However, you realize that you don't want to go where it's taking you. Click on the **Mosaic** icon on the right side of the URL bar (just below the menu bar). In most cases this should stop the transfer, though some WINSOCK.DLLs won't let you do this. Windows NT won't, for instance.

More Getting Around Stuff

Here are a few more ways to move around hyperspace with Mosaic.

Navigate|Back   Returns to the previous page.

Navigate|Forward   Goes forward to the next page in sequence, assuming you have used the **Back** command. The Back and Forward commands move you through the *history list*, the list of documents you've seen in the current session.

Navigate|Reload   Redisplays the current document. Perhaps something becomes distorted. Sometimes, you'll find strange display problems and redisplaying will clear them up.

Navigate|Home   Returns you to your home page.

Navigate|History   Displays a list of all the documents you've been to in this session. Double-click on a document, or click and then click on the Load button to return to that document. Unfortunately, the history list displays the URL addresses instead of document titles—so get used to understanding and decoding URLs!

There's currently no documentation released with Mosaic. However, there's online documentation that's very good. If you have a recent version you can select **Help|Online Documentation**. Or use **Navigate|Menu Editor** to add this to your Hotlist menu: http://www.ncsa.uiuc.edu/SDG/Software/WinMosaic/Docs/WM4_4.html.

So, I Have This URL Thing...

You've been given a URL *(Uniform Resource Locator)*, and told that you really need to check it out. How do you use it. There are a couple of ways.

☞ Type or copy it into the URL text box at the top of the Window. (If this isn't there, select **Options|Show Current URL** to turn it back on.) Then press **Enter**.

☞ Add the address to one of your menus. Then you can get to it whenever you need it, without remembering the address. We're going to look at working with menus later on in this chapter.

Getting Stuff to Your Hard Disk

For instance, say you are looking at the "Ballcourt Marker in the Form of a Monkey" at the Michael C. Carlos Museum at Emory University in Atlanta, Georgia (http://www.cc.emory.edu/CARLOS/carlos.html is the address for the museum's contents page, and http://www.cc.emory.edu/CARLOS/hacha.html is the address for the Ballcourt Marker). You decide you'd like to download the picture. Just hold the **Shift** key and click the left mouse button. A Save As dialog box appears. Click on **OK** and the file, which happens to be in the .JPG format, transfers to your hard drive.

You may want to transfer a whole series of items. In this case, you can select **Options|Load to Disk**. Now, each time you do a normal click on an anchor, instead of viewing the related item, it will transfer to your disk. Again, you'll see the Save As dialog box so you can tell Mosaic where to place it and what to call it.

Building Menus and Hotlists of Favorite Places

Mosaic lets you build and modify *personal menus* (also known as *user menus*). Most of the menus on the menu bar are fixed. But the **Starting Points** menu is a personal menu. There's also the *QUICKLIST*, a list of places you want to go. It doesn't appear on the menu bar; you get to it using the **File|Open URL** command, and selecting it from the **Current Hotlist** drop-down dialog box.

So what's the *hotlist*? It's a list to which you can quickly and easily add the addresses of WWW documents. Let's say you've found an interesting document, one you know you'll want to return to. You select **Navigate|Add Current to Hotlist** and Mosaic places the document's address in your hotlist—whatever that happens to be at the moment. You can make any of your personal menus the hotlist. You may want to have several hotlists, each for documents about different subjects.

Selecting the Hotlist

There are two ways to select your hotlist.

Method One   Click on the first toolbar button or select **File|Open URL**. Open the Current Hotlist drop-down list box. This shows all the personal menus and submenus (strictly speaking, *cascading menus*, menus that come off other menus). Select the one you want to work with. The top line of the Open URL dialog box now shows you the address and title of each document in the menu. Click on **OK**.

Method Two   Select **Navigate|Menu Editor**. In the Personal Menus dialog box select the menu you want to use from the **Current Hotlist** drop-down list box. Click on **Close**.

Adding Your Own Hotlist

Here's a quick and easy way to create a menu of places on the Web that you like to go to often. First, select **Navigate|Menu Editor**. You'll see this Personal Menus dialog box.

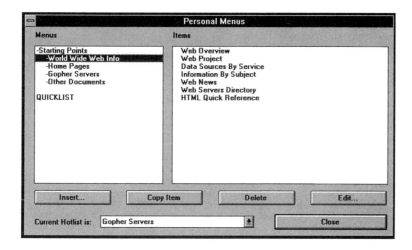

The Mosaic menu editor.

The Menus list box displays all the personal menus, both top-level and cascading menus. At the bottom, it shows the QUICKLIST. There are several ways to modify the menus. You can:

- ☞ Create a new *top level* menu (a menu that appears on the menu bar).
- ☞ Create a new cascading menu (a menu that is a submenu of another).
- ☞ Place a menu item that references a URL address onto a menu.
- ☞ Place a separator line onto a menu.

New top-level menu   Click in the space immediately above the QUICKLIST. Click on the **Insert** button. Type the name of your new menu (such as, ****MY STUFF****) and click on **OK**.

New cascading menu   Click on the menu to which you want to add a cascading menu. For instance, you may want to create several submenus of the menu you have just created. Click on ****MY STUFF**** or whatever you called it. Click on the **Menu** option button, type the name of the menu, and click on **OK**. The new menu appears at the end of the menu, after all the existing items and submenus.

Place a menu item   Click on the menu to which you want to add an item. Type the Title of the WWW document you want to link to this menu. Then type the URL address and click on **OK**.

Place a separator   Click on the menu to which you want to add the separator. Click on the **Separator** option button and click on **OK**. When you open that menu, you'll see that there is a line at the bottom of the menu. The next things you add appear after the line.

You can use these same techniques on the QUICKLIST, with the exception that you can't add submenus to the list (because QUICKLIST is not a real menu).

Is Mosaic Slow?

If you are using Mosaic over a dial-in direct line, rather than a permanent connection, you'll find it slow. It's neat; it's fun; but gee, it's slow. Text pages transfer very quickly, but pictures transfer very slowly.

While you are waiting for your service provider to switch to a 28,800 bps connection (better still, 115,200 bps, but you'll have to wait a while for that), there are a few things you can do to speed up your system. Open the MOSAIC.INI file in Windows' Notepad, search for each line, and make the suggested change.

```
Round List Bullets=yes
```

Mosaic for Windows uses these cute little bullets in lists. They look almost spherical and they take time to transfer, slowing you down. Change **yes** to **no** to replace these with the NCSA logo. (Unfortunately, it's the same logo that's shown for images, so you're never certain if it's an image or bullet.)

```
Anchor Underline=yes
```

If you have a color monitor, you can change **yes** to **no**. This removes the underlines from the *anchors*, the text that you click on to jump somewhere. This speeds up the system, because it doesn't have to keep drawing the underlines.

```
[Document Caching]
Type=Number
Number=2
```

This section relates to what Mosaic does with information that it displays on your screen. It "caches" documents. That is, instead of throwing a document away when you leave it, it keeps it in memory so that if you want to return to it, the page can be redisplayed very quickly. By default, it caches two to five documents, depending on the version you are using, but you may experiment with increasing the number.

You may also want to turn off inline images: the pictures that are in the WWW documents. Select **Options|Display Inline Images** to remove the check mark from this menu item, and select **File|Save Preferences**. This can speed up transmission considerably. On the other hand, you are always thinking, "I wonder what that looks like?" If you want to view a missing picture, you can point at the placeholder, press **Shift**, and click your mouse's right button.

Creating Your Own Home Page

You can create your own home page, if you want. To this page, you can add any text you want, and any links to other sites that you want. And you can do it in that wonderful, little applet, Windows' Notepad.

Remember that HTML files are simple ASCII text files, right? Well, let's create an HTML file, then. Start by opening Notepad. Now, enter this text. You can replace the text with other stuff, but don't change the codes between the < >:

```
<H1>My Very Own Home Page</H1>

<H2>Really Important Stuff</H2>
These are WWW pages I use a lot. <P>

<H2>Not So Important Stuff</H2>
These are WWW pages I use now and again. <P>

<H3>Not Important At All Stuff</H3>
These are WWW pages I use to waste time. <P>
What are these codes?
```

Here's what you just entered:

<H1> </H1>   The heading level. You can have up to six different levels. We've used levels 1, 2, and 3.

<P>   This denotes the end of a paragraph. Simply typing a carriage return in your HTML file will not create a new paragraph in the final document as it's displayed in Mosaic. You must add the <P> code.

Now, save and close the file. Save it using the .HTM extension. Don't call it HOME.TXT, call it HOME.HTM. Put it in the directory you put Mosaic into. Go to Mosaic, and use the **File|Open Local File** command to open the file. What do you see? A formatted WWW document. It's rubbish, of course, but you can see how easy it was to create.

Now we're going to get fancy. Let's add an *anchor*, a link to another document. Let's say, for instance, you are researching *Geek Houses*. You've just discovered a list of Santa Cruz Geek Houses (I'm *not* making this up, really) on the World Wide Web, and found that its address is http://klinzhai.iuma.com/~falcon/geeks/geekhouse.html

This is handy to have for anyone studying these strange creatures—computer geeks—and their social and mating habits, so you decide to add it to your home page. You can add this line to your document, (under the Really Important Stuff heading, of course), and then save the file.

```
<A HREF="http://klinzhai.iuma.com/~falcon/geeks/
geekhouse.html">Geek Houses<A/>
```

When you're finished, you can set this up as your home page. Open your MOSAIC.INI file in Notepad, and find this line:

```
Home Page=http://www.ncsa.uiuc.edu/SDG/Software/Mosaic/
NCSAMosaicHome.html
```

Change it to this:

```
Home Page=file://e:\Internet\mosaic\homepage.htm
```

Save and close the file, then close Mosaic and reopen. You'll see your very own home page. Simple, eh?

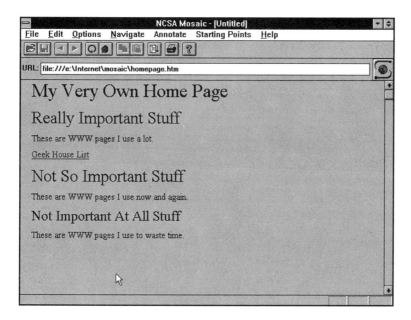

Creating a simple home page is... simple.

Here's a quick way to get addresses. When you find a document on the Web that you think you might want to add to one of your own hypertext documents, select the address in the URL text box in the top of the window, and press **Ctrl-C** or select **Edit|Copy**. You can then paste this into your document.

You can add hypertext links from, say, your research notes to information sources all over the world. You can even get fancy and add graphics and other neato stuff. However, don't expect me to help you. You're going to have to learn lots more codes for that.

Want to know more—lots more—about HTML? You can find all sorts of info online. Select **Starting Points|World Wide Web Info|HTML Quick Reference** and **Starting Points|Other Documents|Beginners Guide to HTML**.

How Do I See This Stuff?

There are all sorts of different data sources on the Internet. You can find graphics of different formats (JPEG, TIFF, GIF), video (Quicktime and MS Video), text and word processing (PostScript, ASCII, Windows Write, Word for Windows), and sounds (digital and MIDI). Mosaic itself cannot display all of these. So, you need *viewers* to do so. In the MOSAIC.INI file, there's a [Viewers] section and a [Suffixes] section. The Viewers section tells Mosaic which viewer you want to use for each file format. For instance, by default it's set up to use the Windows Media Player for Windows digital (WAV) files. The [Suffixes] section refers to file extensions. It tells Mosaic what each file extension means—that .JPEG, .JPE, and .JPG are all JPEG graphics files, for instance.

You may already have programs that can display most file formats you are likely to run into on the Web. You can enter these programs into MOSAIC.INI. Or you can find viewers out on the Web. (Try anonymous FTP to **www.law.cornell.edu** and look in the **/pub/LII/Cello** directory.)

By the way, if you are using the WWW over a telephone line, you may want to forget some file formats. Perhaps getting video over the net seems cool, but it's going to be so slow that it will soon lose its novelty. If you do serious work on the WWW, you may find yourself turning off inline graphics to keep the speed up to a reasonable level, and avoiding down-loading sound, graphics, and video except when you really need it.

The Least You Need to Know

- ☞ Mosaic is a fancy World Wide Web browser for Windows.

- ☞ Mosaic is free program (for noncommercial use) from the National Center for Supercomputing Applications.

- ☞ The latest version is 32-bit. You can run an earlier, 16-bit version if you want.

- ☞ To run the 32-bit version, you'll need Windows NT, Windows 4.0/Chicago, or Win32s, a special utility that lets you run 32-bit programs on Windows 3.1 or Windows for Workgroups.

- ☞ Mosaic lets you create your own menus and add items to menus.

- ☞ HTML is HyperText Markup Language, a system of codes that you can use to turn ASCII documents into WWW documents.

- ☞ Creating a home page with HTML is simple.

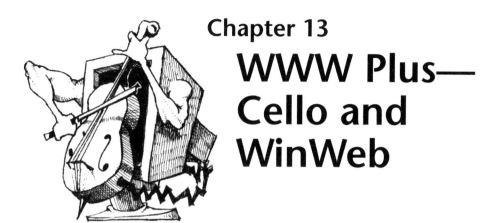

Chapter 13
WWW Plus— Cello and WinWeb

In This Chapter

- ☛ Installing Cello
- ☛ Using Cello's World Wide Web browser
- ☛ Running FTP sessions
- ☛ Running Telnet sessions
- ☛ Running Gopher
- ☛ Using WinWeb

Wouldn't it be nice to find a program that has everything in one place? No need to jump from one application to another to do everything. Well, maybe you should try Cello. Okay, it doesn't have everything, but it's a step in the right direction. It's a program based around a World Wide Web browser, and it has other stuff, too. You can run FTP, Telnet sessions, and Gopher sessions, and send e-mail.

The problem with this approach, though, is that none of the components are as good as the best separate-component programs. Cello does have a neat WWW browser, though you can do more with Mosaic. (Cello seemed to me to be a bit more stable, though; try it and see if you agree.) The FTP and Telnet applications are okay, too, but they're not as good as the ones we are going to look at a little later in this book.

On the other hand, Cello's pretty easy to use—certainly easier than Mosaic. And it's easy to install, so it shouldn't take long for you to check it out. Try it; you may find you like it.

Cello's a Windows program created by the Legal Information Institute (LII), an organization at the Cornell Law School that puts legal information online (such as the Project Hermes Supreme Court decisions). And Cello is freeware; you don't have to pay for it or register it.

The Usual Requirements Stuff

Okay, what do you need to run Cello? This stuff:

Unlike Mosaic, the current version of Cello is 16 bit, so you don't have to worry about loading Win32s if you are running on Windows or Windows for Workgroups.

☞ An IBM PC-compatible PC, a 386SX or better (better is always better).

☞ 4MB RAM (It'll run on less, but not well. If possible, run out and get 16 or 20MB. You can never have too much RAM).

☞ Some flavor of Microsoft Windows 3.1 or better, of course.

☞ Some version of WINSOCK.DLL already loaded. (We covered this in earlier chapters.)

☞ A 256-color VGA board is handy, too, because many of the pictures on the Web are 256-color images.

Let's Load

We're going to assume you've already loaded WINSOCK.DLL and can connect your SLIP, CSLIP, or PPP connection to your service provider. Once all that's done, snag Cello (see Chapter 27 to find out where it lives), and then follow these steps to load it.

1. Create three directories, something like this:

```
C:\CELLO
C:\CELLO\DOWNLOAD
C:\CELLO\VIEWERS
```

To create directories, it's easiest to use Windows' File Manager. If you prefer, though, you can use the DOS MD command.

2. Use PKUnzip to extract the Cello files into your C:\CELLO directory. This is assuming that you downloaded the Cello program and it's compressed in a .ZIP file. If your situation is different, do your own thing—whatever it takes to get the Cello files in the CELLO directory.

3. Read the README.1ST file. You can read it any number of ways, but the easiest way is to open it in Windows' Notepad, Write, or your favorite word processing program.

4. Create a Program Manager icon for Cello. (If you don't know how to do this, see your Windows documentation.)

5. Start your dial-in direct connection.

6. Open Cello by double-clicking on the icon. You'll see a gray "introduction" box over the window; click on the box to remove it.

7. Select **Configure|Files and directories|Download directory**. This is where you tell Cello where to place files that it downloads. Type the name of the directory you created (such as C:\CELLO\DOWNLOAD).

8. Select **Configure|Files and directories|Cache low water mark**. Cello *caches* WWW pages. That is, it saves them on your hard disk in temporary files, so if you want to redisplay a page you recently viewed, it doesn't have to transmit it again.

TECHNO NERD TEACHES...

The *low water mark* tells Cello not to use more disk space if the remaining disk space is below a certain level. The default is 500,000 bytes. So, if you only have 500,000 bytes of disk space left on the hard disk when you view another WWW document, Cello will have to remove one of the earlier ones in order to store the new one.

Where does Cello store these files? In your TEMP directory. You can usually find a line in your AUTOEXEC.BAT file like this:

```
SET TEMP=C:\WINDOWS\TEMP
```

Check to see that this is in your AUTOEXEC.BAT. If you have more than one hard disk, you may want to move the TEMP directory to the one with most space.

9. Select **Configure|Your email address**. Type your full e-mail address.

10. Select **Configure|News server**. Type the IP address or domain name of your service provider's NNTP news server. Cello uses this when you are viewing WWW documents that reference certain newsgroup messages.

I Don't Need Reading Glasses! Whoever created Cello must have been working on a large screen with a high video resolution. The text is way too big on a VGA monitor; it often runs off the edge of the window so you can't read it all at once. Use the **Configure|Fonts** command to change it to whatever suits you.

That's about it. There are, of course, other things you can customize. You can create a signature file that's included with all the e-mail you send from Cello. For example (create an ASCII file called CELLO.SIG and place it in the Cello directory), you can tell it where to place bookmark and style files, and so on. (We'll get to bookmarks and styles in a moment.)

Cello comes with a fairly good Windows Help file. You can start this from within Cello itself (select **Help|Help**), or start it by double-clicking on the file in File Manager (it's called CLOHELP.HLP). You can even create a program icon for it in Program Manager, if you want. When you start the help system, click on **Setting up Cello**, then click on **Cello configuration**, and you'll find yourself in a topic that explains some of the other things that you can configure.

Looking Around with Cello

Let's take a look at what Cello does and how it does it. This figure shows you what you'll see when you first load Cello. The information shown in the middle of the screen is your *home page*, a sort of starting point. It's automatically set up to connect to a file called DEFAULT.HTM in the directory with all your Cello files. It gives some useful introductory information about Cello, and contains links to other documents; this time documents on the WWW itself.

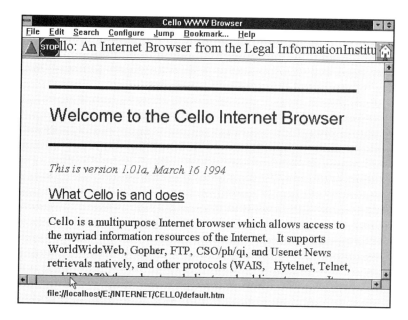

Cello provides a simple WWW browser, with a few add-ons.

Notice the toolbar:

 Click on this button to return to the previous document you were viewing.

 Click here to stop a file transfer or gopher transfer.

 Click on this to return to your home page.

Now, what about moving around in here? As you move through the document, you'll notice some underlined words. There may even be a dotted-line box around them, depending on how you set the **Configure|Links underlined only** menu option. These are the *links* (sometimes called *anchors* in WWW-speak). Click on one and you'll shoot off in cyberspace to another document somewhere.

A little way down in the default home page is a section called **The Legal Information Institute**. In the text, you'll notice the words **Click here to look at our Web server**. Click on the word **look**, and, assuming the network's working correctly, you'll see another page.

The LII WWW server document is a good place to start. It has a variety of useful links, such as one to the NCSA Demo page (which, in turn, has all sorts of useful links to all sorts of useful places).

We'll Never Get Back, Gretel

The WWW reminds me of the story about Hansel and Gretel. It's possible to get so deep into the Web, that if you leave that place, you'll never be able to find your way back. Cello provides a couple of solutions.

When you find a document you know you'll want to return to one day, click on the **Bookmark** menu and the Cello: Bookmarks dialog box will appear. Click on the **Mark Current Document** button, and Cello will add the title of the document you are viewing to the dialog box. Then click on **Quit** to close the box. The next time you want to return to this site, simply click on the **Bookmark** menu again, and double-click on the name in the list box (or click on it once and then click on **Jump**).

If you didn't add a document to the Bookmark list, but later realize you want to return to it, you can—as long as you haven't yet closed Cello. Use the History list. Select **Jump|History** and you'll see a dialog box displaying the titles of the documents you've seen in the current session. Just double-click on the one you want, or click on it and click on **Jump**. The Cello History box is much better than Mosaic's, by the way. The Mosaic one shows the URL (Universal Resource Locator) address, while Cello's shows the document title, which is far more intelligible.

And how about going the other way? To get back home or to the previous document, you can click on the toolbar buttons or use the **Jump|Up** command. (For some reason, there's currently no Jump|Home command—probably an oversight, so maybe they'll add it later.)

URL Do What?

In Chapter 11, we discussed URLs. They are, essentially, addresses that tell the Internet where you want to go when you are traveling around on the Web. For instance, if somebody tells you they've seen the Library of Congress' online Vatican Library exhibit, and that it's at *http://www.ncsa.uiuc.edu/SDG/Experimental/vatican.exhibit/Vatican.exhibit.html*, how are you going to get there? It may take months of digging around before you stumble upon it. What you'll do, though, is select **Jump|Launch via URL**, type the address into the text box that appears, and click on **OK**. And away you go.

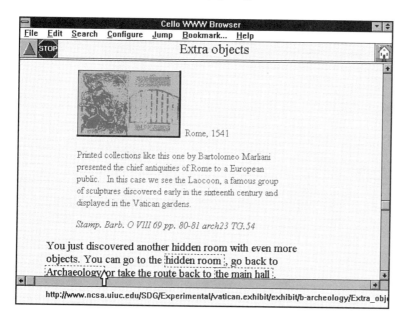

You can visit the Vatican exhibit without even leaving home.

You can collect URLs, by the way. Of course, you can use the Bookmark feature we've already looked at. However, if you'd like to grab an address so you can put it in an e-mail message, or in a word processing file you are storing interesting stuff in, do this. Click on the **Bookmark** menu. When the Bookmarks dialog box appears, click on the **Mark Current Document** button, creating a bookmark. Then click on the new bookmark in the list, and click on the **Copy** button to copy it to the Clipboard. You can now click on **Delete**, if you want, to remove the bookmark.

Now, you can go to any Windows application and paste the bookmark in. It'll look like this:

```
<A HREF=http://www.ncsa.uiuc.edu/SDG/Experimental/
vatican.exhibit/Vatican.exhibit.html>Vatican Exhibit — Rome
Reborn </A>
```

You've actually copied the entire HTML address line; you don't need all of this. Remove this first part:

```
<A HREF=
```

Then remove everything after the second > sign. This remains:

```
http://www.ncsa.uiuc.edu/SDG/Experimental/vatican.exhibit/
Vatican.exhibit.html
```

That's the actual URL address that you can use to travel to the Vatican exhibit.

Getting the Data

In some ways, Cello beats Mosaic. It makes it easier to download data, for instance. Currently, there's no way in Mosaic to copy what's on your screen into a file (maybe there will be by the time you read this, though). Cello makes it simple, using these commands:

SPEAK LIKE A GEEK

Inline graphics vs. retrieved graphics
There are two types of graphics on the WWW. *Inline graphics* are those that appear when you display a document—within the document, mixed in with the text. A *retrieved graphic* is one that is available for download if you choose it, but is not part of an HTML document. Sometimes, clicking on an inline graphic will start a download of a retrieved graphic.

File|Save As   Lets you save the current document as a text file. That means that you'll get all the HTML (HyperText Markup Language) codes included with it (see Chapter 12 for a discussion of HTML).

Edit|View source   Opens the document in Notepad, so you can see what it looks like. You can then save it to your disk, if you want.

Edit|View as clean text   This command is perhaps more useful. It displays the current document in Notepad, with the HTML codes *removed*. You can then use Notepad's **File|Save** command to save the clean file to your disk.

How about downloading various other files—the graphics, sounds, and so on? Cello can tell what these things are. When you click on a graphic or sound that should display, Cello transmits it, places it in your DOWNLOAD directory, and then tries to open the viewer defined in CELLO.INI as the program that works with that type of file. If you are trying to download a file straight to your DOWNLOAD directory, for example, a file from an FTP server on the Web, Cello recognizes it as such and displays the File Save dialog box, so you can give it a name and tell Cello where to put it.

Home Page Creation Made Simple

In Chapter 12, we looked at how to create a home page of your own (an HTML file), containing your own links. The procedure is just the same for Cello as it is for Mosaic. However, take a look at the Cello Help file; it has lots of useful information about creating HTML files. When you've created a new .HTM file, use the **Configure|Files and directories|Home page** command to tell Cello which file to use.

Cello also provides a *really* quick way to create a home page, based on your Bookmarks. You've just seen how to create bookmarks. Did you notice the **Dump to File** button in the Bookmark dialog box? If you click on that, you'll see a typical File Save dialog box, asking you for a file name. Call it something like **HOME.HTM** and save it. Then go to **Configure|Files and directories|Home page** and set HOME.HTM as the home page. Instantly, you have a home page that includes all the entries in your Bookmark dialog box. You can then open the HOME.HTM file in Notepad and edit it, adding and removing items, and perhaps adding explanatory text.

Setting Up Your Viewers

As with Mosaic, you have to set up certain *viewers* in order to see or listen to some of the data you'll find online. For instance, if you want to view a MPEG file, you'll need to get some kind of program that can play the file so you can view the movie. If you want to play a .MID file, you'll need a program that plays MIDI files. You can find these viewers in the CELLO.INI file, in the [Extensions] section. For example, here's how Cello sets up .WAV files to play in Windows' Sound Recorder application:

```
wav=c:\windows\soundrec.exe ^.wav
```

You've heard that the WWW contains video images, but where are they? If you want to find some sample videos on WWW, go to **http:/www.ncsa.uiuc. edu/demoweb/demo. html#exper**. You'll have to have the correct video software loaded and your viewers properly set for your WWW browser.

SPEAK LIKE A GEEK

24-bits The term *n-bit* refers to the amount of data required to save one pixel in a picture. A *1-bit* picture is one that uses one bit of data to save information about each pixel—so the picture is just black and white. A 4-bit picture can have up to 16 colors, because 4 bits can be combined in 16 different ways, each number representing a color. A 24-bit picture can have over *16 million* colors.

This simply tells Cello that when it receives a .WAV file, it should start Sound Recorder to play the file. (.WAV files are digital sound files.) You may already have some of the programs you need, but you can use anonymous FTP to **www.law.cornell.edu** and look in the **/pub/LII/ Cello** directory to find others.

For You Speed Freaks

As you've found out by now, the Web can be slow, especially when you are transferring the really neat stuff that takes up loads of room: graphics, sound, and video. Here are a couple of ways to speed things up, though.

First, turn off **Configure|Graphics|Fetch automatically**. When turned off, a logo replaces all the inline graphics (pictures inside documents that display when you view the document). Unlike Mosaic, though, you won't be able to ask Cello to show you one of these graphics if it wasn't brought in. You'll have to turn the **Configure|Graphics| Fetch automatically** feature back on and redisplay the page (use **File|Reload document**).

You may also want to turn on **Configure|Graphics|Dither**. This tells Cello to convert any 24-bit (very high resolution) inline graphics into simpler *dithered* pictures, so you can display them more quickly. Luckily, there aren't many 24-bit graphics placed inside documents yet, so it's not too much of a problem anyway.

The Other Neat Stuff I Promised

Cello's more than just a WWW browser. You can also:

- ☞ Launch a gopher session
- ☞ Launch a Telnet session
- ☞ Launch a TN3270 session
- ☞ Launch a FTP session
- ☞ Send e-mail messages
- ☞ Send computer files attached to e-mail messages

Musical Gopher

It's nice to have a gopher built-into Cello but it's too simple. You can't, for instance, enter a default gopher site; you have to type the address in each time. To launch the session, select **Jump|Launch gopher session**, type the IP address or hostname into the text box, and click on **OK**. Cello gopher's fairly easy to use; just click on the menu options you want to select. It's not as good as some of the other Gopher programs we're going to look at in Chapter 14, though. I had some problems connecting to FTP servers when using the Cello Gopher program.

Musical Telnet & TN3270

Launching a Telnet session is similar. Select **Jump|Launch telnet session**, and you'll see a dialog box that you have to type the Telnet hostname into. When you press **Enter**, Cello opens a simple window in which you will see your Telnet session. Unfortunately, it's all too simple; you're really better off working with the Windows Terminal and a dial-in terminal

STN3270 A Telnet-like program used for remote logins to IBM mainframes.

account. There's no way to automate your Telnet session by creating function buttons, for instance, and you can't even copy text from the session to the Clipboard. The only tool you have is the ability to end the session with the **Session|Close** command.

As for TN3270 sessions, Cello doesn't have a TN3270 program itself, but it lets you launch one if you have one. You'll use the **Configure|Use your own|TN3270 client** command to tell Cello where the program is, and **Jump|Launch TN3270 session** to start it. Notice also that there are **Configure|Use your own|Telnet client** and **Configure|Use your own|Editor** commands. The first lets you replace the rather simple Cello Telnet program with another (see Chapters 16), and the second lets you use a text editor other than Notepad for the operations on the Edit menu.

Musical FTP

To run an FTP session, select **Jump|Launch FTP session**. You have to enter the FTP hostname, and then Cello will login for you. This is definitely better than using FTP at the UNIX shell, but it doesn't match most of the dedicated FTP programs we're going to look at later in this book (see Chapter 11 and the chapters in Part 3).

In the main, it's easy to use. Click on a directory to see the contents of that directory. Click on a file to transfer the file. If it's a text file, though, Cello figures it out and displays the file in the window so you can read it, a great improvement over UNIX's FTP. Otherwise, it just dumps it into your DOWNLOAD directory.

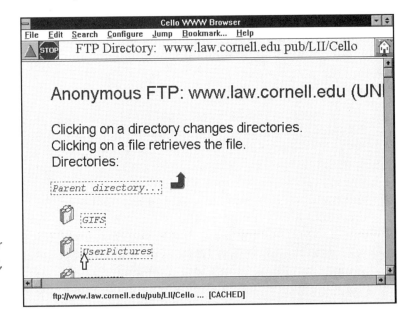

Cello comes with an FTP tool that's better than UNIX, however, not as good as other Windows programs.

Messing with Mail

Cello has a couple of mail options, though they won't always work. (I found I could use it sometimes, not others. The Cello Help file explains this.) You can quickly send an e-mail message to someone using the **Jump|Send email message** command. You'll see a compose window, with your e-mail address already filled in. Enter the address you are sending it to, the Subject, and the message, and then click on **Send**. Of course, this is a *very* simple mail system—no fancy stuff like address books or anything. However, it's handy if you come across something on the Web that you want to tell someone about quickly.

The other option is the **File|Mail file** command. This sends the current document in the window along with a mail message. So if you find some useful info in a WWW document that you know a friend or colleague may need, you can quickly zap it across to him.

Generally, I quite liked Cello. If you want simple, take Cello. If you need flexibility, you may prefer Mosaic. There are a few features in Cello that Mosaic needs, such as a sensible History list showing titles instead of URL addresses (or both, perhaps). However, Mosaic is by far the most powerful browser of the two, in that it has many more features to make working on the Web easier.

News Flash! WinWeb Arrives

Mosaic and Cello are not alone. As I was writing this book, a new Web browser was released, *WinWeb*. It's pretty easy to use, though you won't find as many features as Mosaic. There's a History list, showing you where you've been, and a Hotlist, showing you the Web pages you placed in the list. (The Hotlist is a lot simpler (and easier to use) than Mosaic's system.)

WinWeb has a handy feature for setting the home page, too. Click on an option button to select the EINet home page (the home of WinWeb) or to select the page you are currently viewing. Or simply type the URL address of the document you want to use.

Loading something onto your hard disk is fairly easy, too. Simply select **Options|Load to File**, click on the link from which you want to save, and the Save As dialog box will pop up. This is much the same as the Mosaic system. As with Mosaic, it's the only way to save stuff; you can't copy the current document to the Clipboard or save it as a file.

WinWeb has a nice look and feel to it, though right now, it doesn't have many features. That doesn't mean you wouldn't want to use it. It's easy and seems pretty fast, too. It will be interesting to see how WinWeb develops.

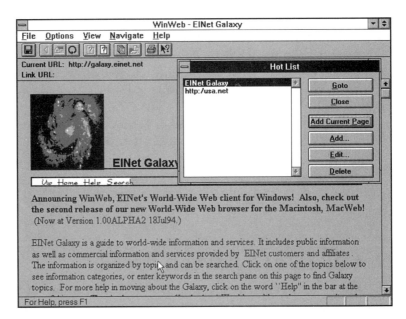

A new arrival to the Web, WinWeb.

The Least You Need to Know

☞ Cello is a free program. It's very simple to install, and is very easy to run, though it has fewer features than Mosaic.

☞ Cello comes with built-in Gopher, Telnet, TN3270, and FTP.

☞ Take a look at WinWeb, a new easy-to-use addition to the WWW.

Chapter 14

Graphical Gophers

In This Chapter

- ☛ Using Simple gopher clients, BCGopher+ and WGopher
- ☛ Working with Gopher Book, the ToolBook gopher
- ☛ Using HGopher, Britain's contribution to gopherspace
- ☛ Using the ultimate gopher, WSGopher

Gopher is one of the easiest Internet tools to use, even when you are working from the UNIX shell. Its system of menus from which you can select other menus or documents makes digging around the Internet pretty easy.

Still, it could be easier, couldn't it? What if you could transfer the advantages of "point-and-click" to gopher, plus a few other convenient features, such as extensive bookmark systems, and lists showing where you've been so you can quickly return?

Well, you'll be pleased to hear that there are several Windows gopher tools around. In fact, you can download five different *free* versions from the Internet. What could be better than that? They're all pretty easy to install, once you have your WINSOCK.DLL up and running. So why not try a few and pick the one that suits you?

BCGopher

The BC in the name of this tool presumably stands for Boston College, as it's owned by the trustees of that eminent establishment. Installing BCGopher couldn't be much easier. It comes in a self-extracting archive file. (See Chapter 27 to find out where to get it.) Place it in a directory and double-click on the file in File Manager; it will automatically extract its contents. One of the files is BCGOPHER.EXE. Create a Program Manager icon for this, and then double-click on the icon to start.

For information on finding these and other programs, see Chapter 27.

Then select **Options|Configuration**. In the Configuration dialog box, you'll probably want to enter your own Default Server name and Default Server Address; use the address given to you by your service provider. You may want to click on the **Connect on Startup** check box, so whenever you start BCGopher, you'll connect to the gopher server and start your session (otherwise you have to select the **File|New Server** option and click on **OK**).

You may also want to select **Differentiate gopher links**. This simply makes the program use different icons for menu items that jump to other gopher sites (they'll appear as little yellow folders with some sort of strange, unrecognizable red symbol on the side). And you should *definitely* change the download directory to something more appropriate. Create a subdirectory of your BCGopher directory to take files that you download from gopherspace.

BCGopher has a good context-sensitive help system. Several dialog boxes have **Help** or **?** buttons that provide information about the dialog box.

Now click on **Close Configuration**, select **File|New Server**, and click on **OK**. BC will connect to your gopher server, and you are ready to start traveling in gopherspace. A clear icon marks each gopher entry: a folder for an entry that takes you to another menu; a sheet of paper for a text file; a Rolodex for a search facility; a picture of a computer disk for a file, and so on. If you lose track of all these, select **Help|What is gopher+** to see a list.

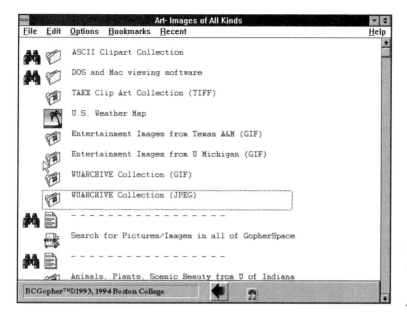

Boston College's BCGopher brings Windows to gopherspace.

Digging Around

Moving around in gopherspace with a Windows gopher is easy; it's just a matter of double-clicking on where you want to go. If it's a menu item that takes you to another menu, that's what you'll see. If it's the sheet of paper, up pops Notepad displaying the text file; you can then use the **File|Save** command to save the file to disk. If you double-click on some kind of binary file, up pops the Save As dialog box, so you can tell BCGopher where you want to place the file. You can use the Configuration dialog box to tell BCGopher what you want to do with each file type—whether you want to load it into a particular application as it's downloaded.

For example, if you download a .GIF file, BCGopher will place it on your hard disk and then attempt to run Lview: a graphics viewer that's available on the Internet. (See Chapter 27 for information about finding viewers.) You'll need to go to the Application Associations section of the Configuration dialog box to change this information, so your downloaded files run the correct applications.

There are a few other important tools for finding your way around. The large black arrow in the status bar at the bottom of the window takes you back to the previous page (as does **Recent|Previous Site**). The rest of the **Recent** menu is very handy, too, as it lists all the places you've been in this session.

You can also place bookmarks. Click on an entry in the window, and then select **Bookmarks|Add**. That entry is added to the **Bookmarks** menu, so you can get there in future sessions. You can use the **Bookmarks|List** command to see complete information about each bookmark, and even modify the information and move the entry up or down in the menu.

Gopher Book

Here's an unusual gopher: Gopher Book. You'll either love it or you'll hate it. It's based on the Asymetrix Corporation's ToolBook multimedia application. (You may have run across this without knowing it; many multimedia programs use ToolBook as a base.) Each gopher menu appears as a page in a book.

Here's how to install. Place the installation ZIP file in a directory, and extract the files. You must use the **-d** parameter. For example, type **pkunzip -d gophbook.zip** and press **Enter**. This extracts the files and places them in the correct subdirectories defined within the ZIP file.

Now go to Program Manager and create an icon for the program. You actually have to run the ToolBook program, and load the Gopher Book "document" into ToolBook. So when you are creating the program icon, the Command Line text box needs to show something like this:

```
c:\gophbook\tbook.exe gopher11.tbk
```

The last part, **gopher11.tbk** is the Gopher Book document (its name will change depending on what version you are using).

Now you can start your Internet Connection, and then double-click on the program icon to start the program. You'll see a window with a closed book inside it. Double-click on the book to open it.

Initially you'll connect to the sunsite.unc.edu gopher server. To select your own service provider's gopher server, select **Options|Configure**, then type the hostname and port into the appropriate text boxes, and click on **OK**. Then select **File|Restart Gopher** and you'll connect to your home gopher.

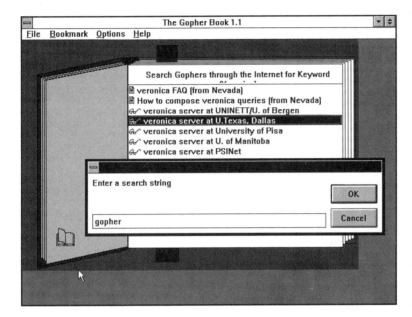

Doing a Veronica search with Gopher Book.

There's really not much to Gopher Book. Double-click on the left side of the book to return to the previous gopher menu. Double-click on an entry to select that entry, to view the submenu or read the document, or whatever.

There's a blue bookmark in the book. Double-click on it to see the list of bookmarks; double-click on one of those to jump to that menu. To place a bookmark on a gopher menu, select **Bookmark|Place** and click on **Yes**.

Gopher Book is very easy to use, but then, it doesn't have many features. You may not like the book format. The idea of Gopher Book is to "superimpose the book paradigm, one we are all familiar with, on the Gopher Information system." Seems unnecessary to me, because we all pretty much understand menus by now, too. Still, Gopher Book is quite popular, probably because of its ease of use.

HGopher

HGopher is a British contribution to gopherspace, and a pretty good one, too (I may be British, but I'm not biased, really). It's certainly more complicated than the last two gophers we just looked at. If Gopher Book is a gopherspace bicycle, then HGopher is a Lexus. It has all sorts of goodies built in, such as the capability to transfer three items at once.

It's easy to install, but it takes a little longer to configure. Copy the unzipped files into a directory, create a Program Manager icon, and double-click on the icon to start. Then select **Options|Gopher Setup**.

Now you're going to see the Gopher Set Up Options dialog box, and you have quite a few things to think about in here:

Gopher Server   The hostname of the gopher server you are going to connect to.

Port   The gopher server's port number.

Selector   A menu item in the first page of the gopher server; it lets you not only connect to that gopher server, but to a particular submenu. You don't have to use this if you don't want to. In fact, you shouldn't the first time you connect to the server, because you don't know the information that goes in here. Later, when you connect to the gopher server, you can click on the right arrow icon of the menu option you want to use, and then select **Info** from the small pop-up menu that appears. The Selector entry is what goes in the Selector text box in this dialog box.

Top Menu Title   Whatever you want to appear in the window's title bar.

Tmp Directory   A temporary directory in which HGopher can save cached menus; it keeps a copy of gopher menus, so it doesn't have to keep getting the same menu over and over. Make sure this directory actually exists.

Save to Directory   Where it saves files that you transfer. Again, make sure this actually exists.

Next come the **Gopher+ Options**. For speed, you may want to select the last option button: **Don't prefetch Gopher+ Attributes**. That means that HGopher will display a small + icon, and if you want to see the gopher+ attributes, you'll have to click on the icon, telling HGopher to go collect them. Selecting the **ASK** options turns on the capability to receive questions from a gopher+ item (it's off by default).

Click on the **Save** button to save your changes, click **OK** to close the Set Up dialog box, and then select **Commands|Go Home** to connect to the gopher server you selected.

How do you know if an item is a gopher+ item? If there's a small icon in the left column which is either a plus sign (means the gopher+ information hasn't been fetched yet; click on it to fetch the information) or a blue rectangle with a green and a red line along the top and left sides (means the gopher+ information is available).

Gopher+   A new gopher format that provides attribute information about a gopher item, such as the type of file, so a gopher client knows which file viewer will be needed to view the file. In some cases, a gopher+ server can provide different views of an item; a couple of different languages, or a couple of different file formats. A gopher plus item can also provide information, such as the document's author, and an e-mail address for the system administrator. Gopher+ items can even ask you questions. Gopher+ is not used much yet, but expect to see gophers doing all sorts of things eventually.

HGophering in Gopherspace

You'll find your way around in gopherspace in much the same way as with the other two gophers we've just seen. However, there's one important difference; you can do three things at once. Let's say you want to read three text files. You can double-click on each in succession, and HGopher gets them all. In the lower left corner of the screen, you'll see three buttons and three little text boxes. Each one controls one of the operations. Click on the button, and you'll have the opportunity to abort the process or view what HGopher has got so far. This is really handy because it lets you view just the top part of a large text file; you don't have to transfer the whole thing to check what's inside.

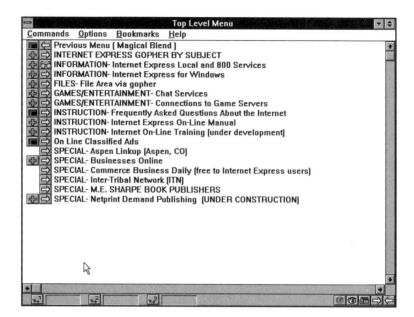

Top Level Menu

Commands   Options   Bookmarks   Help

Previous Menu [Magical Blend]
INTERNET EXPRESS GOPHER BY SUBJECT
INFORMATION- Internet Express Local and 800 Services
INFORMATION- Internet Express for Windows
FILES- File Area via gopher
GAMES/ENTERTAINMENT- Chat Services
GAMES/ENTERTAINMENT- Connections to Game Servers
INSTRUCTION- Frequently Asked Questions About the Internet
INSTRUCTION- Internet Express On-Line Manual
INSTRUCTION- Internet On-Line Training [under development]
On Line Classified Ads
SPECIAL- Aspen Linkup [Aspen, CO]
SPECIAL- Businesses Online
SPECIAL- Commerce Business Daily [free to Internet Express users]
SPECIAL- Inter-Tribal Network [ITN]
SPECIAL- M.E. SHARPE BOOK PUBLISHERS
SPECIAL- Netprint Demand Publishing [UNDER CONSTRUCTION]

HGopher takes time to learn, but is a fancy Windows gopher tool.

There's much more to HGopher. There are other configuration options. You can select the language, network options, various HGopher features, and select and configure different viewers. HGopher is definitely more complicated to set up than BCGopher or Gopher Book, but then, it's more capable. Spend some time reading the Help file that comes with HGopher. It's good, and you're going to need some training to find all the features of this thing.

WGopher

Okay, enough of the complicated stuff. Let's go back to a simple gopher, WGopher, from the Chinese University of Hong Kong (don't worry, they speak English in Hong Kong). Again, it's simple to install (you've probably noticed by now that once you've installed your TCP/IP software, such as Trumpet Winsock, installing the applications you're going to work with is easy).

Simply place WGopher in a directory and create a Program Manager icon for the WGOPHER.EXE file. Then make sure you have a \WINDOWS\TEMP directory (you probably have) and that your AUTOEXEC.BAT file has a line that says **SET TEMP=C:\WINDOWS\TEMP** (the disk drive you are using may be different, of course).

Start your Internet connection and double-click on the **WGopher** icon. Select **Setting|Configuration**, and enter your gopher server hostname and port number. You can also specify a Telnet program, TN3270 program, and Image Viewer (see Chapter 27 for more information). You'll probably also want to select **Home Gopher on Startup**, to connect to your gopher server each time you start the program. Now click on **Save** and select **File|Home Gopher** to begin.

You'll find that WGopher doesn't use fancy icons. It uses text to denote each gopher entry type: [F] for a text file, [B] for a binary file, and [D] for a directory. It puts each Gopher menu in a separate window, so if you travel through several levels, all levels remain on the screen (and can be quickly displayed using the **Windows** menu).

WGopher has a simple bookmark system. Select **Bookmarks|Open Bookmarks** to open a blank window. Now, whenever you find a menu item you want to place as a bookmark, simply select **Bookmarks|Set Bookmark** to add it to the Bookmarks window. (You can make WGopher open the Bookmarks window each time you connect using an option in the Configuration dialog box.)

WGopher's a simple little gophering tool; I think many people will appreciate its simplicity and the ability to work with several windows at once. I also like the WGopher icon, which looks little like a real gopher and more like a character out of Top Cat or Heathcliff. Maybe they don't have gophers in Hong Kong.

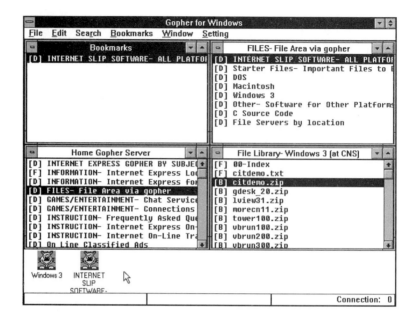

WGopher is easy to use, and has a really neat icon, too.

WSGopher

Okay, now you've had a rest; let's finish up with a more complicated tool: WSGopher. As usual, just throw all the files into a directory you've created for WSGopher, and then create a Program Manager icon for WSGOPHER.EXE. (Come to think of it, the WSGopher icon doesn't look much like a gopher, either—more like a starved cat.) Start your Internet connection, and then double-click on the **WSGopher** icon.

Select **Configure|Home Gopher Server**. Enter your gopher server's hostname (you can actually enter two, in case there's a backup hostname). There's a check box to note whether your gopher server is a gopher+ server, too. You'll have to ask your service provider. When you've entered this information, click on the **OK** button; then select **File|Home Gopher** to connect.

WSGopher has a really good Bookmark system; it's already set up with dozens of different entries to useful gopher sites. You can assign book-marks to various categories: Libraries, Music, Business, Weather, and so on. Click on a toolbar button to open a dialog box, select a category, and double-click on a bookmark to go there or download the item referenced by the bookmark. (The strange thing is that from the Bookmark menu, you can create categories and bookmarks and edit them, but I never did find a menu option to open the dialog box where you actually *use* the bookmarks. I had to use the toolbar button.)

WSGopher actually has the feel of a commercial program more than a shareware or freeware program. It has many configuration options, makes selecting a viewer quite easy, has a nice little utility to delete downloaded files from its download directory, and has an excellent online help system. It also has a sophisticated "extended view" system, which lets you define how WSGopher selects which view to show you when working with a gopher+ item. (You don't have to worry too much about this; gopher+ isn't currently being used to its full potential since it's relatively new.)

There's a surprising range of speeds among these gophers. I found WSGopher to be pretty quick, while Gopher Book was a bit sluggish. What's going on online is not the only thing that slows these programs up, evidently.

Category: Libraries (electronic), 11 bookmarks

Categories: Libraries (electronic)
Title: Barron's Guide to On-line Bibliographic Databases
Server name: gopher.uiuc.edu
Server port: 70
Selector: 1/Libraries/Barron
Item type: Directory   ☐ Gopher Plus

Barron's Guide to On-line Bibliographic Databases
Electronic books, ref works, journals (from U of Minnesota)
Go MLink
Internet Library Catalogs (from Yale)
Internet-Accessible Libraries and Databases
Library Resources on the Internet
Non-USA Library Databases
Noonan Guide to Internet Libraries
Telnet Sessions to Library Programs
Virginia Library and Information Network (VLIN) Gopher
VIRTUAL REFERENCE DESK- from UC Irvine

Fetch
Delete
Move
>>Clipboard
<<Clipboard
OK
Cancel
Help

Status: Loading category 'Libraries (electronic)'

WSGopher has an excellent Bookmark system.

Which gopher do I use? Depends on my mood. Remember, I have some of the commercial gophers, too (WinGopher, in Chapter 21, is especially good). Still, out of this bunch, I think I like WSGopher the most. The system of bookmarks is especially useful. That's not to say *you* will want WSGopher. All these programs are all easy to find and install, so try them, and pick the one you prefer.

The Least You Need to Know

- ☛ Windows Gophering tools are plentiful—and free.

- ☛ The most complicated—and useful—Gopher clients are HGopher and WSGopher.

- ☛ Gopher Book is a simple system based on the book "paradigm."

- ☛ WGopher and BCGopher are two other simple and easy-to-use Gopher clients.

Chapter 15
Keeping Up with Things— News & Mail

In This Chapter

- Using Trumpet for Windows
- Using the Eudora e-mail program
- Using WinQVT for e-mail, news, FTP, and Telnet
- Using the WinVN newsreader
- Using the WinElm e-mail program

It's Him Again—Trumpet for Windows

The Aussie Peter Tattam has been pretty busy. Not only did he bring us Trumpet Winsock, but Trumpet for Windows, too (plus a few other Internet programs). Trumpet for Windows is a nice little e-mail and news program that's easy to install and use.

Start by creating a directory and placing the files into the directory. Then create a Program Manager icon for the WT_WSK.EXE file. Double-click on the icon and you'll see a copyright screen, followed by the Trumpet Setup dialog box.

For information about finding these programs, see Chapter 27.

Trumpet for Windows is well documented, so check the WTDOC.DOC file for instructions for this dialog box. It's straightforward; you have to enter some of the information you gathered from your service provider in Chapter 8. You enter information that tells Trumpet where the NNTP news server is, where the SMTP mail server is, and where you save your mail (POP3). There's also a check box called **Fetch Read-only**. Select this, and when Trumpet reads your mail, it won't remove it from the POP3 server, so you can retrieve it again from another program.

When you click on **OK**, Trumpet is ready to start. It will try to connect to your service provider's system, and grab a list of your service provider's newsgroups. Now for the fun part. Select **Group|Subscribe** and wait a little while for the program to grab the list of newsgroups. Then you'll see a dialog box showing you all the newsgroups you can subscribe to. Click on a name in the **Top Level Hierarchy** list box to see all the groups in that hierarchy. Then click on the ones you want to subscribe to. There's also a useful little search feature; type a few characters into the Search text box, and only the newsgroup names containing those few characters appear in the list box.

Be careful. Remember that newsgroups are addictive, and the easier it is to get an addictive substance, the greater the chance of addiction. Perhaps alt.aliens.visitors, alt.amazon-women.admirers, alt.pictures.binaries.erotica.furry, and sci.aeronautics.airliners all sound intriguing, but consider what effect reading thousands of these things each day will have on your career and social life.

ROT13   A simple code in which each character in a message is replaced with the character 13 places further down the alphabet. It's easy to "crack" but stops people accidentally stumbling across offensive or obscene messages. The plain message looks like garbage until you turn on the ROT13 feature, which converts it back to its original form.

Still, if you decide you are going to risk it, click on **OK**. Your subscribed groups appear at the top of the dialog box. Double-click on one of them, and Trumpet for Windows runs off and gets all the newsgroup messages for you. It shows you a list of messages; you can then double-click on the first one you want to read.

Trumpet for Windows provides plenty of commands to make working with newsgroups relatively simple. You can mark all the messages as read, or change your mind and retrieve them all. Or mark all of them as read, and then retrieve the last 10 or 20 articles. This is handy if you join a large newsgroup and don't want to read all 300 messages, or if you can pull yourself away from newsgroups to go on vacation for a week. You can also reply to a message's author, send a follow-up back to the newsgroup, post your own message, forward a message via e-mail, save the message in a text file, and move a message to a folder for storage. It's all easy and convenient. You can even turn ROT13 on and off.

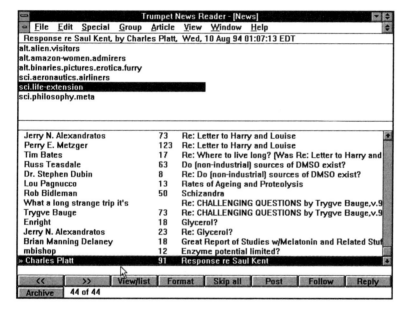

Trumpet for Windows sure beats rn, tin, nn, and trn, the UNIX newsreaders.

And Now for the Mail

Trumpet for Windows has two windows: one for mail and one for newsgroups. Select **Window|Mail**, select **File|Fetch Mail**, and Trumpet for Windows downloads your mail for you. The setup is similar. The window has a top panel listing each folder (use the **Special|Insert folder** command to create folders—when you fetch mail it's placed in the Incoming Mail folder), and a bottom panel showing each message in the folder. Double-click on a message to read it. You can then forward, delete, reply, save in a file, place in a folder—all the usual stuff.

Eudora

Eudora is a commercial e-mail program available from QUALCOMM Incorporated. However, they also release a freeware version; obviously it won't have all the features that the commercial program has, but it's pretty good nonetheless. Its major drawback is that it's distributed without documentation (they want you to buy the real one, after all). Still, you can probably figure most of it out with a little work. It may be worth more than a little work, because it's a nice program (though it's a little sensitive and seems to crash rather easily).

Installation's pretty easy. Place the files into a directory, create a Program Manager icon for WELLDORA.EXE, start your Internet connection, and double-click on the icon you created to start Eudora. When it opens, select **Special|Configuration**, and enter all your setup information. The POP Account is your e-mail address (that is, jobloe@apotpeel.com, for instance). The rest of the information is pretty obvious. You'll get your SMTP Server address from your service provider (see Chapter 8), and you can enter your real name, a return address (if you want to place that in your outgoing mail), and you can tell Eudora how often to check the server for incoming mail. You can even select the font you want to use when displaying or printing your messages.

When you close this dialog box, select **Special|Switches** to see a dialog box listing all sorts of options. One you may want to use for now, until you are sure you fully understand Eudora, is the **Leave Mail on Server** option. This makes sure that when Eudora grabs mail from the server, it doesn't delete it. You can still get to it again, from Eudora or from another e-mail program. Read the other options. Some will be obvious, others not so.

When you close this dialog box, you can use the **File|Check Mail** command to get your e-mail. You'll see a list of message subjects; click on one to open another document window in which you can read the message.

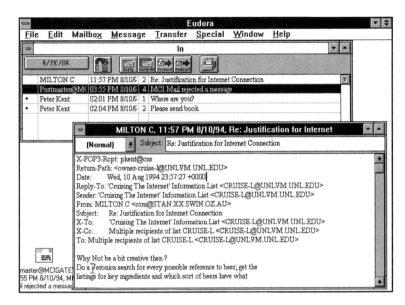

Eudora places lists and messages in their own windows.

Eudora has a great file-transfer system. You can choose to send a file as a UUENCODED file or by using the MIME system. Either way, it's pretty transparent to you. When a message containing a file comes in, Eudora automatically converts it and places it on your hard disk, whether it's UUENCODED or sent using MIME.

Eudora has many nice features. You can create your own mailboxes, and place those mailboxes in folders, creating a hierarchical system by which you can sort your mail. You can change a message's *queuing*, sending it immediately, sending it in a batch at a specific time, or holding it. You can even run the **finger** command on an e-mail address from Eudora, so you can check to see if it's valid. There are all sorts of message-sorting options and search options.

There's an unusual *nicknames* system. When a message comes in, you can select it, select **Special|Make Nickname**, and enter a name. Click on the **Put it on the recipient list** and then click on **OK**. Eudora adds that name to the nicknames list (which you can see by selecting **Window|Nicknames**). Now, when you want to send a message to some-one, you can just select **Message|New Message To** to see the list of nick-names. Select one to use that person's address in the new message. You can also go to the nicknames window and enter notes about each person. If you want to create mailing lists, enter several addresses for each name.

SPEAK LIKE A GEEK

UUENCODED computer files are files that have been converted to ASCII text. You can convert them back by UUDECODING. The MIME (Multipurpose Internet Mail Extensions) system lets you send computer files directly without converting them to ASCII. However, you can't use MIME unless the person receiving the mail is also using a MIME-capable e-mail program.

Eudora is a useful program, so it's well worth your time to figure out how it all fits together. Who knows, you may like it enough to cough up $65 for the full version to get the manual and even more neat features. After all, that's why QUALCOMM puts the program out there, isn't it?

WinQVT

WinQVT is a strange mixture of Internet applications. When you start the program, all you see is a window (showing status messages) with a button bar at the top. The button bar starts the five applications: Terminal (Telnet), FTP, Mail, News, and lpr (a utility that lets you send files from your computer to network printers—not much use for most dial-in direct users, of course).

If you want to try WinQVT, make sure you get the right version. There's one for a Windows Sockets installation, and one for a packet driver (if you are on a network rather than a dial-in direct line). Spend some time reading all the documentation that comes with the program. You have to set up a number of things just right. You must make an entry into the QVTNET.INI file or the Windows Sockets *hosts* file, and add a line to your AUTOEXEC.BAT file. You must do much of the setup of each component in the .INI file.

Unfortunately the documentation isn't very clear on how to *use* the program. There is, however, an online help file that lists what each menu command and button does.

Using WinQVT: All the News Fit to Print

When you start the news reader, you'll see a blank window. Select **Newsgroups|Subscribe**. (In later sessions, you can simply use the **File|Open** command to start a newsgroup session, unless you want to subscribe to another group.) You'll see a dialog box. Simply click on the **OK** button to see a list of all the newsgroups your service provider subscribes to, or type a word first to find only those group names containing that word.

Now, don't freak. It may look like your computer has locked up, but give it five minutes; WinQVT is grabbing the list of newsgroups. (Of course, you are running Windows, so your computer *may have* locked up!) When the list of groups appears, subscribe to the ones you want by double-clicking. Then, to read a group's messages, click on the group, and click on **Load Articles**.

WinQVT's news reader is easy to use, but doesn't have all the features available on other systems. You can mark groups as read, and unmark them. You can post your own messages, or send a follow-up message. And you can save messages to disk. However, there's not much else in the way of newsgroup management.

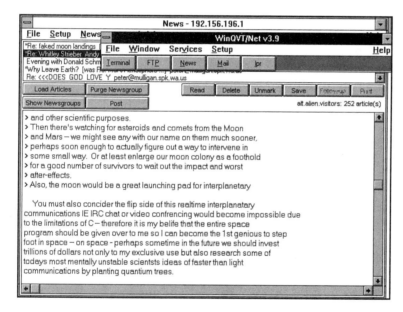

WinQVT's control panel launches each application.

Where's My Mail?

When you start the mail program, you have to select **File|Open** to begin. Again, it may look like your system is locking up, but give the program a while to download your mail. Then you'll be able to double-click on a message that you want to read.

You can then save the message in a file, print it, reply to it, or delete it. That's about it. (Of course, you can send e-mail out, too.) WinQVT does not have a really "feature-rich" mail program, but it's easy to use.

...And the Rest

WinQVT also has FTP and Telnet. FTP is really an FTP window. Once started, you are in a window in which you have to type FTP commands; you may as well be at the UNIX shell. It really can't compare to WS_FTP, for instance.

Telnet is a bit more capable. You can remap your keyboard for a particular system you are connecting to. And you can also setup screen colors and the font you want to use. You can also create a script file, to automate some online procedures, log the session in a text file, and even save an image of the current screen in a file. The Telnet portion of WinQVT is, perhaps, the best part.

WinQVT might be best described as "a decent little program." In other words, yes, it's okay and it's handy, but it doesn't have all the features of other programs that deal with one function at a time rather than five different ones.

WinVN

Back to basics. WinVN sticks with one application: newsgroups. (It lets you send e-mail, too, but you need to be able to do this so you can respond directly to people who have posted messages to newsgroups.)

Don't open too many groups at once, or you'll get lost in the windows. As long as you only open one at a time, you'll have a maximum of three windows open.

WinVN has a simple installation. Place the files in a directory, create a Program Manager icon for WINVN.EXE, start your Internet connection, and double-click on the **WinVN** icon. The first time you start, you'll have to fill in two fairly simple configuration dialog boxes (refer to your information from Chapter 8).

WinVN will ask you if you want to see the entire newsgroup list. If you say yes, it'll take a while, of course. Eventually, you'll see the window fill with the list. Click on the ones you want to subscribe to, select **Group|Subscribe selected groups**, and WinVN moves the group names to the top of the list. There's a handy search command, too, so you can find likely groups.

When you have them all, double-click on a group to see its messages. Each time you open something, it's placed in a different window: one window for the list of newsgroups, one for the list of messages in a group, and one for the current message.

This is probably one of the easiest newsgroup programs I've seen. I also like the way it handles the list, keeping the full list in view and the subscribed groups at the top of the list.

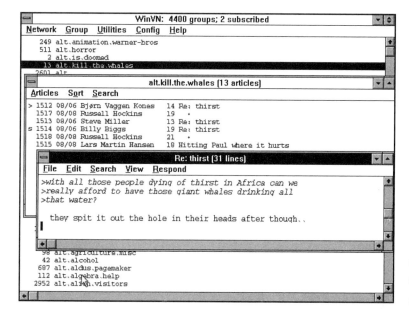

WinVN provides lots of features that make newsgroup reading easy.

You can automatically UUDECODE messages, which is really handy if you are in the habit of downloading pirated and pornographic photographs from the newsgroups. You can view ROT13 articles, save and print articles, jump to the next article with the same subject. You can do just about anything you'd want to do with your newsgroup articles (even get rid of them all using the Catch Up and Exit command).

WinVN is an excellent newsreader, which just goes to show that you don't necessarily get what you pay for. WinVN is as good or better than some commercial products—and it's free!

WinElm

WinElm was created for psychics. There's no user manual and no online help. If you want to know how to use it, you just have to know. If you can manage to get it up and running, you'll probably be able to figure out how to use it, as the commands are all visible on buttons and in a list box. (However, you may not get it running.) Also, it doesn't seem to have been updated since the middle of 1993; so perhaps it's moribund.

If you've used the DOS program ELM-PC, though, you may want to try WinElm. It consists of two parts: the main program (where you do all the work with your messages) and the "mail transport," a small program used to grab the e-mail from your service provider's system.

The system is not very configurable, though. You either have to enter your name, password, and POP3 server each time you log on, or you have to enter it in the Command line of the Program Manager icon you are using to start the system. And the mail handling features are fairly primitive when compared to some of the other programs that are available.

You may want to check out WinElm to see if there have been any changes, but if Release 2 (May, 1993) is the only version available, you're better off with something else.

The Least You Need to Know

☞ There are several nice newsreaders and mail programs available.

☞ Trumpet for Windows is a great program that handles both mail and newsgroups.

☞ WinVN is an excellent newsgroup reader, and it's free.

☞ WinQVT is just okay, although it has a reasonable Telnet program.

☞ WinElm is poorly documented, and you may have trouble getting it running.

Chapter 16
Bits 'n Pieces

In This Chapter

- Using Telnet programs
- Using Internet Talk
- *Really* talking on the Internet
- Using Internet Relay Chat
- Using the **finger** command
- Using the **ping** command
- Using WAIS programs

Well, we haven't quite finished. If you read the preceding chapters, you have all the really important stuff—or at least know where to get it and what to do with it. However, you need a few other things. What about Telnet (not such a small item, really), and a way to chat on the Internet (not so small if you're addicted to it)? What about a way to use the **finger** and **ping** commands (small, but useful)? Read on, and you'll find out all about those and even a way to send your *voice* over the Internet.

Telnet

A lot of useful resources are available via Telnet connections, and there's no reason you can't get to them just because you are using a Windows connection. Check out these ideas.

Use Anything You Want—with Com*t*

If you've been using a dial-in terminal account for a while and have used Telnet extensively, you may run into a problem when you take the dial-in direct route. If you have modified your favorite telecommunications to make your Telnet sessions easier to work with—you may have added keyboard shortcuts, function buttons, scripts, and so on—you are going to have to throw it all away. You can't use your terminal program on a TCP/IP connection! Or can you?

Well, yes, you can—if you get ahold of Com*t*, a little utility that fools your computer's communications ports into working with your network or dial-in direct connection. (See Chapter 27 to learn where to find it.) You will "connect" your communications program to a communications port that isn't being used, such as COM4. Then start your WINSOCK.DLL connection and "dial" your communications program through that port, using the hostname or IP address as the phone number. Com*t* intercepts the program's communications and sends it onto the WINSOCK.DLL, which connects you to the Telnet site. It's just like dialing into a bulletin board, only without the dialing (if you see what I mean).

Watch out for a couple of things. First, many programs won't let you enter text as a phone number. Or they will, but they convert the text to a number using the telephone keypad's number/letter sequence (you know, 1-800-BIG-FOOL). So with many, perhaps most, communications programs, you won't be able to enter a Telnet site's hostname; you must enter the IP address. (With Windows Terminal, for instance, you must enter an IP address.) You can find the IP address by *pinging* the hostname (you can use WS Ping if you want; see later in this chapter). Then use the number that ping returns as the telephone number in your communications program.

I also found that when I loaded Windows' Terminal using a program icon that was set up to automatically load a particular setup (the setup I use when I connect to my libraries local online system) and then opened my COM-T.TRM setup file, I couldn't get the system working. (Hey, I was just being lazy; I had Windows' Terminal all set up to run this other system, and didn't want to create another icon.) If I opened Windows Terminal without the library setup, then opened the COM-T.TRM system, I had no problems, everything ran smoothly.

This is a great system. Once you've installed Com*t*, you can run any telecommunications program you want. Get a fancy program, such as HyperACCESS, CrossTalk, ProComm, Qmodem, or whatever, and you can automate all sorts of things in your Telnet sessions. Even Windows' Terminal will let you create function keys to speed up operations.

NCSA Telnet

Here's another one from the National Center for Supercomputing Applications, *NCSA Telnet*. However, it's not in the same league as Mosaic. NCSA Telnet is a *very* simple program. It's currently unsupported, and may be a little unstable. (You can find out how to get this program, and all the other programs mentioned in the book, in Chapter 27.)

To create a list of Telnet sites that you want to connect to, edit the WINTEL.INI file. Then start the program and select a site from the drop-down menu that appears (or type another hostname in the text box). Once the session starts, you're pretty much on your own. You can copy and paste to and from the session window, select the font you want to see in the window, and choose between the Delete and Backspace key for deleting text during the session. And that's it.

Take a look at WinQVT in Chapter 15. It comes with a good Telnet program, more advanced than either NCSA Telnet or Trumpet Telnet.

Trumpet Telnet

Here's another simple Telnet program. It's easy to install (just place it in a directory and create an icon for it, if you want). But it's *very* simple. You can connect to a Telnet session, and that's all—except, you can connect to several sessions at once, and put each in a separate window that you can minimize or hide behind another.

Yakety Yak Revised

Remember way back in Chapter 1, when we were talking about talking on the Internet? Well, a few programs will let you do just that—use the Internet's talk and chat facilities from Windows.

WinTalk

WinTalk shows just how a graphical-user-interface program can be so much more flexible and easier to use than a command-line program. WinTalk has a little smiley face icon that sits on your "desktop." When you want to talk with someone, click on the icon, then click on **Talk** in the menu that pops up. Select the person from a drop-down list box and click on **OK**. A window opens up with two parts: one part is where your typing appears, and the other part is where the other person's typing appears.

You'll remember that in UNIX talk, these windows are one on top of the other. They are in WinTalk, too—but you can change that and put them side by side, if you want. You can also change the panel and text colors, and enter a word-wrap value. There are other configuration items, too. Do you want a dialog box to appear when someone calls you, or should the program play a sound? Or both? What sound do you want played? Select any .WAV file you want. What sort of requests should you accept: invitations to talk from any local user, any user at all, or nobody? And when you refuse a call, what message should the person extending the invitation see?

WSIRC

WSIRC stands for Windows Sockets Internet Relay Chat. If you're an IRC junkie, there's no need to go cold turkey just because you set up a dial-in direct Windows system. Use WSIRC to get your fix.

The version I've looked at was an early one, and a little unstable. By the time you read this, though, perhaps it will be a bit easier to use. It provides three windows: one large one in which most of your "work" is done, a small one at the bottom where you type, and a vertical strip along the right side where certain information appears, such as lists of the IRC channels. The help file is useful, too, as it has a list of IRC commands and servers (the program doesn't automate entering commands, you still have to type them in).

Internet VoiceChat

Do you have relatives in Moldova? Peru? Albania? I bet those long distance calls are mounting up, aren't they? You may have thought about using Internet's Talk tool to *chat* to friends and relatives overseas. It's much cheaper.

Not exactly personal though, is it? I mean can you type emotions and reactions? Listen in on Internet Relay Chat or a Ytalk or Talk session and you'll notice people typing goofy stuff like **smile**, **chuckle**, and **sigh**. If your grandchildren are five thousand miles away and their parents type **the kids say hi!**—well, it's not quite the same as the real thing, is it?

Well, try Internet VoiceChat. If you have a sound card and a microphone all correctly hooked up to your Windows computer, and if the people you are calling do, too, Internet VoiceChat will let you actually *talk*. Real words. Laughter, chuckles, all that stuff. And at $1.25/hour or whatever you are paying for your Internet connection, it's much cheaper than long distance calls!

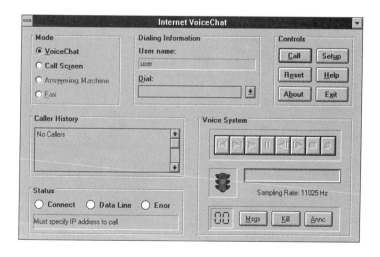

Internet VoiceChat's control panel lets you set up a real conversation.

This is shareware, and if you register it, you get more neat stuff, such as the answering-machine mode. You know how an answering machine works don't you? Someone calls. You're not there. They hear your message. They leave a message. Neat.

The author, Richard Ahrens, promises a Fax mode later, which will let you send .GIF and .BMP images (pictures of the grandchildren, perhaps). Future plans include a CB mode for conference calls and voice actuation; the program will sense when you start talking and automatically begin recording. The current version won't work with Trumpet Winsock, but a new version that will work with Trumpet Winsock will be released soon.

Finger

Finger's a handy tool. You can use it to check that an e-mail address you have is correct, or to get information from someone's .plan file (see Chapter 5). There are a couple of Windows finger applications you should check out, **Finger** and **WS Finger**. Both are simple to use, but there's a problem with the current version of WS Finger because the window it uses is so narrow, it sometimes truncates lines of text.

```
╔═══════════════════════════════════════════════════════════════════╗
║ ─           Finger - typhoon.atmos.colostate.edu             ▼│▲ ║
╠═══════════════════════════════════════════════════════════════════╣
║ │Host                                                              ║
║ Login name: forecast                  In real life: Forecast status║
║ Directory: /users/Forecast                                        ║
║ Never logged in.                                                  ║
║ No unread mail                                                    ║
║ Plan:                                                             ║
║ ****************************************************************** ║
║ STATUS OF GRAY'S ATLANTIC   1944- | Nov 24 | Jun 7 | Aug 5 |Observed
║ SEASONAL HURRICANE FORECAST  1993 |  1993  |  1994 |  1994 |      ║
║ FOR 1994                     Mean | Fcst.  | Fcst. | Fcst. |      ║
║ ================================================================= ║
║ Named Storms                 9.3 |   10   |   9   |   7   |    1  ║
║ Named Storm Days            46.1 |   60   |  35   |  30   |  2.0  ║
║ Hurricanes                   5.7 |    6   |   5   |   4   |    0  ║
║ Hurricane Days              23.0 |   25   |  15   |  12   |    0  ║
║ Major Hurricanes (Category 3-4-5)  2.2 | 2 | 1 |  1   |    0  ║
║ Major Hurricane Days         4.5 |    7   |   1   |   1   |    0  ║
║ Hurricane Destruction Potential  68.1 | 85 | 40 | 35   |    0  ║
║ ****************************************************************** ║
║                                                                   ║
║                                                                   ║
║                         ▷                                         ║
╚═══════════════════════════════════════════════════════════════════╝
```

Getting the typhoon forecast with Finger 3.1.

WS Ping

Ping is a useful command for a few reasons, even if you don't understand all the network gobbledygook it provides. You can use it to make sure your network connection is working. You can use it to make sure the host you are trying to reach actually exists and is reachable. And you can use it to convert a hostname to an IP number; you ping the hostname and get an IP number back. Try WS Ping, an easy to use and flexible Ping program.

Where does all this WS stuff come from, WS Ping, WS_FTP, WS Finger? WS stands for Windows Sockets, the method by which windows programs can communicate with a TCP/IP connection.

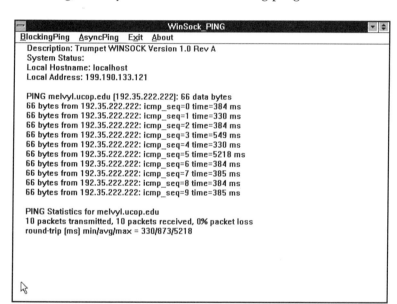

WS Ping checks your Internet connections for you.

Where's WAIS?

WAIS (Wide Area Information Server) seems to have all but disappeared from the Windows scene. Throughout this book, I've only mentioned it once, I think, when talking about America Online—that service has combined gopher and WAIS. The other commercial and shareware products generally don't include a WAIS tool.

There are a couple of shareware WAIS programs for Windows, though, one from EINet and one from the U.S. Geological Survey. Unfortunately they both have the same name: WinWAIS! (At least, one is called EINet winWAIS and the other is called WAIS for Windows [WinWAIS].)

They are both a little confusing, but WAIS itself can be a little confusing if you are not used to working with it. Of the two, the EINet version is probably easier to use. Both programs come with online help, and EINet winWAIS also comes with some image viewers.

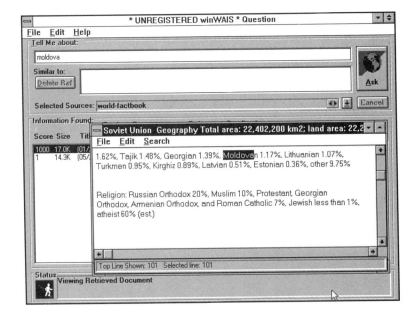

EINet WinWAIS lets you search a Wide Area Information Server.

The Least You Need to Know

- ☛ Com*t* lets you use any telecommunications program with a TCP/IP connection.

- ☛ NCSA Telnet and Trumpet Telnet are very basic Telnet programs, without the frills.

- ☛ See WinQVT for a good Telnet program (see Chapter 15).

- ☞ WinTalk is a nice Windows front end for talk sessions.

- ☞ Internet VoiceChat lets you actually talk with other Internet users—real voices!

- ☞ WS IRC is a new program that lets you use Internet Relay Chat from Windows.

- ☞ WS Finger and Finger let you run the **finger** command. WS Finger truncates the text, though.

- ☞ Use WS Ping to check connections and convert hostnames to IP numbers.

- ☞ EINet WinWAIS and WAIS for Windows provide a graphical user interface for your WAIS searches.

Hey, now's a good time to take a break. Relax. Close your eyes. Roll your head around. Your neck is a well-cooked piece of asparagus.

Part III
The Cough-Up-
the-Dough Route

Okay, so there are good reasons for not digging around and installing shareware, freeware, and public domain software on your system. The main reason is installation hassles. If you read the last part of this book, you will know that installing your own dial-in direct account can sometimes be a hassle. You may be tempted to buy an all-in-one system. Pay yer money and get running. Take a look at the systems in the next few chapters. They range from the merely okay to the truly excellent, from pretty cheap to a little pricey. One of them might suit you.

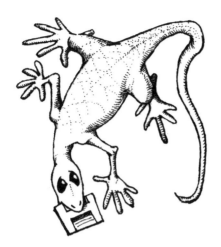

Chapter 17
The Lizard's Loose—Internet Chameleon

In This Chapter

- ☞ Looking at the Internet Chameleon applications
- ☞ Creating a login script for Chameleon
- ☞ Testing the login script

Internet Chameleon by NetManage is one of the better-known commercial systems for Windows Internet access. It's an all-in-one package, or almost, anyway. (It doesn't include a World Wide Web browser but you can load and run Mosaic once you connect with Chameleon if you want.) Unlike working with shareware and public domain software, there's no need to worry about loading WINSOCK and then finding all the bits 'n pieces you need. Just cough up your $199, load Internet Chameleon, and you are ready to roll.

NetManage claims that you can install the product and get it running in five minutes. That's a little optimistic. Maybe the box should say "five-minute installation if you are connecting to a service with a preconfigured setup and everything goes well." It took me several hours to get it running, including a couple of calls to technical support, mainly because the documentation was weak when it came to writing logon scripts.

Also, there are a few bugs. I had the system freeze once or twice, and on several occasions, it crashed Windows, jumping straight back the DOS prompt. But let's face it, how many Windows programs *don't* kick you out now and again?

We're going to start by taking a look at the product and the different components. If you decide to use Internet Chameleon, make sure you read the end of this chapter, where I explain how to create a Login script. (For information on where to find Internet Chameleon, see Chapter 27.)

So What's in It?

Here's what comes with Internet Chameleon:

☞ **Custom**   This is the program you use to make the connection to your service provider, to load, in effect, WINSOCK.DLL. Just open the application and click on Connect and away you go.

☞ **Finger**   Automates the finger command.

☞ **FTP & FTP Server**   An FTP application to make transferring files easier. The FTP Server lets you make files on your system available to others via FTP.

☞ **Gopher**   A File-Manager type Gopher menu system.

☞ **Mail & Mail Utilities**   E-mail made easy.

☞ **NEWT News**   Simplifies your access to newsgroups.

☞ **Ping**   Test the connection to other hosts using ping.

☞ **Telnet**   Login to other computers on the Internet.

☞ **TFTP**   A Trivial File Transfer Protocol program. You can use TFTP to transfer files between systems without any directory or file listings, but you probably won't use this much; use FTP unless you run into a system that doesn't support FTP (rare).

☞ **Whois**   Use the Internet Whois system to track down other Internet users.

The major complaint that I have about Internet Chameleon is the poor documentation. Remember to check the online help; it's more detailed than the book. However, the two contradict each other in places, so you'll have to play around to figure out which is correct. There are a few basic usability problems with the programs. Still, it shouldn't take too long to figure out how to use all these tools, and they certainly beat the UNIX command line.

FTP

Chameleon's FTP application could use some improvement (I found WS_FTP much easier to use, and it's free!). Move around in directories by double-clicking on the file folder icon. Get files by clicking on the file and then on the arrow button next to Copy (the one pointing to your Local directory). Read text files by clicking on a file and then on the arrow button next to the View label (the one pointing to the file). You can also use Append to add a text file to the end of another one, create and delete directories, delete and rename files, and get information about files.

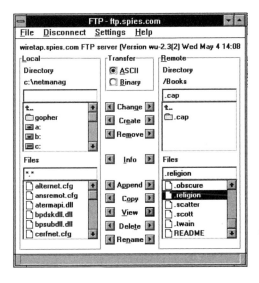

Chameleon's FTP application is easier than the UNIX command line, but could be better.

Chameleon Mail

Use Chameleon Mail for a few days and I'll guarantee you won't pine for Pine—or for Elm for that matter, and certainly not for UNIX mail. I'm assuming, of course, that if you've read this far, you are not one of those "the-command-line's-faster-than-a-GUI-and-anyway-there's-nothing-you-can-do-with-Windows-that-I-can't-do-with-a-batch-file" dinosaurs.

If you like the idea of being able to click on a button to reply or forward a message, to copy text to and from other programs, of seeing all the commands listed in menus or described in the status bar when you pass the mouse over the toolbar button, you'll like Chameleon Mail. (Again, it could do with some improvement; they need someone with experience in user interface design. Hey, I know someone who could do it! NetManage, give me a call!)

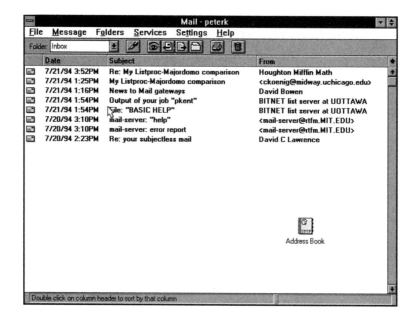

E-mail made simple. Internet Chameleon has an easy-to-use e-mail system.

Chameleon Mail has a very basic address book; it'll save addresses, but you can't include a note or description. In fact, it saves less information than Pine's address book, which seems a little sad. Still, it's easy to use. Click on the **Names** button when you are ready to add the To address to a message; double-click on the names you want to send the message to; and click on the **OK** button. You can create groups, so you can mail to a number of people at the same time.

You can do all the normal mail stuff, of course, though you get the wonders of a Windows program to help you along; click on buttons and select menu options to carry out commands. Cut and paste is a real help when working with e-mail; you can cut stuff out of documents and paste it into a message or vice versa.

You can reply to and forward mail, print and delete messages, copy messages into a text file, and so on. Plus, there are a few extra niceties. Messages that you write are placed in the outbox, so you can write them when you are off-line, and send them later, when you go online.

And Chameleon Mail will get your mail from the POP server when you start the program, when you tell it to do so, or at an interval that you set—every 10 minutes, every hour, or whatever.

Shove 'Em in 'Ere

Do you find that you can't delete e-mail? I mean you *can*, but you just can't bring yourself to do so? After all, that message from Bert in the next office asking you if you want to go for a beer might one day be useful, so why get rid of it now—you can always do so later.

Folders are what you need. Create mail folders—one for messages from the boss, one for friends, one for each LISTERV group of which you are a member, and one for "garbage that you should probably delete but don't want to decide right now." Once you've created your folders, you can quickly and easily move mail to the correct folder while reading it. Click on a button to see a list of folders and double-click on the one you want. You can quickly move to any folder to read the messages using a drop-down list box at the main Mail window.

> When Chameleon retrieves messages from the service provider's POP server, it doesn't necessarily delete them. If it doesn't, the messages stay there and will be retrieved again, over and over, until you delete them. To make sure Chameleon deletes them, select **Settings|Network|Mail Server** and click on the **Delete retrieved mail from server** check box.

Finally, Real File Transfer! (Perhaps)

Chameleon lets you send actual computer files attached to your e-mail messages. Simply click on the **Paperclip** button, and then select the file you want to attach from a dialog box. When you send the message, the file goes with it. Of course, there's a catch. The person receiving the file has to be able to accept such a message, and most Internet users don't have programs that will, at least for the moment. If you receive attached files, you can even view the file without extracting it from the message (as long as its extension has been "associated" with a Windows application).

You can also UUENCODE messages. Remember this? You take a file you want to transfer—a desktop publishing file, a sound, a picture, or what-ever—then you use the UUENCODE program to convert it to a text file. Then you send the text file, and the person at the other end, being the sort of knowledgeable type that you hang out with, knows just what to do with it. He quickly decodes the file with UUDECODE, converting it into its original format, and "Bob's your uncle" (as they say in England), it's all done. The original file is now on the recipient's computer disk.

Problem is, things don't seem to work like this very often. The other person sends e-mail back telling you that when he tried to play the sound file, his sound board spat out the file, or the desktop publishing program opened up the document file but it was full of strange Greek poems.

Chameleon can help, though. To UUENCODE a file and add it to a message, simply select **Uuencode** from the Message menu, and select the file you want from a dialog box. When you receive a UUENCODED mes-sage, simply select **Uudecode** from the Message menu, and Chameleon Mail will convert it for you.

Chameleon's Gopher

Internet Chameleon's Gopher is a simple gophering application. If you spend a lot of time in gopherspace, take a look at WinGopher (Chapter 21) for a fancy gopher. Chameleon Gopher is a File Manager-like program; double-click on icons to open up "directories" (or menus) of other options. Double-click on file icons to display the contents of the file.

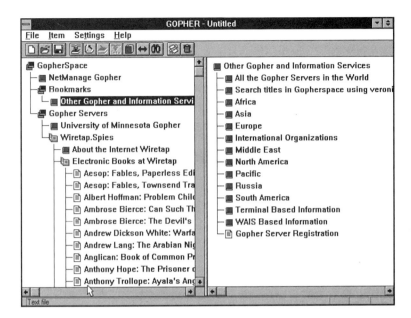

A simple File Manager-type gopher; double-click to open up directories and display files.

When you first open the program, you are not connected to a gopher server on the Internet. It's not until you double-click on one of the servers in the program window that it goes out and connects. You can add your own connections. Select **Item|Add Gopher Server**, type the name you want to appear in the program window on the "tree" structure, and enter the hostname. For example, you may enter **Wiretap.Spies** as the name and **wiretap.spies.com** as the hostname. (This is a good server to connect to, as it contains all sorts of weird stuff.)

A different icon indicates each file type and menu option type: a page of text (text file), a picture of a file drawer (search), an icon showing a page with a picture of a boat on it (.GIF files), and so on. Don't worry about forgetting what all the icons are; select **Help|Symbol Legend** to see each icon and its description.

This gopher uses a simple way to display files. It checks to see what application that type of file is associated with in Windows' File Manager. For example, .TXT files are associated with Notepad. That is, if you try to run a .TXT file, Notepad opens. So Chameleon Gopher tries to open Notepad to display a text file.

NEWT News

Of all the Internet Chameleon programs, NEWT News is probably the best. When you first open NEWT News, Internet Chameleon's newsgroup reader, you'll have to enter the name of the host. Then NEWT runs off and gets a list of all the newsgroups the host subscribes to and displays the list in a window. It's a simple matter to scan through the list, double-clicking on the ones you want. Then select **File|Exit** (or, if that menu item is disabled, as it was in my system, double-click on the window's control menu).

NEWT will go out and update your list of newsgroup messages. Once there, it's pretty obvious what to do. Double-click on a message to read it, click on the various icons to save the message in a file, write a response, write a new message, or print the message.

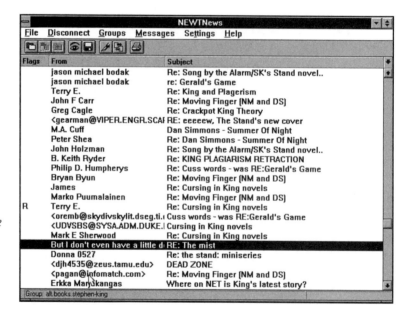

If you've ever used the rn or trn newsreader programs, you'll appreciate NEWT News.

Chameleon Telnet

There's a limit to what can be automated for Telnet sessions, because each Telnet host operates differently. So Internet Chameleon's Telnet application is a simple blank screen in which you see the session, plus menu options that help you connect to a host and automate each session yourself. Once connected, though, it will look pretty much like you are connected using Windows Terminal or some other communication's program. That's not the fault of Internet Chameleon's designers, of course, it's just that when you connect with Telnet, you are, in effect, a terminal on that other computer.

There are a few nice touches. You can save the session in a text file, create a "button pad" to which you can attach commonly used commands (rather like the buttons at the bottom of the Windows Terminal window), change colors and fonts, and so on. It also has a neat utility for "remapping" your keyboard during the session, so you can configure the keyboard to work with the particular host you are connecting to.

Whois

Remember Whois from my last book, *The Complete Idiot's Guide to the Internet* (Chapter 14)? It's a system for tracking down other users on the Internet. It's not perfect—there are no system wide directories of all Internet users—but it can come in handy now and again. (Okay, so you may never use it. However, if you want to, it's there.)

It's a small program. Just enter the name of the Whois server you want to search, the name you are looking for, and press **Enter**. Within a few moments, you'll have a list of matches. If you find someone that interests you, note down his "handle" (the information in parentheses after the name), and then search for that; you'll get more detailed information about the person.

Ping

You saw ping back in Chapter 3 (though if the "Joy of UNIX" title scared you off, maybe you didn't). Anyway, Internet Chameleon's ping program provides a simple way to send a ping message to another host, to check the connection. You can set up ping by selecting options from a dialog box— the number of times you want the ping message sent, the size of the data sent, the interval, and the timeout. Then click on **Start** and it does its stuff.

Sticky "Finger"

Internet Chameleon's Finger program is a simple way to gather information using the **finger** command. Just type in the hostname and username, press **Enter**, and off it goes, traveling across continents to get you the latest NFL scores or drink's machine stock information. (See the following illustration. And, for a list of finger sites, see Chapter 3.)

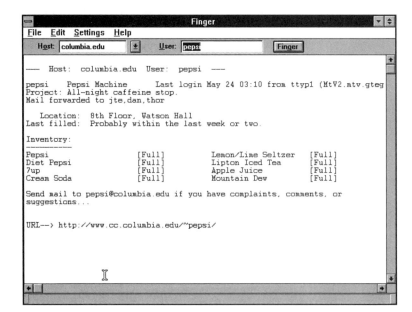

The Finger program lets you quickly collect and print finger data.

Loading the Lizard

I'm not going to waste your time providing full installation instructions for Internet Chameleon. The documentation is, for the first few pages, understandable. Just take your time, and refer to the table of information you created in Chapter 9.

Unfortunately, the documentation's pretty weak when it comes to writing a logon script, which you'll have to do if you are not using a service provider for which a script has already been created. So let's take a quick look at scripts.

Creating a Login Script

Currently, Internet Chameleon comes with preconfigured setups for AlterNet, ANSRemote, CERFnet, InterAccess, MRnet, NETCOM, OnRamp, Portal, and PSINet. If you don't find a preconfigured login script for Internet Chameleon in the NETMANAG directory (you can see by selecting **File|Open** in the Custom application), check with your service provider. If they haven't written one, you'll have to write your own. Here's how.

First, open the file called SLIP.INI. It's in the NETMANAG directory, and you can open it in Windows Notepad or any word processor. (If you use a word processor, make sure that when you finally save it, you do so in ASCII format.)

Now, look for a section that matches the name you entered into the Name text box in the Add Interface dialog box. For example, if you used the name SLIP0, look for [SLIP0], if you used the name CONet, look for [CONet]. Here's what I found when setting up Chameleon to run with Colorado Springs' Internet Express.

```
[Internet Exprss]
SCRIPT=login: $u$r word: $p$r
TYPE=SLIP
```

What's all this mean? Well, **Internet Exprss** is simply the name I gave to this setup (it appears on the top line of the Custom application). The next line is the actual script. **SCRIPT=** means, as you've probably guessed, that the following information is the script that will be used when logging on.

Next you'll see **login:**. This is telling Chameleon to look for the word **login** (followed by the colon). There's a space, and then **ur**, which means send the username (**$u**) followed by a carriage return (**$r**). Another space follows, then **word:**, which means look for **word:**, the word *word* and a colon. (Actually what it's really looking for is **password:**, but just the last part of the word is enough.) Another space, and then **pr**, which means send the password (**$p**) followed by a carriage return (**$r**). The username and password (**$u** and **$p**) are taken from the setup information you entered into Chameleon's Custom application earlier.

Scripts are case-sensitive. Don't enter **USERNAME:**, for instance, if the system actually displays **Username:**. Instead, enter **Username:** or **name:**. You must enter exactly what appears during the login procedure.

We don't need to worry about the last line, **TYPE=SLIP**. This simply tells Chameleon that this service is using SLIP. We're just concerned with the script itself.

Now, there's a problem with this script. Internet Express doesn't ask for a login, it asks for a username. So I have to replace **login:** with **name:**.

Of course there's also more. Take a look at the test session I ran (in Chapter 8). As you'll see, I have to type **slip** and press **Enter**. So, to tell Chameleon what to do I add this to the script:

```
continue $c$r
```

The word **continue** is what Chameleon will look for (as you'll see in the test session, the full prompt is **Type "c" followed by <RETURN> to continue**). I didn't place a colon after the **continue**, because there is no colon in the actual login routine. I also checked the session to make sure the word **continue** didn't appear anywhere earlier in the routine; if it did, Chameleon would get confused.

cr tells Chameleon to send the Startup Command that I entered into the Login Settings dialog box during the setup (**$c**), followed by a carriage return (**$r**). The Startup Command is, in this case, the word **slip**.

When Chameleon logs onto a system, it displays the session in a window, so you can see what's going on. However, it only follows the procedure up to the last thing you enter in the script. So if I leave **slip** as the last thing, I won't see the full procedure; I'll miss the line where my service provider tells me my IP address. Also, I can have Chameleon grab the IP address, to make sure I entered the correct one.

To do all this, I just add this information:

```
Your $- -i
```

This tells Chameleon to look for the word **Your** (take a look at the test session in Chapter 9 and you'll see, near the end, **Your address is 199.190.133.121.**) Then I tell Chameleon to ignore everything that follows

($-), until Chameleon sees my IP address (-i). This final command also tells Chameleon to grab the IP address and use it instead of the one I gave it when I entered all my configuration data. So if I entered the wrong number, Chameleon will substitute the correct one.

So my final script looks like this:

```
[Internet Exprss]
SCRIPT=name: $u$r word: $p$r continue $c$r Your $- -i
TYPE=SLIP
```

To summarize, Chameleon will look for the Username: prompt (**name:**), and send my login name (**$u**) followed by a carriage return (**$r**). Then it will look for the Password: prompt (**word:**) and send my password (**$p**) followed by a carriage return (**$r**). Then it waits until it sees the **Type "c" followed by <RETURN> to continue** prompt (**continue**) and sends the slip Startup Command (**$c**) followed by a carriage return (**$r**). Finally, it waits to see **Your**, and ignores everything until my IP address appears (**$-**), and then grabs the address (**-i**).

Script Scrutiny

Now we can check it all out, to make sure the script works. Close the SLIP.INI file, and open the Chameleon Custom application. Click on the **Connect** menu option, and Chameleon will start to dial your service provider and run the script. As it does so, it will display the Log window, which shows you the session. This is what I see when I click on Connect (you can see in bold the entries that Chameleon makes from the script):

```
Welcome to the CNS Network
        If you are a new user, please login in as
                    userid    "new"
                    password  "newuser"

Username:pkent
pkent
Password:********

Permission granted
_[2J
```

```
_[5;1H                          Community News Service (CNS,Inc.)
_[7;1H                                       in affiliation with
_[8;1H                                       ==TELEPHONE EXPRESS==
_[13;1H                                      If you need assistance,
_[14;1H                              please call CNS at 719-592-1240
_[19;1H               Type "c" followed by <RETURN> to continueslip
slip

Switching to SLIP.
Annex address is 165.212.9.10.  Your address is
199.190.133.121.
```

That's it; I'm connected. Chameleon will grab the IP address, and replace the IP address I had given it with this one. The one I entered when configuring Chameleon is the same as this, but you may remember from Chapter 8 that my service provider gave me the wrong IP address; they told me the address was 199.190.122.121. I caught the mistake, but if I hadn't caught it, Chameleon would have caught if for me.

To Buy or Not to Buy?

Should you get Internet Chameleon? Well, if you want to get all the software in one place, and if you want technical support, Internet Chameleon might be a good idea. Once you set it up, you can always mix and match, replacing the pieces you don't like with shareware or public domain software that you prefer.

However, be aware that, in many ways, Internet Chameleon acts like beta software. Its user interface has serious drawbacks; it's almost like nobody asked any users what they thought about it before the software shipped. The documentation is also poor; it's incomplete, as well as being misleading and confusing in places.

Internet Chameleon beats the UNIX command line hands down, but it's not the best designed software around.

The Least You Need to Know

☛ Internet Chameleon is an almost-all-in-one package for around $200.

☛ While Chameleon is much better than the UNIX command line, it has some design problems.

☛ Chameleon has programs that handle mail, newsgroups, FTP, Telnet, ping, finger, and Whois searches. It also has a gopher client.

☛ You can install Internet Chameleon in a few minutes if you have a ready-made configuration file.

☛ If you don't have a configuration file, you'll have to write a log on script. Follow the instructions in this chapter carefully.

Fix your eyes on the center of this page and wait for a 3-D image to appear. Be patient.

Chapter 18

Cruisin' the Net with NetCruiser

In This Chapter

- ☛ Installing NetCruiser
- ☛ Using the World Wide Web
- ☛ Working with e-mail and newsgroups
- ☛ Using NetCruiser's FTP, Telnet, and Finger tools

Now you're going to look at a program that, although not perfect, is bound to be very successful: NetCruiser. It's going to be successful because it provides most of the Internet's important features on a dial-in direct line, but insulates you from the hassle of installing them. Although each feature is only a subset of what the feature can do in a full-fledged version, NetCruiser makes them so easy to use that many people won't care. (Let's face it; with all the millions of newcomers to the Internet, most of them won't know!) See Chapter 27 for information on acquiring NetCruiser.

If you've read everything in this book so far, you know what a hassle it is to install some of this fancy stuff. Sure, installing most of the programs in this book is relatively easy. The complicated bit is installing the WINSOCK.DLL and dialer so you can make your TCP/IP connection in the first place.

NetCruiser has an incredibly easy installation program that takes care of all that. It literally takes about five minutes to enter your information. Don't worry about IP addresses and all that nonsense. They want the important stuff: name, postal address, and, most importantly, credit card number. Then NetCruiser does the rest: dialing up their system, registering you, and logging off. That's it. The whole operation takes less than ten minutes.

Why is it so easy? You can only use NetCruiser with one service provider, NETCOM. They've written software to suit their system. They didn't need to give their program the capability to run on any system, so they could automate everything.

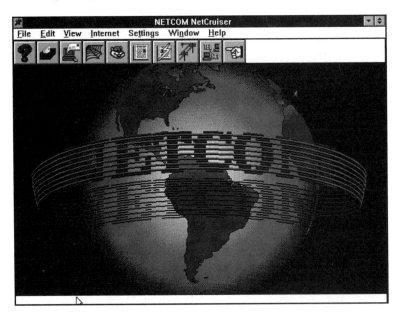

The NetCruiser main screen—the starting point.

Once registered, you double-click on the **NetCruiser** icon, enter your password, and find yourself at the NetCruiser screen ready to take on the world. From here, you can read mail or newsgroups, or use the WWW, FTP, Telnet, or Finger tools. All these tools have nice big toolbar buttons that are clear and understandable. Click on a picture of a house to return "home," on a picture of a spider's web to start the World Wide Web browser, and so on.

NC WWW

NetCruiser's World Wide Web browser is a very good system, containing most of what you'll find in Mosaic, but in an easy-to-use format. When you start NetCruiser's Web, though, make sure you use the **Settings|WWW Options** command. Here you'll be able to select a home page and download directory; turn inline graphics off (*very* important—you can waste a lot of time waiting for inline graphics); change anchor colors and formats; and modify the document formats (the fonts used for different types of text).

Once you are working, you can do all the usual things: create bookmarks, search the currently displayed document (though this feature isn't doing repeat searches correctly), and copy the document into a text file. There is a problem, though; the file's saved with all the HTML codes intact, so it may not be much use to you. (For more information on HTML codes and what they look like, see Chapter 12.)

You can go directly to a page if you know its URL address. Just type it into the URL box and press **Enter**. You can also open an HTML file from your hard disk.

NetCruiser's Web browser at work.

Mail

The e-mail system is fairly basic, but again, easy to use. When you view an incoming message, you can reply to it, forward it, save it to disk, delete it, or move on to the next message. You can't create folders, but there are two folders already set up for you: Inbox and Saved Mail.

There's a simple address book; you can add a person's name, e-mail address, and some comments. You can, in theory, also create mailing lists, putting several e-mail addresses under one group name (though this feature wasn't working on the version I looked at).

This is a simple e-mail system, certainly not as sophisticated as some of the systems we looked at in Chapters 6 and 15, and not even as sophisticated as some of the UNIX mail systems, such as Pine. It's a lot easier to use, though.

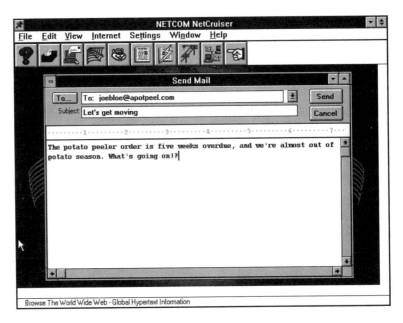

NetCruiser provides a simple—and simple to use—e-mail system.

Newsgroups

NetCruiser provides a nice way to select newsgroups. Select the **Internet|Choose USENET Newsgroups** command to see a dialog box. You'll probably want to use the **View** menu to remove the status bar and toolbar, otherwise, you may not be able to see the entire dialog box. Then click on a button to select a category—Arts & Entertainment, Computing, Home and Family, and so on. Click on the group you want to subscribe to, and click on the **Subscribe** button. The only thing it's missing is a way to search the list.

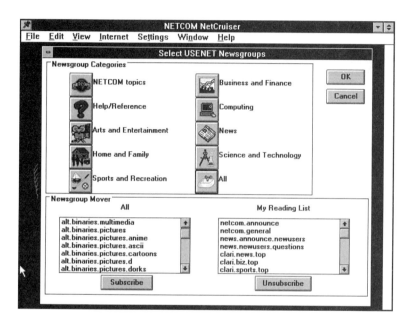

NetCruiser provides the easiest way to select newsgroups of any newsreader.

Once you get into the newsreader, you are going to find the NetCruiser style very easy to use with most of the important features. You can reply to or forward messages via e-mail, post a follow-up message, or save the message in a file. You won't find all the fancy features available in a newsreader such as WinVN (see Chapter 15).

Gopher

NetCruiser's gopher uses an unusual system. When you select the gopher tool, a map of the United States appears, with a drop-down list box at the top. If you simply click on the **OK** button, you connect to the NETCOM gopher server. However, you can click on a state in the map, to place a list of gopher servers in that state into the list box. Or click on Canada or Mexico to get a list of foreign gopher servers (don't click on the sea—all you'll see is the title bar change to **Gopher To: Water**).

Once connected, you'll get an easy-to-use gopher. You can create book-marks, download files, and navigate around. NetCruiser has built-in viewers, so you can read documents and view files. You'll have to download the graphics files first, and select the **File|View Graphics File**. There's a bug here—make sure NetCruiser stores the file with the right extension or you won't be able to view it.

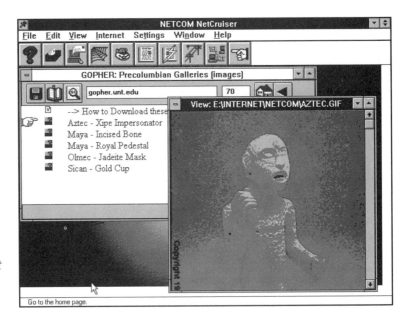

Checking out the Dallas Museum of Art with NetCruiser's gopher.

Telnet

Telnet starts off with the same map you see when you start Gopher. You select a Telnet site—or enter your own—and click on **OK**. You'll then find yourself in a window, where the session will unfold. There are no real controls for your session; once you've started, you are on your own (you can, however, modify the font you see, and select the terminal type).

The most disappointing thing about this application is that you'll have to keep your directory of Telnet sites elsewhere—while you can select an address from the list, you can't add to the list. And anyway, the list is only hostnames; it doesn't contain descriptive names.

FTP

FTP is okay, but not as good as WS_FTP (see Chapter 11). You'll see the same map from which you can select an FTP site. Or enter one of your own (again, no way to add FTP sites and descriptive titles). When you get into FTP, you'll see a window with two panes: the remote site's directories in the top pane and the files in the directory in the bottom pane.

You can view text files in a window. Each time the remote site sends text (each time you change directory, for instance), you'll see a text window pop up, which is a little irritating. There's a feature that lets you download graphics files and view them immediately. Why won't this work for Gopher, one wonders? (Probably will, eventually.)

There is a nonofficial way to add your own hosts to these lists (though you can't add descriptive titles). Open Notepad and edit the .HST files (they are in the NETCOM directory). You'll find FTP*.HST files (for FTP and Telnet) and GPH-*.HST (for gopher).

There are also tools for creating and deleting directories, and for deleting files. However, these are only for the *remote* system, whereas you are more likely to need them for your own system. Most FTP sessions are anonymous FTP sessions, and you won't be able to mess with the FTP site's directories and files anyway.

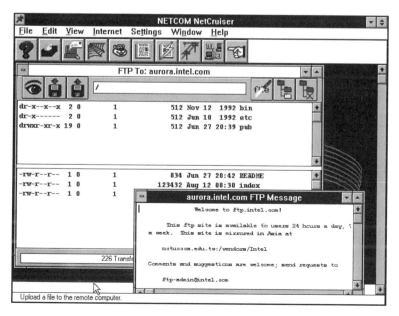

FTP's okay, but could be better.

Finger

Finger. What can I say about Finger? It's a simple program, and NetCruiser has it covered pretty well. You start off at the map again, though you can type a host. The Finger window opens, you type the username, press **Enter**, and wait a little while for the Finger information to arrive.

NetCruiser is a *very* nice system. It's easy to use (the Online Help system could be a little clearer, though), fairly quick, and seems to be stable, too. It's going to be very popular with many Internet users because it's so easy to set up.

If you want the ability to use the programs of your choice, programs with more capabilities, you'll have to set up your own dial-in direct account. Unlike Internet Chameleon, for instance, you can't run other TCP/IP programs while NetCruiser is running. (With some other commercial products that come with WINSOCK.DLL, once the connection is made to the Internet, you can run any TCP/IP software that's compatible with the WINSOCK.DLL.) If you need all the features available, then you'll have to look elsewhere. NetCruiser has sacrificed features for ease of use.

The Least You Need to Know

☞ NetCruiser is *very* easy to install—you are setting up a dial-in direct account, but you'd never know it.

☞ NetCruiser has e-mail, newsgroups, WWW, Telnet, FTP, and Finger.

☞ NetCruiser's tools are all easy to use, though they don't have all the features available in some other programs.

☞ If you want to use NetCruiser, you must sign up with NETCOM, a large service provider.

## Chapter 19

Internet in a Box: Boxed Cyberspace

In This Chapter

- ☞ "Writing" logon scripts for Internet in a Box
- ☞ Using AIR Series/Internet in a Box's applications

Have you seen the ads for Internet in a Box? It's been advertised since late 1993, but at the time of writing, it still wasn't available. It should be out by September, 1994, though, so by the time you read this, it will probably be available. It's worth the wait; it's a really nice piece of work.

The first thing you'll notice is that Internet in a Box is very easy to install. If you've read the earlier chapters where I described how to write login scripts—for Internet Chameleon (Chapter 17), UMSLIP (Chapter 9), and Trumpet Winsock (Chapter 10)—you'll know what a hassle it can be. There's no way around it because each system is different, so you must create a script.

Internet in a Box, though, automates the process. You don't *write* a script; you enter information into a dialog box, telling the program what to look for and what to do when it sees it. Once you know what your login procedure looks like (see Chapter 8), you can create the script in less than five minutes, with ease.

The Internet in a Box programs, by the way, are also sold in various combinations as the *AIR Series—AIR Connect, AIR NFS,* and so on. *Internet in a Box* is the consumer product (sold directly to the public); the AIR Series is the corporate product (sold to companies).

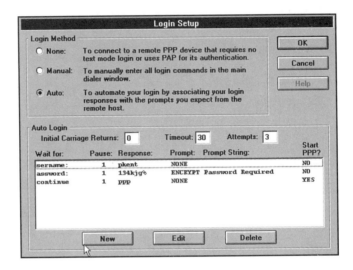

Finally, creating a login script is simple.

What, then, will you find when you start? Internet in a Box is based on Spry, Inc.'s AIR Navigator series of software. It runs on PPP connections, so it's pretty fast. It comes with these programs:

- ☞ AIR Mosaic (World Wide Web)
- ☞ AIR Mail (e-mail)
- ☞ AIR News (newsgroups)
- ☞ AIR Gopher
- ☞ Network File Manager (FTP)
- ☞ AIR Telnet
- ☞ Image View (graphics viewer)
- ☞ UUCODE (UUENCODE and UUDECODE)

AIR Mosaic

AIR Mosaic is a very capable World Wide Web browser. It looks very much like NCSA Mosaic, which is no surprise—it's developed from that product. It's actually easier to use than Mosaic, though. It has most of the tools you need; you can create hotlists, and add destinations to those hotlists. It has a neat directory-type structure in its Hotlists dialog box to display each hotlist category and the documents associated with it, and makes creating new menus really easy. Just click on a hotlist, click on a check box, and close the dialog box; the hotlist will appear as a new entry on the menu bar.

There's also a Kiosk button. The Kiosk mode is in NCSA Mosaic, though it's not obvious. (You have to start the program using the **-k** switch in Mosaic.) Kiosk mode lets you set up your computer in a public place—a lobby, library, or trade show, for instance—and allows anyone to walk up and fool around on the Internet. In Kiosk mode, the menu and tool bars are removed, so users can't do anything that will do any harm.

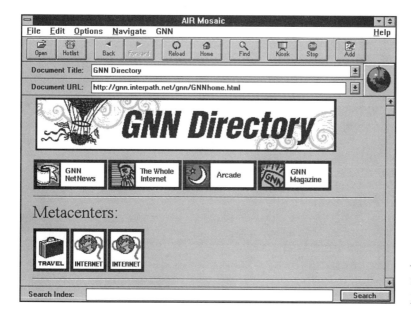

AIR Mosaic, an improved version of NCSA Mosaic.

AIR Gopher

AIR Gopher uses a File Manager-type window, with directories on the left side and subdirectories, documents, and files on the right side. You don't need as many double-clicks as with other gophers; a single click on a directory displays its contents in the right pane.

AIR Gopher has several viewers already set up. If you double-click on a graphics file, the file transfers and displays in the Image View program. UUENCODED files travel to the UUCODE program; Telnet nodes automatically launch AIR Telnet, and so on. And Image View is much more than just an image editor. You can use the program to edit the downloaded files in a number of ways: rotate, flip, resize, adjust the color balance and gamma correction. It even lets you create a slide show of downloaded graphics.

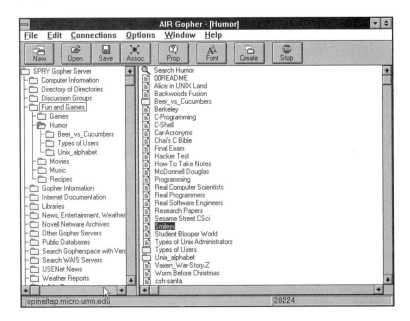

AIR Gopher is a File Manager-type gopher.

File What?

Network File Manager is Internet in a Box's version of FTP. It's an unusual way to do it, and I'm not sure I really like it. When you double-click on the icon, two applications open: File Manager (the regular one that comes with Windows) and Network File Manager.

The problem with this setup is that on a small screen all the application "overhead" stuff—title bars, menu bars, toolbars, scroll bars, and status bars—take up a lot of wasted space. There's very little left over for doing work. I'd rather have a WS_FTP-type application (have you noticed I favor WS_FTP?) with everything in one place, and plenty of room to see what is going on in the directories, on your disk, and theirs.

Apart from that gripe, the program works pretty well. You can double-click on a text file to view it in Notepad. One really nice feature is drag-and-drop; when you find files you want in the FTP site, drag them from the lower window, up into a directory in File Manager. (You'll probably end up using drag-and-drop, because the nonmouse method is a bit awkward.) You can also create an FTP log, showing exactly what happened in the session. As with all the Internet in a Box applications, Network File Manager has a well-designed toolbar that is easy to understand and use.

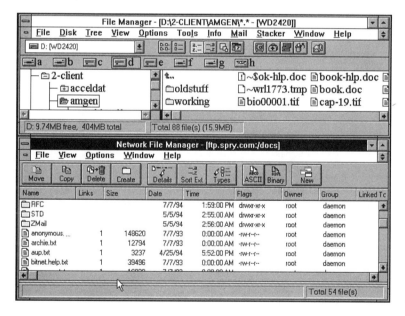

Network File Manager (FTP) works in conjunction with File Manager.

AIR News

AIR News is one of the easiest news readers I've come across. When you first open it, you'll be presented with a window showing you all the newsgroups available to you, and several other windows with newsgroups that you are already subscribed to: a window for Education, one for Television (*Ren and Stimpy*, *The Simpsons*, *Seinfeld*, useful stuff like that), one for

Music, and so on. Of course, you can create more of these windows. And when you want to subscribe, click on the newsgroup, click on the **Subscribe** button, and double-click on the name of the window you want to place the newsgroup into.

Unfortunately, there's no way to search the list of newsgroups for likely subjects. You can turn the list of newsgroups into a "tree," making it easier to dig down through the newsgroup hierarchy and find what you are looking for. Double-click on the **sci** top level, for example, to see folders labeled aeronautics, agriculture, answers, anthropology, and so on. Double-click on one of those to see more, lower, levels.

AIR News has plenty of other features, too. Apart from the usual functions of a news reader, you can also define the font used in messages, save your "workspace" when you close so when you come back you'll be in the same place, and choose whether to view messages in the same window as the message list or in another.

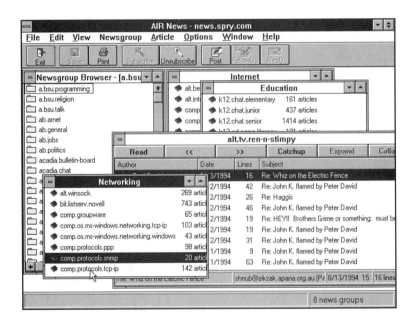

AIR News, one of the best news readers you'll find.

AIR Telnet

Internet in a Box's Telnet application is excellent. You can create a library of Telnet sites, and select one by hostname or description. Once into a session, you can choose from a variety of terminal settings—emulation type, number of lines and columns, the backspace key, and so on. You can also remap your keyboard, and save the configuration for use in other sessions.

You can also change the fonts and colors used in the screen, save the current screen into an ASCII text file, and send the entire session to a printer or text file. For every Telnet site, you can save all these settings, so each session is automatically configured just the way you want it when you connect.

The great advantage of Internet in a Box is its ease of use, especially its capability to create its own logon scripts with minimal input from you. Many users will be able to set up the software without even looking at a manual. All the well-designed applications have easily understandable toolbars, menus, and procedures. Where it fails, though, is that it's only a partial solution. (That's where pretty much all of the "kits" fail, not just Internet in a Box, of course.) There's no WAIS, ping, finger, or Archie. The loss of Archie, in particular, seems to be an important one. There's no Internet Relay Chat, no Talk. I'm sure these elements will be added in the future, but for now, you'll have to do without them (and you can't add them to the AIR Series separately).

For most Internet users, though, Internet in a Box is a really good choice—easy to install, easy to use, and with most, perhaps all, of the features you'll need.

The Least You Need to Know

- ☞ Internet in a Box is easy to install, as it automates the script-creation process.

- ☞ All the applications are easy to use, with sensible, identifiable, toolbars.

continues

continued

☛ Network File Manager is an okay FTP application, which works in conjunction with File Manager. It uses drag-and-drop to transfer files.

☛ AIR News is one of the best news readers on the Internet.

☛ AIR Mosaic is developed from NCSA Mosaic, though it's easier to use.

Chapter 20

Internet Made Simple: America Online

In This Chapter

- Working with America Online's Internet Center
- Sending Internet mail
- Reading newsgroups
- How America Online makes finding mailing lists easy
- Using America Online's Gopher/WAIS hybrid

I must admit; I'm not sure if I truly like America Online. AOL, as it's known in the online world, is an online service similar to CompuServe, Prodigy, and GEnie. Right from the start, AOL was designed to be easy to use, and it certainly is. It has a neat graphical user interface—there's a version for Windows, DOS, and the Macintosh—that is simple to work with. That, along with a good advertising campaign, has provided AOL with phenomenal growth over the last year or so.

So why am I unsure about this service? Because it's slow. Until very recently, AOL users had to connect at 2400 baud, a ridiculously slow speed when you consider that services such as CompuServe are working at 14400 baud. And even now, 9600 is as fast as it goes. Also, AOL's phenomenal growth has created phenomenal slowdowns, as everyone and his dog are trying to connect at the same time.

When you sign onto AOL, you are automatically set up to run at a painful 2400 baud. As soon as you get on, use the **Go To|Keyword** command and type **9600**. Find a 9600 baud number, and follow the instructions on how to reconfigure your software.

It's popular on AOL to laugh about the high cost of working on CompuServe—CI$ as it's known on AOL. Indeed, AOL has much lower hourly rates than CIS. However, it has much higher online times! While CIS lets you work with offline navigators (systems with which you do most of your work offline, minimizing online time and expense) with AOL, everything's done online. (There are currently no true offline navigators for the Internet, but you can expect to see them appear over the next year or two.)

As for that neat interface, yeah, it's nice, but no nicer than many of the interfaces now available for other systems. All the online services have realized that in order to get and keep users, they need to make their systems easier to use.

So what's AOL doing in this book? AOL has the jump on the other online services again; this time, they've added Internet access, and made it easy to use. All the online services have Internet e-mail, of course, but AOL's gone further, adding newsgroups, Gopher, and WAIS, with more to follow.

AOL's the first, but it won't be the last. CompuServe should have some kind of Internet access by the end of 1994 (it already has newsgroups), and everyone will follow. For now, though, AOL leads the pack. And you can try AOL for free for ten hours. Can't beat that. (For information on getting the AOL software and free trial, see Chapter 27.)

Where Do We Go from Here?

Getting to the AOL Internet Center is simple. Once you've logged on, select the **Go To|Keyword** menu command, type **Internet**, and press **Enter**. (You can also use the **Go To|Edit Goto** menu to add **Internet** as a menu option.) When you finally get there, you'll see the window in the following illustration:

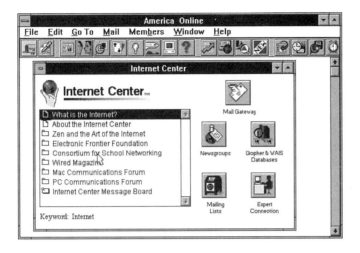

AOL's Internet Center, the starting point for its Internet services.

Getting the Message Out

The AOL Mail Gateway isn't really anything terribly special—all online services have Internet e-mail these days. You can send mail from CompuServe to AOL, from Prodigy to GEnie, and so on. However, AOL makes Internet mail a little easier. It has a nice, simple mail program, but perhaps more importantly, it provides lots of information about how to send e-mail, for example, how to address messages to various networks connected to the Internet.

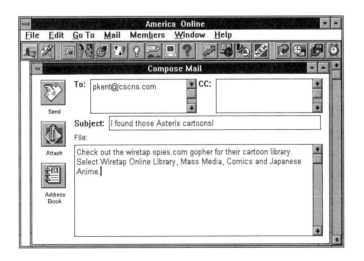

You want simple? Here's simple. The AOL e-mail system is very easy to use, though not exactly "feature rich."

As for finding Internet addresses, AOL doesn't have a connection to any of the systems that maintain lists of Internet users. The information AOL displays about finding addresses states, rather misleadingly, that there is no way to track down addresses on the Internet.

Of course, this isn't the world's best Internet mail program. There's no way to send files across the Internet, and no way to even UUENCODE or UUDECODE them—though you can kludge it by encoding on your computer and then uploading the ASCII file to a message.

TECHNO NERD TEACHES...

Free? Nothing's Free!   Well, almost free. Unlike most of the online services, AOL doesn't charge any extra fees for receiving Internet e-mail. That makes it easy to connect to hundreds of mailing lists, for instance, without worrying about who you're going to rob to pay the bill.

Newsgroups

AOL has a good newsgroup system. You can just cruise through the system, reading messages wherever you want. Or you can "subscribe" to the ones that interest you, and AOL groups them together. AOL subscribes to about 12,000 groups, more than most service providers.

TECHNO NERD TEACHES...

AOL seems to be a little prudish in its choices. While the Internet has dozens (hundreds?) of newsgroups related to sexual subjects—from alt.binaries.pictures.erotica to alt.sex.fetish.spanking—it's difficult to tell what AOL has subscribed to. AOL seems to have made the ones it does subscribe to hard to find. There's no alt.sex listing in the Alternative Newsgroups Topics window, for instance, though you can subscribe to a few of them through Expert Add window if you know the names.

If you search for the word **binaries**, you'll see a large list of various newsgroups. The list doesn't include alt.binaries.pictures.erotica.blondes— or any of the other sexually oriented newsgroups—even though AOL does carry this. This is of note because traditionally the Internet has been a free-for-all, a judgment-free environment in which you can find information and discussions about anything. It looks like AOL is sanitizing the Internet for presentation to the public at large—while still giving "those in the know" access to the naughty bits.

Subscribing to the ones you want is easy. Just click on a group to see a short—very short—description of what the group's about. Then click on the **Add** button to place the group in your list of groups.

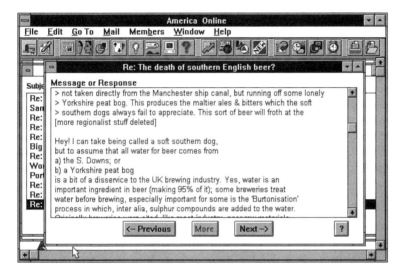

AOL's Newsgroups feature is probably its strongest.

You can search the list of newsgroups for a keyword, and you can also use the "expert" feature—if you already know the name of the group you want, you can just type it into a text box rather than search for it. And the Latest Newsgroups window provides a quick way to find out if a new group has been added since you checked all the lists.

If you are used to working with a UNIX newsreader, you'll find AOL's a pleasant change. However, it could be better. It certainly doesn't match something like NEWT News, the reader that comes with Internet Chameleon (see Chapter 17). For instance, once you've read a message, that's it—

AOL sometimes seems to take a long time to display information in a window. For instance, when it displays a newsgroup list in a window, the timer icon appears and you can't do much until it's finished. However, if you press **Esc**, AOL will stop updating and let you get on with reading the messages. Then, when you want to see more of them, you can click on the **More** button.

it's gone. You can't go back and retrieve it, as you can with some other readers. Nor can you flag messages to make sure they remain in the list even after you've read them.

Although it's nice to see AOL provide a way to look for newsgroups by subject instead of by name, some users will find this frustrating. Newsgroups are created on a hierarchical system, with each level containing other levels below it. AOL provides no way to follow the hierarchy down, so you can see all the groups that are related by subject.

Mailing Lists

AOL also helps you find mailing lists. Of course, this is not a true "feature"—any service that lets you receive e-mail lets you subscribe to a mailing list. However, AOL makes it easier, because it provides a directory of mailing lists that you can search to find the subject that interests you, and see a short description of each one. (As I mentioned earlier, it doesn't charge for Internet e-mail, so it makes it much cheaper to subscribe.)

For instance, by searching on the word **television**, I was able to find the **flamingo** group. This is "for unmoderated discussion among fans of the series "Parker Lewis" (formerly "Parker Lewis Can't Lose") on the Fox television network," a really useful subject that I've been trying to find for ages. My family won't be seeing much of me anymore. (If we need any evidence that cyberspace won't necessarily provide a quantum leap in humanity's intellectual evolution, the **flamingo** and **90210** mailing lists surely provide it.)

AOL also gives a precise description of how to subscribe to each group. While it's not complicated, many new Internet users misunderstand this information, to the chagrin of mailing-list subscribers who get tired of receiving "how do I subscribe?" messages.

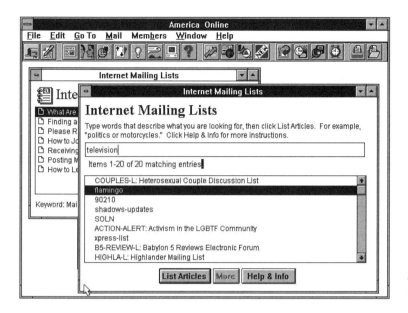

AOL makes finding a mailing list easy.

Gopher & WAIS on AOL

AOL has a hybrid system that merges Gopher menus with WAIS (Wide Area Information Server) database searches. It's an easy, point-and-click way to find lots of interesting information, though you are limited to the menus and structure provided by AOL. You can't connect to a gopher address you've found in a book or were given by a friend. As an AOL message puts it, "AOL added more structure to make it easier to navigate the system of Gopher menus. We selected certain gophers that we think are especially interesting or useful and listed them as 'Editor's Choices.' Gopherspace is notoriously unstable so we tried to choose Gophers that are more reliable than most."

Still, there are plenty of categories from which to select, enough to keep most casual users quite happy. And what about those WAIS searches? You'll remember that WAIS provides a way to search databases stored on computers all over the world. Well, whenever you see an "open book" icon, you can double-click on it to open a search box. You can then type a word you are searching for, click on the **Search** button, and away it goes, searching the databases.

You can also do Veronica searches, to look around in gopherspace for useful menus and menu options. However, having built a menu using Veronica, there's no way to save it for future use. Almost all other gopher browsers will let you do this, but with AOL's Veronica, you'll have to redo the search each time you want to find the information again, because AOL doesn't support the bookmark feature that most gophers have.

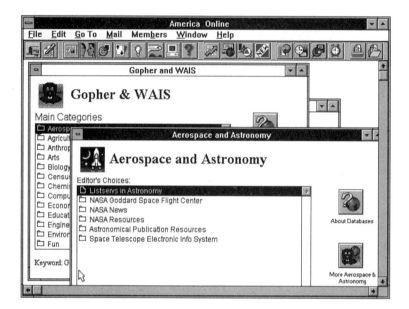

Gopher and WAIS combined together in an easy-to-use point- and-click interface.

If You Know What You're Doing— Expert Connection

There may be more by the time you read this. Last time I looked, AOL had an Expert Connection button, but clicking on it simply displayed a message that promised "a number of new Internet connections, including FTP and Telnet." These should be working sometime "in the coming year," whatever that means. (AOL was advertising Internet access for a long time before it actually had it, so perhaps they're stuck in a time warp.)

It's Good, but Is It Internet?

AOL's Internet Center has a lot to commend it. It's very easy to use, and it provides lots of simple explanations that lead you through various proce- dures. You'll also find plenty of information about the Internet available in the Internet and Network Information window.

However, is it true Internet? Well, not quite. It's only a small part of what's available. At the time of writing, there was no FTP and no Telnet (though these should be added soon). No true gophering (though the system they've set up is very good—you just can't customize it). No way to track down Internet addresses through Whois and Fred. No Archie (though maybe they'll add Archie when they add FTP). No World Wide Web, no Jughead, no IRC, or Talk. AOL's Internet Center is really the Internet Sampler. And what AOL provides, though easy to use, is not very flexible. You get what they give you, and that's it.

Still, if all you want is access to newsgroups and mailing lists (and don't mind not being able to get to messages you've already seen), plus the ability to goof around in gopherspace now and again, it's a pretty good system. It's relatively low-priced—$3.50 an hour, though you can find Internet service providers who charge less—and comes with very easy-to-use software. The newsgroup feature alone will make AOL worthwhile to many people.

The Least You Need to Know

- ☛ America Online provides a simple, easy-to-use Internet interface.

- ☛ Reading newsgroups with America Online is very convenient. It doesn't have all the features of other news readers, though.

- ☛ Sending e-mail is easy, and AOL provides clear instructions on how to subscribe to mailing lists.

- ☛ There's a nice gopher/WAIS hybrid tool, but it's not configurable; you can only go where they let you go.

- ☛ There's plenty missing. Maybe FTP and Telnet will be added soon, but there's no World Wide Web, Fred, Whois, Jughead, IRC, or Talk. And what there is isn't very flexible.

This is what a polar bear looks like pressed up against the windshield of your car. Just so you know what's going on if that ever happens.

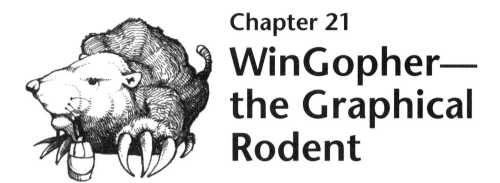

Chapter 21

WinGopher—
the Graphical
Rodent

In This Chapter

- ☞ Digging around gopherspace with WinGopher
- ☞ Installing WinGopher
- ☞ The WinGopher Test Server
- ☞ Creating WinGopher login scripts

Ever wondered why Internet software is badly documented, hard to install, and difficult to use? Me too. (Okay, it's partly because most of the software is shareware or public domain, but what excuse do the commercial publishers have?)

Well, it doesn't have to be that way, and WinGopher proves it. WinGopher's documentation and installation procedure should embarrass other Internet software companies; it's not perfect, but it's certainly a step in the right direction.

You get a good feeling about the product right from the start, and, I'm glad to say, the feeling stays with you when you use the program. This product makes gophering from the old standard, boring UNIX gopher feel as satisfying as picking your nose with boxing gloves on.

TECHNO NERD TEACHES...

Okay, they were good to me! Yes, I admit it, I also got a good feeling from the free Internet account that NOTIS, publisher of WinGopher, gives to writers and editors! These guys obviously know what they are doing.

WinGopher is more than just a Gopher client; it also comes with Telnet and ping applications, though there's no true FTP. You can do FTP through some gopher menus, of course, but it doesn't have an FTP application that lets you connect directly to an FTP site.

There are two versions of WinGopher: plain old WinGopher, and WinGopher Complete. If you have your TCP/IP software up and running already—perhaps you have Trumpet Winsock or another product, such as Internet Chameleon—all you really need is WinGopher. If you don't have any kind of TCP/IP software yet, you need WinGopher Complete, which comes with a copy of Distinct TCP/IP, a product from, you guessed it, the Distinct Corporation. Being the thorough guy that I am, I'll look at WinGopher Complete.

Installing WinGopher

Installation is very quick, very easy. There's a Quick Start card—though it defeats its purpose by referring you back to the Installation Guide. The instructions in the guide are pretty straightforward, and it should take ten minutes or less from opening the box to dialing into NOTIS's own system.

Where's Home?

Unlike Internet Chameleon's Gopher program—which isn't really connected to a gopher server until you double-click on one—each time WinGopher opens, it connects to what it terms the Main Gopher Server. Think of this as the "home" gopher. You'll probably want to set up your service provider's server as the Main Server, though you don't have to. If you find you use another one somewhere much more often, you can make that the Main Server instead. (To change the Main Server, select **Options|View/Change Options|Server Options**.)

Which address do you enter? You can try the hostname from your e-mail address. Better still, go into your account using the curses gopher, take a look at the top of the first page of your service provider's gopher server, and it should show the hostname. (If you enter an incorrect hostname, WinGopher won't be able to start. It will ask you for the hostname of another server, and you'd better get it right, or it will close.)

Do-It-Yourself Gophering

When you first log on to your system with WinGopher, you'll notice *collections* of places to go in gopherspace. You can think of these collections as menus. As you can see in the following illustration, each collection contains directories and files related to a particular subject, such as economics, government sources, images, phone books, news (that's real news reports, not newsgroups), education, and so on. Notice The Internet Hunt icon. That will take you to information about the game called The Internet Hunt, as I discussed in Chapter 2.

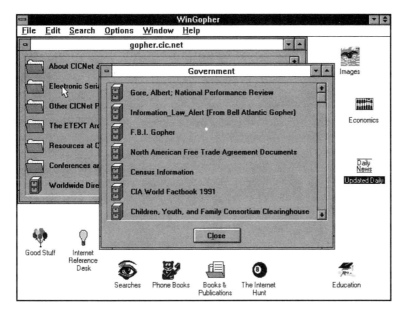

Double-click on an icon to open up a collection of gopher information sources.

You can add items to these collections, and create your own, using the various menu commands.

A quick warning about these stories. They really are pretty gross. I'm no prude, but I found them disgusting. So disgusting that I know my editors won't even let me tell you the subject matter. Stay away if you are easily offended!

Disgusting Reading Material: A Real-Life Example

Let's say you've just heard about a disgusting collection of tasteless, offensive stories and poems. You've been scanning through one of the many Internet directories available at your bookstore, and discovered the Gopher address for this collection: ftp.spies.com. The directory also notes that this is in the /Library/Fringe/Gross directory.

This seems like something useful to have on hand, so why not add it to the Books collection? You open the collection (**Options|Collection Manager**), and create a collection item (**Edit|Collection Item**). All you need to do is select the item type (in this case a directory), type in the name you want to give the item in the Books window (Nasty Stories), and enter the Host and Path.

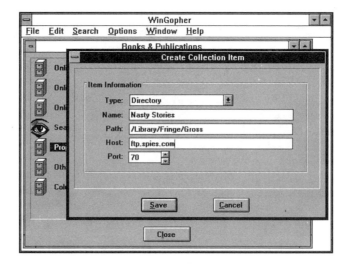

You can quickly and easily add gopher addresses to any WinGopher collection.

When you click on the **Save** button, that item is added to the collection window. Double-click on the item, and away you go, off on your search for entertainment.

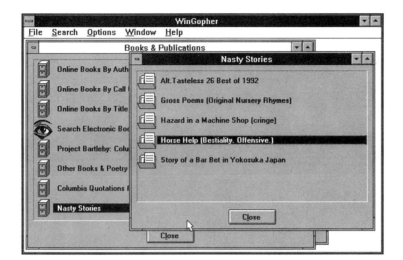

Double-click on Nasty Stories, and there they are waiting for you.

Getting to the Goodies

Getting around in WinGopher is simply a matter of double-clicking on the little file-cabinet pictures to connect to a particular gopher site—another window opens up containing various items. Remember, each window is the equivalent of a menu in the curses gopher.

You might see more file-cabinet icons or file-folder icons. Double-click on one and another window (another menu) opens up; the file folders are directories within a particular host.

Maybe you'll see a picture with a folder and a sheet of paper sticking out. Double-click and a text file will open in the WinGopher Text Viewer.

The picture of an eye lets you search a gopher index. The picture of a sunset over the sea transfers a graphic image to your hard disk, and displays the image in the WinGopher Image Viewer. (Check out the Images collection already set up for you. You'll find sources of images from NASA and the Soviet Union, satellite images, PhotoCD pictures, and lots more.)

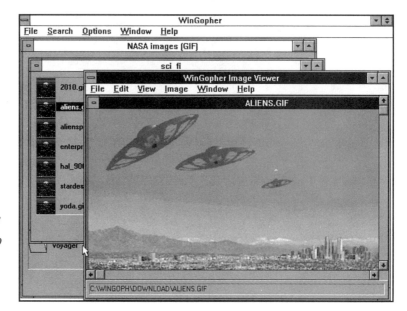

Double-click on a GIF image file to copy it to your hard disk and open it in the Image Viewer.

Hey, these images are lousy! Yes, of course they are; they are 256-color images or better, and you are using the standard 16-color video mode. Whadd'ya expect? Go buy a better video card, or change video modes to one with more colors if your existing card will support it. You can change video modes by clicking on the **Windows Setup** icon in the Main program group.

Double-clicking on the picture of the musical scale loads a sound file onto your computer and then opens the Windows Media Player application so you can listen to it. And there are other icons, for phone books, binary files, video files, Telnet sessions, and so on. You can get around in gopherspace without ever touching the keyboard.

When WinGopher is transferring a large file onto your hard disk, don't do anything else in Windows. Don't try to open an application or change disks in File Manager, for instance. Windows doesn't handle multitasking of communications programs very well, and WinGopher (at least running under Distinct TCP/IP) seems especially sensitive to these problems.

So Where Has Vron Gone?

It's not immediately apparent in WinGopher how to do a Veronica search. But she's there, along with Jughead. Simply open the Searches collection, and you'll find a list of Veronica servers around the world. Double-click on one of them, type what you want to search for, and off it goes.

You'll also find an entry for a Jughead server, though in my version it wasn't hooked up properly. Of course, you can connect to the Jughead servers I listed in Chapter 4 and search from there.

Bits 'n Pieces

WinGopher comes with a couple more pieces; there's WinGopher Telnet, a simple program that lets you run a Telnet session in a window. Remember, though, that when you are running Telnet, you are connected to another computer and using that computer's software. So there's not a lot that a Telnet application can do to improve the program—you're playing by the other computer's rules now. WinGopher Telnet is very basic. All WinGopher Telnet will let you do is change the terminal type, colors, and character set.

There's also Distinct TCP/IP Ping, which you get if you buy WinGopher Complete. Again, a simple program to use the **ping** command to check if you can connect to another host. It's not a great ping application, though. It doesn't let you create a list of hosts, and the only configuration option is to set the ping interval.

How about FTP? Well, you can download files through gopherspace, but WinGopher doesn't have a true FTP function that would allow you to connect directly to an FTP site.

If you want a more advanced Windows Telnet tool, take a look at Internet Chameleon's Telnet (Chapter 17), and WinQVT (Chapter 15), which let you remap your keyboard to match the system you are linking with.

The WinGopher Test Server

The WinGopher Test Server is a free service, using an 800 number that you can dial into to make sure your software's working, and get information about service providers. You won't be able to travel around the Internet from here; you'll only be able to view a few files and directories that NOTIS has made available.

If you don't have a service provider yet, the Test Server's Access Provider Information directory will help you find one. If you do have a service provider, check out the Access Provider Information directory just to see if there are configuration files available for your system. When I checked, NOTIS had information for 20 service providers; they say they'll add more.

I must admit, WinGopher isn't perfect, but what software is? I had a few crashes in my version. If WinGopher crashes, it doesn't close the Distinct TCP/IP software, so you have to close Windows and reopen. Still, I was very impressed with the product—with its ease of use and installation. A crash here or there is worth putting up with for a user interface this well designed.

TECHNO NERD TEACHES...

Want a free gopher hat? NOTIS is looking for information about the ways in which companies are using WinGopher. You send them the info; they send you the baseball cap with a gopher on the front. Take a look at the Win a Free WinGopher Hat directory.

If you're lucky, you'll find configuration files for your service provider. You can see in the next figure the files for a service provider called Infinet Systems. Double-clicking on the first icon displays the text file. You can then save the file if you want, using the **File|Save As** command. Double-clicking on the second and third icons lets you copy the dialup script and socket file to your hard disk. The first is the script that Distinct TCP/IP uses when dialing into the service provider; the second is the configuration information—host addresses and so on.

Once you have the dialup script and socket file, just follow the WinGopher instructions. In a break with Internet tradition, they're pretty straightforward. What will the oldtimers say?!

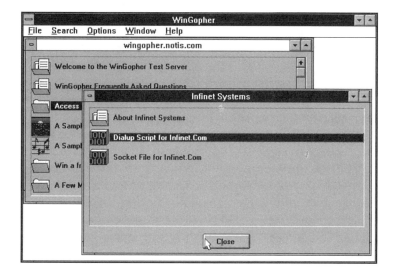

Just double-click on an icon to view it or copy it to your hard disk.

No Script for Your Service Provider?

If you can't find information for your service provider on the WinGopher Test Server, check on your service provider's system, or call them. If they don't have anything, you're out of luck, on your own. You'll have to create your own files. The WinGopher documentation is not as clear as it should be here, unfortunately. Luckily for you, I've done it already—my service provider wasn't set up, either.

There's a bug in the Text Viewer's File|Save As command in WinGopher 1.0a. You may think you are saving the file in the WINGOPH directory—you may even double-click on the directory in the Save As dialog box—but it's probably going into the WINDOWS\TEMP directory. I got around the problem by creating a subdirectory in WINGOPH called DOWN-LOAD and double-clicked on that directory in the Save As box.

Remember the sample
session you created in
Chapter 8? You're going to
need it now to create this
script.

Script-Writing: An Exercise for the Adventurous

The first thing you need to do is create the script, something the WinGopher Complete manual doesn't cover. The Distinct TCP/IP documentation that comes with the product covers it, though not very well. The scripts themselves, however, are fairly well documented internally. Each script is saved in a text file; open one up and you'll see lots of notes explaining what's going on.

Start by opening the Distinct Network Configuration application and selecting the **SLIP/PPP|Script** menu option. When the SLIP/PPP Script dialog box opens, make sure to select the Use Dialup Script check box, choose a script from the drop-down list box, and click on the **Edit** button. I'd suggest opening the NOTIS script, the one that's used when you log onto the WinGopher Test Server. (The following instructions assume you used that script.)

The script opens in Notepad. Immediately save it with a new name, using the **File|Save As** command, using the name of your service provider, for instance.

Here's what you'll need to change; search for each entry in the script:

SEND ("ATQ0V1E0S0=0\013")   Actually you may not need to change this. This is the modem initialization string—the information sent to your modem to tell it to get ready. This is okay for most modems, so leave it alone for now. If you run into problems later, you may need to change this.

SEND ("ATDT1-800-299-1619\013")   This is the phone number. You need to replace the 1-800-299-1619 with the number you dial to get to your service provider (including any special codes such as 9 for an outside line an *70 to turn off call waiting).

SEND ("^M^M")   This comes soon after the WAITFOR ("CONNECT") line, and means that the program should wait until it sees **CONNECT**, then send two carriage returns. This is probably okay for most systems. However, your system may require that you send something else, in which case, you would replace the ^M^M. If you have to type something—let's say, **h**—you would enter **h\013** between the quotation marks.

WAITFOR ("ogin")   This tells the program to wait until it sees the text **ogin**—the **login** prompt. You may need to change this. For example, if your system has a colon after the word login, change this text to **login:**. Perhaps your system asks for your **username:**, instead; then replace **ogin** with **sername:**.

Why ogin? Why do these scripts—and scripts for other products—miss the first character of the word being looked for (**ogin** instead of **login**)? Because the scripts are case sensitive. If you enter **Login** and it's really **login**, the script won't work, so the people writing the scripts, if they are unsure of the case of the first character, just leave it out.

SEND ("guest\013")   After seeing the ogin: prompt the script sends the word **guest**, the login name for when you are using the WinGopher Test Server. Replace **guest** with your real login name.

WAITFOR ("ssword")   This line tells the program to look for the **ssword** prompt (password). If necessary, replace it with the actual password prompt that appears on your system—**ssword:**, for instance. (One wonders whether it was prudery that made the author of this script leave two characters off the beginning of the **ssword** prompt.)

SEND ("canyon\013") After seeing the ogin: prompt, the script sends the word **canyon**. This is the password used for accessing the WinGopher Test Server, so you need to replace it with your actual password.

TECHNO NERD TEACHES...

Wait! Isn't sending your password a security faux pas? Well, yes, it is. So if you want to enter the password yourself each time, replace the **SEND ("canyon\013")** line with these three lines:

```
ASKTEXT ("Enter login name")
SENDTEXT
SEND ("\013")
```

This tells the program to display a message (Enter login name), then to send the response that you type, followed by a carriage return, and continue with the script. Okay now?

We've almost finished the script. But the NOTIS script doesn't have a command to send the **SLIP** or **PPP** command, the command that tells the system to go into the correct communications mode. Your system may not need to do this. If it does, though, you'll have to add a command or two.

In my test session in Chapter 8, you can see that I have to wait for the **Type "c" followed by <RETURN> to continue** prompt and then send the word **slip**. I can do this by adding the following commands to the script, right after the last one we looked at.

```
WAITFOR ("continue")
SEND ("slip\013")
```

This tells the program to wait until it sees the word **continue**, and then send the word **slip**. I checked the session, by the way, to make sure that **continue** doesn't appear earlier in the script, or it would mess it up.

There are a couple more important lines in the script:

```
SRVRADDR ()
CLNTADDR ()
```

If you look back at my test session in Chapter 8, you'll see that near the end of the session, the host sent this line:

```
Annex address is 165.212.9.10.  Your address is
199.190.133.121.
```

In this case, the first is the server address (SRVRADDR) and the second is the client address (CLNTADDR). So the SRVRADDR() and CLNTADDR() lines tell the program to grab these numbers. That means you'd better make sure you have them the right way around, or it will flip them, assigning the numbers as the wrong addresses.

Take a look at the Distinct TCP/IP documentation if you need more help. Each script command is pretty well described, and there's a sample script you can look at.

Finally, close and save the script, and select the new name in the SLIP/ PPP Script dialog box.

Configuring the TCP/IP Connection

Now we need to do the TCP/IP configuration. I found the WinGopher documentation a little unclear here, so let's quickly run through it. You'll have to open the Distinct Network Configuration program; here's what you'll need to define (check Chapter 8 for the information you should have collected from your service provider):

Select the Host|Define menu option   This is where you'll enter all the Internet addresses you've been given by your service provider. The ones already in the list are for connecting to the WinGopher Test Server (you can remove them if you want, using the **Host|Remove** command). You may want to use the **mypc** entry. When you click on **mypc** in the list, you'll see **mypc** appear in the Name text box and a number in the Internet Address boxes. Put your Internet Protocol (IP) address in here and click on **Save**. Then put your service provider's first domain name server address in the Internet Address boxes and a name in the Name text (just type **name server** if you want, or the name of your service provider). Click on **Save** again to save this. Repeat for any other name server addresses you may have been given. If your service provider gave you a gateway address, add that, too. Then close the dialog box (click on **Continue**).

Select the Host|Domain menu option   In the Local Domain Name text box, type your service provider's domain name (cscns.com, for example). Then, from the drop-down list box, select the service provider's first name server address, the one you just added to the Define Host box. If you've been given more than one name server, select an Alternate Server, also.

Select the Host|Local menu option   This is the name you gave your IP address (**mypc**, for example).

Select the SLIP/PPP|Hosts menu option   In the Local serial name text box, select the name you gave your IP address (**mypc**, for example). In the Remote serial name text box, select the name you gave your service provider's address. By the way, entering these items removes the check marks from the two check boxes, which disables the **SRVRADDR ()** and **CLNTADDR ()** lines we looked at in the script earlier. So you can actually choose to get these numbers two ways, have the script grab the numbers, or select the names you gave them in this dialog box.

Select the Host|Subnet menu option   If your service provider gave you a subnet mask (most service providers probably won't), enter it in here by clicking on the right end of the bar in this dialog box. Click several times, on different parts of the bar, until you see the number you want. If your service provider didn't give you a subnet mask, you can just leave this set to 255.255.255.0. (To return it to this number, click on the left side of the bar.)

Select the Gateway|Default menu option   If your service provider gave you a gateway address (not mail gateway, just gateway), use this option to select it.

That's the complicated stuff. The other items are fairly straightforward. Enter the modem information (**SLIP/PPP|Communications**), and make sure that you select **Enabled** in the **SLIP/PPP** menu. Then select **SLIP/PPP|Dialup** and make sure to select the dialup option button. You'll also find a feature in this dialog box that other TCP/IP programs need: the capability to tell the program to hangup after so many idle minutes. I keep leaving my machine for a few moments while connected, getting distracted, and coming back hours later, only to find my net worth reduced by a few wasted dollars. This feature limits that reduction to a few wasted cents.

The Least You Need to Know

- ☞ WinGopher is a well-designed tool for traveling in gopherspace.

- ☞ Double-click on an item to open a menu or copy the file to your hard disk.

- ☞ WinGopher has a .GIF image viewer and a .TXT text viewer. For other files, you'll have to load them onto your hard disk and then open them in the appropriate application. (You can define .AVI (video) and .WAV (sound) players if you have them.)

- ☞ WinGopher also comes with simple Telnet and Ping applications.

- ☞ Installation is straightforward, especially if you can find configuration files for your service provider.

- ☞ NOTIS provides a WinGopher Test Server. Use it to make sure you have installed WinGopher correctly, and to find information about service providers and configuration files.

**It's OK to write on this page.
You paid for it.**

Part IV
Quick and Easy "Pink SLIP"— Using The Pipeline

Okay, you've noticed there's a disk at the back of this book. And maybe you haven't even read the first gazzillion pages of this book—rather, you jumped directly to the disk.

The disk contains a program that you can install in about five minutes. In another five minutes or so you can connect to a system called The Pipeline, based in New York. This program provides a neat, simple way to work with The Pipeline. PC Magazine said that The Pipeline's software "left the other interfaces eating its dust."

In this section, you'll learn all about The Pipeline. However, if you prefer to just jump in and get started, turn to the page facing the inside back cover of the book for quick instructions.

## Chapter 22

Introducing The Pipeline: Your Direct Line to the Internet

In This Chapter

- Introducing The Pipeline
- Installing the software
- Connecting to The Pipeline
- Subscribing to The Pipeline
- How to logon again

We've covered a lot of ground in this book, and provided you with a lot of options. I've explained how to do more with a basic dial-in terminal account, and how to change over to a dial-in direct account if you feel you need to do so. I've told you about many different tools you can use once connected—commercial, shareware, and freeware. Now, I'm giving you another option; one you can try out within a few minutes.

What Is The Pipeline?

The Pipeline Network, Inc., a service provider based in New York in the Financial District, was founded by James Gleick, the best-selling author of *Chaos: Making a New Science* and other books. The distinctive thing about The Pipeline is its software. You can dial into The Pipeline and use it like any other dial-in terminal system, but you can also use some really neat software that makes working with the Internet pretty simple.

The Pipeline is a sort of hybrid connection. It's not a true dial-in terminal connection using a simple serial communications protocol, and it's not a true dial-in direct connection using TCP/IP. It's what The Pipeline calls *Pink SLIP™*, invented by The Pipeline's head programmer Uday Ivatury. This is a packet-transfer protocol, which means that instead of sending a stream of related data, The Pipeline sends data broken down into packets. When the packets arrive at your computer, the software puts them back together.

The great advantage is that a variety of different kinds of packets can be sent at the same time. The software can figure out how to put them together correctly so you can do different things at one time. You can start a file download, for instance, and then go digging around in gopherspace or take a look at your newsgroups. Try doing that with zmodem or xmodem!

About the Software...

The Pipeline's software is deceptively simple. When you first connect, you'll see a fairly sparse main screen: a menu bar, six buttons and a short list of subjects. However, once you get to know the system, you'll find that there's a lot there. You can use FTP, Telnet, e-mail, newsgroups, gopher, and World Wide Web. You'll also find WAIS (Wide Area Information Server) searches, finger, the capability to search various "phone books" around the Internet, and more.

The Pipeline software is very popular. *PC Magazine* recently said that "Pipeline left the other interfaces eating its dust..." and called it a "top-notch Internet interface." It's such a neat system that other service providers are licensing it from The Pipeline, so pretty soon, the system will be available all over the place. You can only use the software we've bundled with this book with The Pipeline service provider, however.

There are two ways you can try it out. You can dial directly into The Pipeline's New York telephone number or dial into a local SprintNet number. Once you've subscribed, you can also use the service via "remote login." (I'll explain all these options in a moment.)

Once connected, you can try it out for 15 minutes (and you can log on again if the first 15 minutes wasn't enough to see everything you want). If you like the system, you can subscribe on-line. Or you can find out about a service provider in your area that is using The Pipeline system software—or will be soon. For more information about rates (including SprintNet charges) and other service providers, see Chapter 27. (During your demo login, The Pipeline will pay the SprintNet charges.)

The Pipeline is planning a significant upgrade to its software very soon. While most features will work in much the same way as I've described in this book, there will be a few important changes, including the addition of a World Wide Web browser. The new software is being tested as I write, so it should be available soon. See Chapter 23 for information on upgrading your software on-line.

Let's Start—Installing the Software

Follow this procedure to install the software:

1. Close Microsoft Windows and then reopen Windows.

2. Place the disk in your floppy disk drive.

2. In Program Manager, select **File|Run**.

4. Type **a:\setup** or **b:\setup** (use the appropriate one for the disk drive you are using) and press **Enter**.

5. The installation program will begin. It's straightforward. Just follow the instructions.

Starting The Pipeline Software

Follow this procedure to configure the program before logging on.

1. Double-click on the **Pipeline** icon in Program Manager.

2. You'll see a large dialog box with two buttons. Click on the **I do not have a user name yet. Let me use the "Demo" account** button.

3. Now you will see the Phone Setup dialog box.

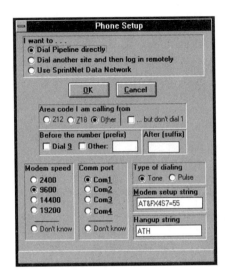

*The Phone Setup
dialog box.*

You have three ways to dial into The Pipeline:

Dial The Pipeline directly   You'll want to use this if you are in
the 212 or 718 area code (The Pipeline is in 212), though you can
use it from any other area code, too.

Dial another site and then log in remotely   You can't use this
method for your demo session, but if you decide you'd like to
subscribe to The Pipeline, you may want to try it. If you have a
dial-in terminal account with another service provider, you can
dial into their system, go to the UNIX prompt, and use the **rlogin**
command to connect to The Pipeline. The advantage? If you are
calling long distance, it's much cheaper to work this way than go
through SprintNet.

Use SprintNet Data Network   SprintNet is a system that people
from all over the country can dial into using a local access number (in most major cities). If it's long distance to call your own
service provider or The Pipeline, use SprintNet. During your demo
session, The Pipeline will pick up the tab.

3a.   If you are going to **Dial The Pipeline directly**, click on the **212** or
      718 or **Other** option button. If you click on Other, the software
      will assume you need to dial 1 before the long distance number (if
      you don't, click on the **but don't dial 1** check box).

If you need to dial 9 to get an outside line, click on the **Dial 9** check box. If you need to dial anything else to get an outside line, click on the **Other** check box and type what needs to be dialed into the text box to the right of Other. In rare cases, you may need to dial something after dialing the phone number; this goes in the **After (suffix)** text box.

3b. If you are going to **Use SprintNet Data Network**, click on that option button. The dialog box will change. You can now click on the **Show List** button to see a dialog box that shows two options, **High speed numbers** and **Low speed numbers**:

If your modem works at 2400 baud or less, double-click on the **Low speed numbers** item. If it's faster, double-click on the **High speed numbers** item. You'll see a list of states. Double-click on your state to see a list of cities. Double-click on your city to see a list of numbers. Double-click on the number you want to use to close the box and place the number in the Phone Setup dialog box.

Take a close look at the number. If there's an area code in there, remove it (unless you know you need the area code to reach that number).

Later, if you subscribe to The Pipeline and decide to use the remote login feature, you can select the **Dial another site and then log in remotely** option button. Ignore the area code and the "Before the number" stuff. (This may not make sense yet, but don't worry, you'll see how it all works in a moment.)

4. Select the **Modem speed** you set your modem to work with.

Connecting direct to The Pipeline   The Pipeline currently has 14400 bps modems, though they will soon upgrade to 28800.

Using SprintNet   SprintNet is currrently upgrading its modems. In some areas, the maximum speed you can use is 9600 bps, in others it's 14400. If you try 14400 and find you can't connect, come back and change to 9600.

Dialing another site and logging in remotely   Use whatever speed you normally use to connect to the service provider.

5. Select the serial communications port your modem is connected to; click on the appropriate **Com** option button.

6. If your phone lines are pulse lines, click on the **Pulse** option button. They are probably tone lines, though, in which case you should leave **Tone** selected.

7. Don't mess with the **Modem setup string** or **Hangup string** unless you know what you are doing! These should be okay in the vast majority of cases.

8. Click on the **OK** button to close the dialog box and see the Pipeline window.

9. Click on **Connect!** in the Pipeline menu. You'll see the **Connect** dialog box. This shows your **User name** (it's *demo* for the demo session), and the **Password** (also *demo* for this session). Notice the **Show** button. When you click on this, it changes the password so you can view it. Click again and it hides the password.

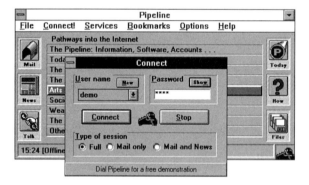

The Connect dialog box.

10. Leave the **Type of session** set to **Full**.

11. If you want to see the login procedure, double-click on the status bar at the bottom of this dialog box, and it will open up to show a session window.

12. Click on **Connect** and the session begins. The program dials into the system and logs you on (except if you're using Remote Login; if so, see the alternative step 12).

If you subscribe to The Pipeline and decided to use the Remote Login procedure, things will work a little differently in step 12.

12. When you click on the **Connect** button, you'll see the **Enter Your Choice** dialog box. Type your service provider's phone number in here, plus any other necessary numbers (9 to get an outside line, *70 to turn off call waiting, and so on).

If you see the message **Error: Sprint TERMINAL missing,** you've probably set the modem speed too high for SprintNet.

Now continue the steps...

13. Click on **OK**. The system dials your service provider.

14. When the system connects, you'll see a message box. Click on **OK** to remove it.

15. A Terminal window will open. In that window, you'll see your service provider's system asking you to log in. (If necessary you can select **Options|Emulation** to pick the correct terminal type.)

16. Enter your username and password as if you were logging onto your service provider's system normally. (As you *are*, of course.)

17. Get to the UNIX shell, however you have to do that on your service provider's system. (In my case, I have to select the UNIX shell from a menu option.)

Note that the **-l** is a lowercase letter l. And if pipeline.com doesn't work, try **remote.pipeline.com**. And if you still can't get in, check with your service provider to see if this format of the **rlogin** command will work on their system.

18. At the UNIX shell, type this: **rlogin -8 -l** *username* **pipeline.com** and press **Enter**. (Fill in your own username.)

19. The system will contact The Pipeline. You'll see the Password prompt. Click on the **Activate!** menu option.

20. The Terminal window will disappear, and you'll be logged onto The Pipeline.

If you don't see as much as you want to in 15 minutes, there's nothing to stop you from logging on and trying for another 15 minutes.

Where Now?

One way or another, you are now into The Pipeline system. You'll see a message telling you that you have fifteen minutes to look around, and that there are certain things you can't do while in demo mode. Close the message box (press **Alt-F4** or use the **Close** command in the Control menu) and start looking around.

Just play around, if you want, or refer to the next few chapters for information. (Those chapters assume you have full rights, not just demo rights.) Now we're going to show you how to sign up for a Pipeline account, explain how to log on the next time, and move onto the next chapter.

Sign Me Up!

If you want to sign up with The Pipeline (you can find full terms in Chapter 27), select **Services|Subscribe**. You'll see a dialog box into which you can enter your name, company name, phone number, address, and the username you want to use for your account. Click on **OK** and you can sign up right then and there (you'll have to enter a credit card number). Or click on the **Don't create an account** check box and someone will contact you later to confirm your account and set up a password and username. (Or call them directly, to speed up the process.)

Once logged in, you can use the **Options|Password| Save Password** command to save your password so you don't have to type it in every time you log on. You shouldn't do this if other people have access to your computer! (Or, at least, people you don't trust. Maybe—just maybe—your family's okay.)

Next Time You Call...

The next time you open The Pipeline program, you won't see the same configuration dialog boxes. Instead, you'll be in The Pipeline main menu window. If you want to change your dialing and modem configuration (to select a different way to call in, for example), select **Options|Dialing and modem setup**.

When you are ready to dial in with your new account name and password, select **Connect!**. The Connect dialog box will pop up; click on the **New** button. You can now type in your username and your real name. Close the New User dialog box, and your name will be in the **User name** drop-down list box. Now enter your password into the **Password** text box. If you want to be sure you are typing the correct password, you can click on the **Show** button to show the password as you type. (When you do so, the button changes to Hide. Clicking on **Hide** will take it back to showing asterisks as you type the password.)

If you are using the **rlogin** method, you'll see the dialog box asking for your telephone number again. Enter your number, and click on **OK**. That number will be saved, so the next time you log on, you won't have to type it in. From here on, everything's the same as before. So log on, and read the next chapter.

The Least You Need To Know

☞ Run SETUP.EXE on the disk to install the software.

☞ Run the program from the icon and fill in the configuration data.

☞ Click on **Connect!** in the main window to start your connection.

☞ You can connect directly to The Pipeline's New York number, via SprintNet, or via **rlogin** on your current service provider's system.

☞ See Chapter 27 for information about rates and service providers using this software.

**Attention Star Rangers:
Wipe this page with lemon juice
and watch this week's Captain Space
Commander Clue appear!**

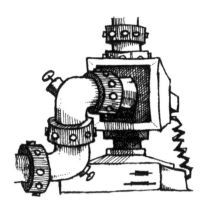

Chapter 23

Diving into The Pipeline

In This Chapter

- ☞ Learning about The Pipeline window
- ☞ Customizing The Pipeline
- ☞ Upgrading to the next software version

The Pipeline's main window is based on the gopher system. Those "bars" you see in the middle (the ones under the **Pathways into the Internet** heading)—each one is a gopher menu. You know how to use a Windows gopher by now (unless you skipped the rest of this book and came straight to the disk!). You double-click on an entry or select it and press **Enter**. That entry will take you to another, just like in the old UNIX gopher client.

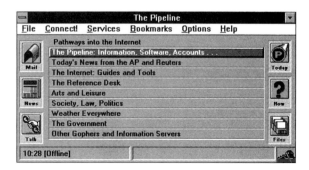

The Pipeline window is based on a gophering system.

Each time you open a gopher menu, though, another window pops up. In the preceding figure, notice the icons in the left column, and in the status bar. The status bar provides a handy reminder of what these icons do when you double-click on them.

List	Displays another gopher menu (in another window).
Text	Lets you read the text file.
Search	Lets you search for information.
Picture	Downloads and displays a graphics file.
File	Downloads the file.
Connect	Starts a Telnet connection.

The Pipeline and its gopher windows.

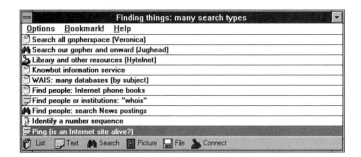

The Pipeline puts everything in a separate window, so after a while, everything gets very cluttered. There are two ways to deal with this. First, select **Options|Pipeline windows|Show floating window list**. This displays a small window showing all your open windows. The floating window remains "on top" all the time. Click on the title bar to see all your Pipeline windows, and double-click on an entry to bring that window to the front.

Next, use the **Options|Pathways into the Internet|How many open lists at once** command to limit the number of gopher lists open at any time.

If you find the background color of the Pipeline window obnoxious, change it: Double-click on an entry and use the Options menu to change the background color. It will "stick" so all subsequent windows have the new color. You can also pick a different font if you want.

More? Of Course There's More!

The Pipeline may be based on the gophering concept, but there's more. First, notice the buttons (you have noticed the buttons, haven't you?). Click on a button to go to a particular service:

 Mail   The e-mail system (the same as selecting **Services|Mail**).

 News   The newsgroup system (the same as selecting **Services|News**).

 Talk   Lets you talk with someone else (the same as selecting **Services|Talk ("chat")**).

 Today Displays today's news and weather reports (the same as selecting **Services| Today's News and Weather**). By the way, once you get online, this icon changes, being replaced by a weather icon that more closely resembles the actual weather in New York (as if you care!). The icon may show a cloud with rain, for instance.

 How   Displays an online help system that describes how to carry out common tasks. This is not the same as the **Help** menu option.

 Files   Lets you search for or download a file (or both at the same time) using Archie and FTP (the same as selecting **Services|Get files ("FTP" and "Archie")**).

Then there are the menus. Here's what each menu item does:

☞ The **File** menu enables you to manage users, work with files, and leave the program. It contains the following commands:

Add new user   Lets you create a new user account, so everyone in your family or neighborhood can use your computer to reach The Pipeline. (Each account has to be set up with The Pipeline, and costs extra.)

Display picture file Lets you display a graphics file in The Pipeline's Viewer.

Exit Closes The Pipeline program, closing the connection if you are in a session.

☛ The **Connect!** command dials into The Pipeline and logs on.

☛ The **Goodbye!** command closes your connection.

☛ The **Services** menu gives you a list of things to do in The Pipeline. Here's what you'll find:

Mail Displays the e-mail system.

News Displays the newsgroup system.

Talk ("chat") Lets you call someone else on the system to chat with them.

Today's News and Weather Displays a document with today's news and weather reports (the weather's for NY, though, not much use if you are in South Dakota).

Find current news (UPI) Lets you do a WAIS (Wide Area Information Server) search in the United Press International news system for a particular subject.

Get files ("FTP" and "Archie") This system lets you search for a file, or download a file, or both at once.

Chat (IRC) Lets you connect to an Internet Relay Chat server (see Chapter 1).

Find someone on the Internet Searches for e-mail addresses.

Search all Gopherspace (Veronica) Lets you use Veronica to search for a subject in gopherspace.

Connect to another system (Telnet) Starts a Telnet session.

Open a plain terminal Lets you run a session at the UNIX prompt, in case you want to use an Internet feature that isn't built into The Pipeline's user interface.

Subscribe/Renew This is where you subscribe to The Pipeline, or renew your subscription.

Bookmarks   Opens the Bookmarks menu, so you can go directly to somewhere or something, without digging your way through the Internet to get there.

☛ The **Options** menu lets you configure the way The Pipeline runs.

Dialing and modem setup   You've seen this already; it's where you enter the information for connecting to The Pipeline.

Password|Save Password   Saves your password so you don't have to enter it each time you log on. Dangerous if other people can get to your computer!

Password|Change Password   Lets you change your password.

Pipeline windows|Show floating window list   Displays a small window listing the open Pipeline windows. The floating window remains above all other windows. If you are working in another application, click on the title bar to bring all The Pipeline windows to the front. Double-click on an entry in the window to bring that window to the front.

Pipeline windows|Minimize all windows together   If you select this option, each time you minimize one of The Pipeline windows, all minimize together. And when you restore one, they all restore together.

News (forums)|How many entries at most   Lets you limit how many messages will be downloaded from your newsgroups. Some newsgroups are *very* active, and build up to large numbers very quickly. This number is a total for all newsgroups, so the more groups you work with, the higher the number you need.

News (forums)|Organization name   You can add an organization name by which you will be identified when you send messages to a newsgroup.

Pathways into the Internet|How many open lists at once   Use this to limit the number of windows that remain open while you are working in gopherspace. A handy way to limit clutter.

Pathways into the Internet|How many list items at most   This lets you limit how many items can appear in a gopher menu, so that very long menus can be displayed more quickly (by truncating them).

Download directory   Lets you define where The Pipeline should place files that you download.

Word processor for big files   When you open a mail or news document, The Pipeline displays it in the mail or news window itself. However, if the file is too big, the system has to place it in a word processing program. So this menu option lets you define where you want the document displayed if it is too big for the normal window. By default, you open such documents in Windows Write.

Font for printing   Lets you specify which font you want to use for printing.

☞ The **Help** menu, not surprisingly, gives you access to The Pipeline's online help system.

Contents   Displays The Pipeline's Windows Help Contents page.

Help|"How do I..."   Displays a Windows Help page with typical questions about The Pipeline.

Help|About the Pipeline   Displays the program's About dialog box, showing the version number.

Now Where Was I?

The Pipeline has a very simple bookmark system. The Bookmark menu contains a series of bookmarks that you can select to go directly to a place on the Internet. No need to dig your way down various gopher menus, or run an FTP session, or start the Telnet service, or whatever. Just select the bookmark, and The Pipeline does the work for you.

How do you add items to the bookmarks? Here and there, you'll see Bookmark check boxes and Bookmark menus. Simply click on the check box or menu, and The Pipeline adds the location to the Bookmark menu. Simple. (The next version of The Pipeline will have a different system, in which you can categorize bookmarks, and display them in a small dialog box. Upgrade your software to the latest version once you get online.)

Help Me!

You can get The Pipeline's help program at any time by selecting **Help|Contents** or **Help|"How do I..."**. There's also *context-sensitive* help, that is, help about where you are currently. Press **F1** to get help for the item the cursor is currently on. As for more help, there are a few other places you can go.

The Help button Click on the question-mark button in The Pipeline main window to see a gopher window containing a list of documents that answer common questions (how to find information about Internet resources, how to find other Pipeline users, how to find other answers, and so on). This is an interactive system. Not only does it provide text answers, but you'll also be able to get directly to the tools you need from here. For instance, if you select **Find a name, place, anything else on the Internet**, you'll see a gopher menu that contains links to Veronica, Jughead, Hytelnet, and various Internet "phone books."

The Pipeline: Information, Software, Accounts If you select this option from The Pipeline main window, you'll get into a gopher menu that leads you to more information about using The Pipeline.

The Great Upgrade: An Exercise for the Eager

Upgrades are the lifeblood of the software business, though in The Pipeline's case, upgrades are free. Still, now and again, you'll get the chance to upgrade your software with neat new features. Follow this procedure.

1. Double-click on the first entry in the main menu (The Pipeline gopher menu): **The Pipeline: Information, Software, Accounts....**

2. When the next gopher menu opens, double-click on **Pipeline Software**. The window that opens is where you can find the latest software, both released versions and, sometimes, beta versions.

3. You will see entries such as these examples:

    ```
    Upgrade to Version 2.0 (313K) v20.zip

    Entire distribution disk (1.44M) pipeline.zip

    An unzip program unzip.exe

    The Version 3 beta test
    ```

    The little icons to the left of each entry indicate what each line is: if the icon is a disk, it means that when you double-click on the line, a download will begin. If the icon is a file folder, it will open another menu, and if it's a page, it will display a document for you to read.

4. When you find the upgrade file you want to download, double-click on it.

5. A small dialog box appears, showing you the file's name. You can change the name if you want.

6. Click on the **OK** button and the download begins. (The Pipeline places the file in the download directory defined using the **Options|Download directory** command.)

7. Once downloaded, "unzip" the file. (Confused? Read the Techno Nerd Teaches box.)

TECHNO NERD TEACHES...

If you don't have PKUNZIP, notice that one of the options in The Pipeline Software window is **An unzip program unzip.exe**. If you download this file, then run it as a program, it will extract PKUNZIP for you. (You can run it by double-clicking on it in File Manager—make sure you put it in its own directory first.) Once extracted, you can use PKUNZIP to extract The Pipeline software. Place PKUNZIP.EXE in the same directory as The Pipeline software, select PKUNZIP.EXE in File Manager, select **File|Run**, type **pkunzip** *pipelinefilename* and click on the **OK** button.

8. Once you've extracted The Pipeline files, find the text file and read it. This will explain how to upgrade your software.

The Least You Need to Know

☞ The Pipeline is based on a gophering system; the entries in the middle of the window are all gopher menus.

☞ Double-click on an entry in the middle of The Pipeline window to select that gopher menu.

☞ Click on a button or select a menu option to select another form of the Internet service.

☞ To upgrade your software, select **The Pipeline: Information, Software, Accounts** followed by **Pipeline Software**.

(zen text)

Chapter 24

Working with The Pipeline E-mail

In This Chapter

☞ Sending and reading e-mail

☞ Working with mail folders

☞ Working with the address book

If you haven't used any of the Windows e-mail programs we've looked at in this book, you're in for a real treat: a graphical-user-interface, double-click, iconized, button-enabled, e-mail system.

You can use The Pipeline e-mail system both on- and offline. When you connect, the software grabs all your messages, saves them on your hard disk, and sends any that you've written. Then you can log off and deal with the mail without paying connect charges. Notice also that when you connect to The Pipeline, there are three **Type of session** option buttons. You can have a **Full** session (logon and stay on), **Mail** session (logon, grab e-mail, logoff), or **Mail and News** session (logon, grab e-mail and newsgroups, logoff).

To see the e-mail window, click on the **Mail** icon in the main window, or select **Services|Mail**. It's a simple e-mail system: in the top of the window is a list of messages. Simply click on a message to read it. Notice the buttons at the bottom of the window. Click **New** to write a message to someone, **Reply** to send a response to the message you are reading (and click in the **quote** check box to include the original message in the response), **Forward** to send the message on to someone else, **Save** to save the message in a folder, and **Delete** to trash it.

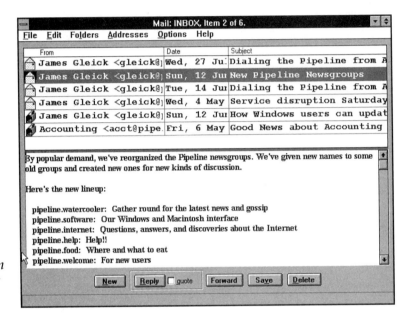

		Mail: INBOX, Item 2 of 6.

File   **Edit**   **Folders**   **Addresses**   **Options**   **Help**

From	Date	Subject
James Gleick <gleick@]	Wed, 27 Ju	Dialing the Pipeline from A
James Gleick <gleick@]	Sun, 12 Ju	New Pipeline Newsgroups
James Gleick <gleick@]	Tue, 14 Ju	Dialing the Pipeline from A
James Gleick <gleick@]	Wed, 4 May	Service disruption Saturday
James Gleick <gleick@]	Sun, 12 Ju	How Windows users can updat
Accounting <acct@pipe	Fri, 6 May	Good News about Accounting

By popular demand, we've reorganized the Pipeline newsgroups. We've given new names to some old groups and created new ones for new kinds of discussion.

Here's the new lineup:

pipeline.watercooler: Gather round for the latest news and gossip
pipeline.software: Our Windows and Macintosh interface
pipeline.internet: Questions, answers, and discoveries about the Internet
pipeline.help: Help!!
pipeline.food: Where and what to eat
pipeline.welcome: For new users

[**New**]   [**Reply**] ☐ quote   [**Forward**]   [**Save**]   [**Delete**]

Click on a message in The Pipeline's e-mail screen to read it.

About Those Folders...

You can create folders to hold your mail. Click on the **Save** button, and you'll see a small pop-up menu. This lists the folder names; selecting a folder moves the current message into that folder. If you want to create a folder, select **Create**. (Or select **Folders|Create folder**.) Type an eight-character name and click on **OK**.

Now, when you want to move a message into that folder, just click on the **Save** button and then on the folder name. To view the contents of a folder, select it from the **Folder** menu.

What Are You Sending?

Sending e-mail is simple enough. Click on the **New** button or select **File|New**. In the window that appears, type an e-mail address, or select one from the drop-down list box. Type a subject, and type your letter.

There are a few handy options. The **Save copy in Sent Mail** check box tells the program that a copy of the message should go into the Sent Mail folder. If you want to enter an *emoticon* (you know, a smiley), you can select one from the **Edit** menu—there's a smile :-), a wink ;-), and a frown :-(. Of course, you can also use the usual Windows **Cut**, **Copy**, and **Paste** commands (on the Edit menu).

There's another useful command. Click on the **Insert** button (or select **Edit|Insert file**), and you see a small dialog box with two buttons: **Plain text** and **Program or picture file**. The first option displays a typical File Open dialog box, so you can open a text file; the text from that file is inserted into the message. The other option will UUENCODE a binary file and place it in the message. When the message gets to the other end, what happens? If it's another Pipeline user, the system will automatically UUDECODE the message back to its binary format. If it's not a Pipeline user, of course, he'll have to know how to use UUENCODED messages.

Whenever someone sends you a UUENCODED message, The Pipeline automatically converts it back to binary and places it in your download directory. You get a mail message telling you about it.

Where's It Going?—The Address Book

The address book is very easy to work with. If you receive a message from someone who you think should be in your address book, just click on that message in the list, and select **Addresses|Add sender to address book**.

If you want to type in a few addresses, though, select **Addresses|Open address book**. You see a list of your entries. Click on the **Add** button, type a name into the **Alias** box (no spaces), tab into the **refers to** box, and type the e-mail addresses. Press the **Spacebar** between e-mail addresses; the program beeps and replaces the space with a comma. Enter as many addresses as you want, and click on **OK**. To close the dialog box, click on **Done**.

Now, when you are sending a message, you can select an alias from a drop-down list box. If you have, say, 15 addresses associated with an alias, The Pipeline automatically sends the message to all 15 people.

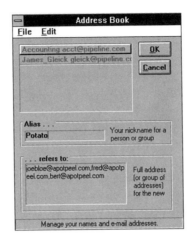

*The address book lets
you enter single
addresses and
mailing lists.*

More Useful Stuff

Before we leave e-mail, let's just take a look at a few more useful features:

- ☞ **File menu:**

    Save to file   Saves the current message in a text file.

    Examine outgoing attachments   Shows you which UUENCODED files have attached to the message.

- ☞ **Edit menu:**

    Find Subject or Sender   Lets you search your message list for a particular message.

    Repeat last search   Searches the list again.

- ☞ **Options menu:**

    Fonts   Lets you select the type of fonts you want to use in the e-mail system.

    Colors   Lets you modify the colors used.

    Hide headers and line breaks   When selected, you won't see each message's header rubbish (all the stuff about where the message came from and where it's been).

    Beep for new mail   Your computer beeps if The Pipeline downloads new mail.

Show message for new mail   You see a message when you get new mail.

Save outgoing mail (Sentmail)   The **Save copy in Sent Mail** check box is always checked, so a copy of all outgoing mail saves automatically (you can clear the check box for individual messages).

Confirm deletions   Displays a message asking you to confirm that you really want to delete or cancel a letter.

Signatures|Use built-in signature   Tells The Pipeline to send your signature file automatically at the end of each message.

Signatures|Create or change signature   Lets you create or modify your signature file.

The Least You Need to Know

- ☛ The Pipeline has a simple address book in which you can create mailing lists.

- ☛ You can insert text from a file into a message, or attach a UUENCODED file.

- ☛ There's a system of folders, so you can save messages according to subject or sender.

- ☛ You can add an automatic signature, and enter smileys from the Edit menu.

**You could fit alot of haiku
on this page.**

Chapter 25

Newsgroups: Heard It Through The Pipeline

In This Chapter

- ☛ Working with newsgroup folders
- ☛ Adding groups to your folders
- ☛ Reading newsgroup messages
- ☛ Working with newsgroups off-line

The Pipeline has subscribed to 7,500 newsgroups, a huge number (many service providers subscribe to "only" about 4,000 or 5,000). If you are ready to risk reading the newsgroups, click on the **News** button in the main windows, or select **Services|News**.

News Folders You Can Use

The Pipeline's newsreader consists of folders, each folder containing related newsgroups. When you first open the newsgroups, you'll see the Your Newsgroup Folders dialog box that shows you the folders; you already have five folders set up.

From here, you can **Open** a folder (so you can read the messages), create a **New** one (selecting which newsgroups should be in the folder), **Edit** an existing one (adding and removing newsgroups), and **Delete** a folder (if

The Pipeline saves the list of newsgroups on your hard disk. You can update the list, to make sure you have the latest (you don't right now—newsgroups are being added all the time). In the main window, select **The Pipeline: Information, Software, Accounts**, and select **Update my Newsgroup lists** for information on how to do this.

you live in Podunk, Texas, you may want to delete the New York folder). By the way, you can create, edit, and delete folders while offline, saving connect charges. You only need to go online to actually download the messages (and you can do that using the **Mail and News** session option in the Connect dialog box).

Creating Your Very Own Folder

Here's how to create a newsgroup folder. Click on the **New** button. You'll see a large dialog box (see the following figure). Type the folder name into the **Name for this Folder** text box. Then start adding newsgroup names. There are several ways to do that:

☛ Type a name into the **Name of news group** text box, and click on **Add**.

☛ Type a word in the text box, and click on **Search**. The program finds matches in the newsgroup list and places them in the large list box. Double-click on the ones you want to add. (The list contains not only newsgroup names, but short descriptions, too, making the search more effective.)

☛ Click on one of the folder tabs at the top, and double-click on a newsgroup in the resulting list.

When you're done, click on the **Done** button. When you edit a folder, you see the same dialog box and follow the same procedure.

You can create newsgroup folders offline, then go online to grab the messages.

Getting the Goods

When you are ready to read your newsgroup messages, double-click on a folder (or click on the folder and click on the **Open** button). The News Folder window opens, showing you all the groups in that folder. The ones with [+] before the names have unread messages in them; those with [-] don't. (The [-] sign means either that the newsgroup has no messages in it, or the newsgroup doesn't exist at all—you may have mistyped a name.)

Double-click on a group to see the list of messages in the right list box. Then click on a message in the list to read it (it'll take a few moments to transfer everything). Note that you won't always see the message. If it's not

If a newsgroup shows a [+] sign, but when you double-click on it, no newsgroup articles appear, it may be that you have the **Options|News (forums)|How many entries at most** set too low. Increase it to around 150 and try again. (This option limits the total number of newsgroup articles that will be transferred—so if the first few newsgroups have more than the maximum, you won't see the messages for the next newsgroups.)

transferred, it means that it's not on the mainframe, even though the header is there. This happens quite often, sometimes because The Pipeline removes the message after posting, while the header remains.

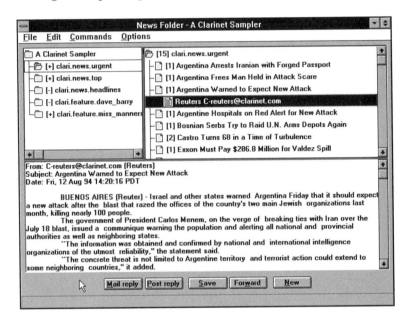

The News Folder window lets you read and respond to newsgroups.

If you've been away a while and find that the newsgroup has way too many messages for you to handle, select **Commands|Mark these articles as "read"** to remove all the messages. Then select **Commands|Catch up with the latest articles** to get the most recent articles back.

The buttons at the bottom of the screen let you mail a reply to the person who sent the newsgroup message, post a reply (that is, send a response to the newsgroup itself), forward the message to someone else via e-mail, save the message in a text file, and send your own message to the newsgroup. As usual, you can use the Cut, Copy, and Paste commands, and there's also a Print command in the File menu.

The **Commands** menu also has some important commands:

Mark these articles as "read"   Select a newsgroup and then this option to mark all the articles as read, so you won't see them again.

Get already seen (older) articles   This lets you go back and view messages that you've seen or marked as read. A dialog box appears, showing you what message number you've read to. For example, if it says you are up to message 3019, and you want to see a message that was about 10 down the list, enter 3005 and click on **OK** to retrieve the last few messages.

Catch up with the latest articles   This reloads the last messages that The Pipeline's news server grabbed off the net.

Expand all subjects   Expands the message "tree," showing all the messages within a particular topic.

Search|Search Topics   Lets you search for a particular topic.

Search|Search Author Info   Lets you search for a particular author.

Offline Assistant   A few useful tools for working offline—as you'll see in a moment.

Many newsgroups have UUENCODED files containing, in particular, graphics. While The Pipeline's newsgroup reader cannot decode files—they appear as normal text—you can mail them to yourself. When the Mail system sees them, it automatically decodes them for you. (If it's a multipart UUENCODE—one that's been broken into pieces, cut and paste each piece into a mail message and mail it to yourself.)

All the News—Fast and Easy

Remember the **Mail and News** session option when you connect to The Pipeline. You can use this to work with newsgroups offline. Here's how.

First, connect to The Pipeline using the **Mail and News** option (the option button near the bottom of the Connect dialog box). The software logs on, grabs your e-mail, and updates your newsgroup listings, and then logs off automatically.

When the program's logged off, click on the **News** button in the main windows. Select a folder and click on **Open**. Then double-click on a newsgroup to see the list of messages. You can now select the messages you want to read. Click on a message to select it. (A selected message has a red border around it.) You can also use the **Commands|Offline Assistant** menu commands. **Mark articles in a thread** marks all the articles within a thread; a thread is indicated by a folder, which may have several articles within it. **Mark all articles** tells the software that you want to read all articles in a newsgroup. And **Unmark all articles** removes the marking from all of them. Close the window using the Control menu (or by pressing **Alt-F4**).

Now, the next time you log on using **Mail and News**, the software goes to your newsgroups and grabs those messages, so you can read them off-line.

The Least You Need to Know

- ☞ You can add newsgroups to folders while offline.

- ☞ You can read newsgroup messages while online.

- ☞ You can also download the message titles, select the messages you want to read while offline, and have the program download just those messages.

Chapter 26
Out and About on the Net with The Pipeline

In This Chapter

- Using Archie
- Using FTP
- Using Telnet
- Talking through The Pipeline
- Using the UNIX shell
- Finding news and weather
- Using Veronica searches

We've covered the basics of The Pipeline in the last few chapters, but before we leave, let's take a look at a few more miscellaneous Pipeline tools to get you moving along that Internet infohighway.

FTP: All the World's a Software Store

Let's take a quick look at how you grab files from FTP sites around the world using The Pipeline.

Click on the **File** button in the main window, or select **Services|Get files** ("FTP" and "Archie"). You'll see the Find and Receive Files dialog box (this illustration shows what it looks like after you click on the

Advanced button). You can use this in one of two ways: you can enter a sitename to start a full FTP session, or you can enter just the name of the file and have Archie look for it.

If you enter only the file name, you will be using Archie to search the Internet for the file. You can click on the **Advanced** button to get to a few more options. Click on **Partial match is all right** if the text you entered may not be the full file name. Select the **Maximum number of hits** (the number of file entries that will appear in a window when Archie finishes). You can select the Archie server that you want to use from the **Available host machines** drop-down list box (you don't need to, though).

When you click on **OK**, The Pipeline calls up Archie and does the search for you. It then displays a window listing all the files it finds. You can simply double-click to download the one you want.

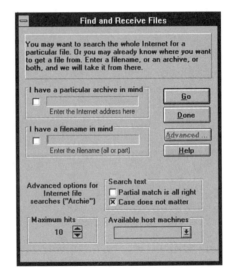

*The Pipeline com-
bines FTP and Archie
in one box.*

If you want a full FTP session, enter a site name. If you also know the directory you want to work in at that FTP site, you can enter the directory into the file name text box. When you click on **GO**, the session begins; you'll see the directories in a window. Double-click on directories to see the contents of the directories, or on a file to download that file to your system.

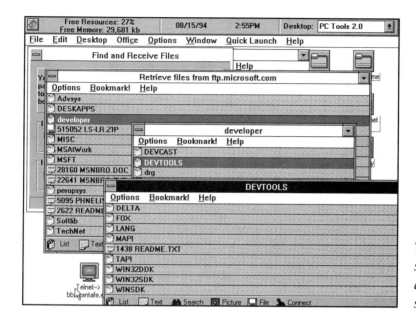

The Pipeline's FTP session places each directory listing in a separate window.

The Pipeline Telnet

To run a Telnet session, select **Services|Select to another system ("telnet")**. You'll enter the Telnet site address into a dialog box (you can also choose to add it to your bookmarks, so you can get to it quickly next time), then click on **OK**. You'll drop into a terminal window in which the session will take place.

Note that you can modify various items from the **Options** menu. You can change colors and the font, select a terminal emulation, and also set up a log. You can save the log to a file, and you can also "scrollback" through the session in the window. The Telnet window's **Edit** menu also lets you Cut, Copy, and Paste, and paste in smileys.

Talk

If you'd like to "talk" to other Internet users, click on the **Talk** button in the main window, or select **Services|Talk ("chat")**. You'll have to enter a person's username and hostname (or just username if you are talking with another Pipeline user). The Pipeline will call that person for you.

You have a call coming in!

To find the names of other Pipeline users you can talk to, double-click on **The Pipeline: Information, Software, Accounts**, on **Pipeline People**, and then on **Show who else is online now**. You can even double-click on a name to see information about that person—his real name, phone number, comments, and so on (only stuff he wants you to see, of course). You are not on the list until you double-click on **Update my personal information** and enter all the necessary info.

When the person answers, you'll be able to "converse" in a two-panel window, with your text in one panel, his in the other.

Internet Relay Chat

Here's another chat service: Internet Relay Chat. Select **Services|Chat (IRC)**. You learned all about IRC in Chapter 1, and The Pipeline provides the same basic interface that you learned about there. You'll be in a terminal window and have to use the system in the normal way (see Chapter 1 if you need more help). A new graphical IRC system is being added to The Pipeline soon.

Back to the UNIX Shell!

If you really feel the need, you can go to the UNIX shell using the **Services|Open a plain terminal** option. I doubt whether many users actually find their way here, or, if they do, know what to do with it. However, there may be times that you want to use a service that is *not* built into The Pipeline interface. Maybe you just find yourself pining for UNIX, or wanting to remind yourself why you are using a graphical user interface. In such a case, come to the terminal window and get out your UNIX book (better still, get out *The Complete Idiot's Guide to the Internet*).

The session runs in the same Terminal window that The Pipeline uses if you run an rlogin session through your service provider (see Chapter 22) or if you use Telnet or IRC. You can modify the background and foreground (text) colors, change the font that's used, and select the terminal emulation. Another handy item: you can scroll back through your session to see what happened earlier.

News & Weather

The Pipeline has a couple of quick ways to get to information about the weather and news. Select **Services|Today's News and Weather** to see the same window that appears if you click on the **Today** button in The Pipeline main window. Sometimes this has news, but usually it just has a New York weather report. If you want your own weather, double-click on **Weather Everywhere** in the Pathways into the Internet list and you'll be provided with a gopher menu with links to all sorts of things: U.S. weather maps, earthquake and hurricane reports, auroral-activities, forecasts for cities in all 50 states, and more.

The **Services|Find current news** option lets you do a Wide Area Information Server search on a Clarinet news newsgroup (a newsgroup about news). A dialog box pops up; type in a subject you want information about, click on the **Search** button, and off it goes, coming back a few moments later with information.

There's the **Today's News from the AP and Reuters**, a mainline for news junkies. Double-click on this entry in The Pipeline main window and a gopher window pops up, containing about 20 news stories, plus links to more gopher menus with more news stories!

A Date with Veronica

You can use Veronica—to search gopherspace—directly from The Pipeline main window. Select **Services|Search all Gopherspace (Veronica)**. Type what you are looking for into the dialog box that appears, and click on **OK**. When Veronica has finished, she'll display another Pipeline gopher window, containing the entries she found.

What Else?

You can find all sorts of things in The Pipeline. The nice thing is, it only takes a few clicks or double-clicks to get moving. Spend a little time double-clicking on each of the Pathways into the Internet in turn, looking through the menus and submenus. When you run across something you know you'll want to come back to one day, use the Bookmark option to add them to your Bookmark menu (or, if you upgrade to the next version, the Bookmark dialog box).

You'll find an enormous range of resources, and all work in pretty much the same way: double-click on an interesting item. If it's a menu another window opens, if it's a GIF file, it's downloaded and displayed in a graphics viewer. If it's a text file, you can read it in a text window; if it's a searchable resource, you can type in a search keyword.

The Least You Need to Know

☛ To search Archie, enter just a file name into the Find and Receive Files dialog box.

☛ When Archie completes its work, you can select the file you want and download it.

☛ To run a full FTP session, enter a site name—and an optional directory name—into the Find and Receive Files dialog box

☛ You can chat with other Pipeline users with the Talk system.

☛ Spend some time double-clicking around The Pipeline to see what's there.

☛ Remember to use the Bookmark feature to find your way back to places of interest.

Chapter 27
Finding the Goodies

In This Chapter

- ☞ The Macmillan Computer Publishing Internet site
- ☞ Buying commercial programs
- ☞ Where to FTP for the freeware and shareware programs

In this chapter, you'll find sources for all the products—commercial, public domain, and shareware—that I've mentioned in this book. Remember, though, prices and source information will change. This information was correct (it's always difficult to know for sure on the Internet) at the time of writing.

The Macmillan Computer Publishing Internet Site

Macmillan Computer Publishing (the big company that Alpha Books is a small part of) is getting its own Internet site soon. You'll be able to access the Macmillan Computer Publishing host by anonymous FTP, Gopher, and WWW. It's going to be a great place, where you can download sample chapters for books that interest you, read reference articles, and even order books online.

The Macmillan folks are going to do you a big favor. They're going to make sure that all the freeware and shareware programs I talk about in this book are available there for FTP, and update their stash periodically so you'll always know where to go to get the recent versions.

Here's the catch. The site isn't up yet. It's due to be up and running a couple of months after the release of this book. As we went to print, the site was being set up. When it does go live, though, you'll be able to reach it through World Wide Web at **http://www.mcp.com** or FTP at **ftp.mcp.com**.

Ask Your Friendly Service Provider

You should always check with your service provider if you are looking for a bit of software. Not only is it convenient to get stuff out of the file library on your host—no need to worry about FTP sites being clogged up with other people trying to grab stuff—but in some cases, your service provider or system administrator may be able to help you. Why spend an hour or two writing a login script, for instance, if your service provider has already created one? Use the existing one, and all you need to do is modify one or two things—the username and password, of course, and maybe the phone number.

The Rest of This Chapter May Be Wrong...

Hey, I can't be responsible for changes—you know that. Prices and dealer participation may change without warning, void where prohibited, plus tax and shipping. In some cases, addresses and phone numbers may change. Most importantly, though, FTP sites may change; they often do. Sometimes the FTP site is still there, but you can't get onto it because another five zillion people are trying to do so at the same time.

So what do you do? Well, remember the Macmillan Computer Publishing site. If you can get on, we'll have the software there. If you can't get on there, or you want to get to the source of the program, check to see if the

FTP site you've been trying displays a list of *mirror* FTP sites when it tells you that you can't log on. If so, try a few of the mirror sites. Somewhere on those sites there should be an area that stores exactly the same files as the original site.

If you can get onto the site, but can't find the files you are looking for, they may have been moved; try digging around. Spend some time picking likely directory names and looking inside. Remember to read the INDEX files that many directories have (sometimes they won't be called INDEX; there might be a text file with some other name). The Windows FTP programs make reading these files very easy.

If you still can't find what you need, try Archie, Veronica, and Jughead. These tools often turn up places you can go to grab files that seem to have disappeared off the edge of the cyberworld.

Commercial Products

First, let's take a look at the commercially distributed products I mentioned.

Pronto

CommTouch Software, Inc.
1206 W. Hillsdale Blvd.
Suite C
San Mateo, CA 94403
800-638-6824
415-578-6580
Fax: 415-578-8580
Pronto*Commtouch.COM

Talk to Your Service Provider! There are just a handful of well-known, widely used Internet access programs. If you buy one, ask your service provider if they've created configuration files or logon scripts for the program—it'll save a lot of time and hassle.

CommTouch Software, Inc. sells Pronto, the e-mail and newsgroup program we looked at in Chapter 6. Single copies sell for $149.

At the time of writing, a version that works with newsgroups as well as with e-mail was not ready, but should be by the time you read this, as should a version that works with dial-in direct connections.

MKS Internet Anywhere

Mortice Kern Systems, Inc.
35 King Street North
Waterloo, Ontario Canada N2J 2W9
519-884-2551
FAX: 519-884-8861
MODEM: 519-884-2861
inquiry@mks.com

Another UUCP mail product, similar to WinNET Main & News. The program costs $149.

Internet Chameleon

NetManage, Inc.
10725 North De Anza Blvd
Cupertino, CA 95014
408-973-7171
FAX: 408-257-6405
info@netmanage.com

NetManage, Inc. distributes Internet Chameleon. The product is $199. NetManage also sells other versions of its TCP/IP software, in different combinations.

Internet in a Box/AIR Series

SPRY
316 Occidental Avenue South
Seattle, WA 98104
800-777-9638
206-447-0300
FAX: 206-447-9008
info@spry.com

SPRY distributes this product in two ways. In one incarnation, it's known as *Internet in a Box*, and you can buy it in bookstores and software houses ($149 list price). O'Reilly & Associates sells this version. In its other incarnation, it's known as the AIR Series, and sold directly by SPRY, the company that actually writes the software. The AIR Series has a variety of combinations: AIR Connect, AIR NFS, AIR Navigator, and so on. SPRY regards Internet in a Box as a consumer product and the AIR Series as a corporate product.

WinGopher

NOTIS Systems, Inc.
1007 Church Street
Evanston, IL 60201-3665
800-556-6847
708-866-0150
FAX: 708-866-0178

WinGopher is a product of NOTIS Systems. WinGopher Complete costs $129. If you already have a dial-in direct or permanent connection and don't need the TCP/IP Winsock software, you can buy WinGopher for $69.

Service-Provider Specific Programs

A few of the products we mentioned only work with a particular service provider—if you want to use the product, you must use the service (WinNET is a little different, as we describe below).

The Pipeline

The Pipeline
150 Broadway
Suite 1710
New York, NY 10028
Phone: 212-267-3636
Fax: 212-267-4380
Email: info@pipeline.com
Modem: 212-267-6432 (login as *guest*)
Telnet, gopher, FTP: pipeline.com

The Pipeline software bundled with this book is for use with a service provider called The Pipeline, Inc. The Pipeline is selling this system to other service providers, so you may find a local provider using the software. To find out if there's a service provider in your area using system (there are a number all over the country, and the list is growing quickly), you can contact The Pipeline at staff@pipeline.com. If you are an Internet service provider and want information about using the software for your customers, contact licence@pipeline.com.

If you want to continue working with The Pipeline Network, Inc., here are their current rates (check with them for the latest rates—things change);

$15/month with 5 free hours, $2/hour for extra hours
$20/month with 20 free hours, $2/hour for extra hours
$35/month, no limit on hours

These charges are only for connect time, not for phone charges. If you are not within local-call distance, you have three choices:

Long distance calls   You'll have to figure out what that costs.

SprintNet   If you use SprintNet, you'll pay $5/hour between the hours of 8 a.m. and 5 p.m. during business days and $2.50/hour any other time (evenings, weekends, holidays). These times are New York time. This charge is in addition to The Pipeline charges.

rlogin   If you use the rlogin method I described in Chapter 22, you'll pay whatever you have to pay your service provider for the time you are logged on through their system, almost certainly less than SprintNet, plus The Pipeline charges.

America Online

America Online
8619 Westwood Center Drive
Vienna, VA 22182
1-800-827-6364

You can get a free 10-hour test of America Online. Call to order the software you need. The software itself is free. The service, once you've used up your 10 hours, is $9.95/month for 5 hours, and then $3.50/hour for every hour over 5 (no restrictions on time of day).

NetCruiser

NETCOM
3031 Tisch Way, 2nd Floor
San Jose, CA 95128
800-353-6600
408-345-2600
FAX: 408-241-9145
info@netcom.com

NetCruiser is a NETCOM product and can only be used with that service provider's system. There's a $25 registration fee (which gets you the software). Then you pay $19.95 a month. For that, you get 40 "peak" hours and as many hours as you want on weekends and from midnight to

9 a.m. during the week. If you use more than 40 peak hours, you pay
$2/hour for those extra hours.

WinNET News & Mail

Computer Witchcraft, Inc.
330F Distillery Commons
Louisville, KY 40206-1919
800-589-5999
502-589-6800
help@win.net

Computer Witchcraft, Inc. designed this product for use with the WinNET
service, which provides e-mail and newsgroups. The charge is $8/hour with
a $9.95 monthly minimum. WinNET is in both MCI's Friends and Family
and Sprint's The Most plans, so if you are using those services you may be
able to save on your long distance rates. If you use WinNET's 800 number,
you will pay an extra 18 cents a minute for calls made between 8 a.m. and
5 p.m. EST during the week, 12 cents a minute for calls at other times.

   WinNET News & Mail is also available as shareware, for use with UUCP
mail accounts (other versions, perhaps a dial-in terminal version, may be
available soon). The registration price is $99. See later in this chapter for
more information.

32-bit/16-bit   Many of the
programs listed here have
both 16-bit versions (for
Windows 3.1 and Windows
for Workgroups) and 32-bit
versions (for Windows NT
and the soon-to-be-re-
leased-Windows-4.0-
Chicago-thing). Also, there
are often versions available
for other computers, such
as the Mac.

You can get the commercial version of WinNET
News and Mail by sending e-mail to
request@win.net. In the Subject line, put **WinNET**.
You'll get a reply containing UUENCODED program files, which you'll have to UUDECODE.

Public Domain, Shareware, and Freeware

Here's information about the public domain,
shareware, and freeware products, most of which
you can download from the Internet. See earlier in
this chapter for information about the **Macmillan**

FTP site. We plan to have these programs in our FTP site, so you can grab them from there. However, I'm also providing information about other sites, so you can get them if the Macmillan site is not yet operating when you buy this book, or if you want to make absolutely sure you have the very latest version.

Qwkmail Programs

If you want to use a Qwkmail program, check with your service provider. Qwkmail has to be set up on the service provider's system in order for you to use it, and if it has been set up, they may have a library of Qwkmail programs.

For a list of programs, FTP to the **ftp.wustl.edu** FTP site, change to the **systems/ibmpc/msdos/offline** directory, and get the **qwkp9406.zip** file (or something similar—the number will change with the date of the document). This file, updated periodically, contains several text files that tell you everything you ever wanted to know about Qwkmail, including the name of literally dozens of Qwkmail programs and contact information for the programs' authors. You'll also find a few Qwkmail programs in this directory (look for the files with qwk somewhere in the name, and read the index file in this directory). You may also use Archie to track down Qwkmail programs. I found dozens listed when I did a search recently.

Public domain software is software that is available without restriction; you don't have to pay, and you can do what you want with it. **Freeware** is software that you can use for free, but someone owns the copyright, so you can't do whatever you want with it. You can't sell it or modify it without permission, for instance. **Shareware** is software that you can try for free, but for which you should pay a registration fee if you decide to continue using it. Often paying the registration fee gets you another, more advanced, version of the software, and detailed documentation.

WinNET News and Mail

This program is available for free when you sign up with the WinNET service (see earlier in this chapter). However, if you want to run it on a system you are already connected to, you can get a shareware version ($99 registration fee). At the time of writing, the only shareware version available was one for UUCP connections, though there may be other versions

Talk to Your Service Provider! Before you go digging around on the net looking for a public domain or shareware product, take a look on your own service provider's system. Quite often, you'll find libraries of such software, and the service provider may even have created configuration files and login scripts.

released soon, perhaps for dial-in terminal accounts. (UUCP—UNIX to UNIX Copy Program—accounts let you use the Internet for e-mail and newsgroups, but nothing else.)

To get a copy of the software, first send e-mail to **request@win.net**. In the Subject line, put **help**. You'll receive a list of software that you can download. Check to see if there is a dial-in terminal system available. If you want the UUCP version, send e-mail to **request@win.net**, and put **UUCP** in the Subject line. You'll get a reply containing UUENCODED program files, which you'll have to UUDECODE.

UMSLIP

UMSLIP is a program from the University of Minnesota that lets you set up a dial-in direct connection for your DOS computer. You can find it at the **boombox.micro.umn.edu** FTP site in the **/pub/pc/slip** directory. Get the file named **sliparc.exe**. This program is free to students at the University of Minnesota, $50 for others.

Minuet

This DOS multifunction program is available at the **boombox.micro.umn.edu** FTP site, in the **/pub/pc/minuet/beta16** directory. It's shareware, so there's a registration fee.

Slipdisk

This is an archive file with some handy DOS programs. You can find it in various places. Search for **slipdisk** using Archie, or try the **ftp.cs.tamu.edu**

FTP site, in the **/pub/DCE/misc** directory, or try the **ftp.cerf.net** FTP site in the **/pub/software/msdos/internet** directory. The slipdisk "package" contains PC Gopher, a mail program, a Telnet program, and so on.

WinSock

I mentioned two WinSock programs in the book:

- ☞ **Microsoft TCP/IP for Windows for Workgroups** is available from the **ftp.microsoft.com** FTP site, or by calling Microsoft Sales at 800-426-9400. The current version does not include a dialer. The files are available for free from the FTP site.

- ☞ **Trumpet Winsock** is a shareware program ($20). You'll find this all over the place. You can get it from the **ftp.ncsa.uiuc.edu** FTP site, in the **PC/Mosaic/sockets/** directory. The latest version should be in the **biochemistry.bioc.cwru.edu** FTP site, in the directory **/pub/trumpwsk**.

Win32s

If you want to run the 32-bit version of Mosaic in Windows 3.1 or Windows for Workgroups, you'll need to load something called Win32s, distributed by Microsoft. You can get it from the **ftp.microsoft.com** FTP site, in the **d:/softlib/mSLfiles** directory. At the time of writing, the latest version was in a file called **pw1118.exe**.

You can also find this software at the **ftp.ncsa.uiuc.edu** FTP site (the home of Mosaic). It's in the **/PC/Mosaic/** directory (though under a different name, because NCSA added a text file to the package—at the time of writing it was **win32s.zip**).

If you have problems installing the Win32s software, there's a Microsoft Knowledge Base document you may want to get hold of. Go to the **ftp.microsoft.com** FTP site, change to the **/developr/win32dk/kb/q106/ 7** directory, and get the file called **15.txt**.

Web Browsers

Here's where to get the Web browsers I talked about earlier:

☞ **Mosaic for Windows** is free. Its home site is the **ftp.ncsa.uiuc.edu** FTP site, in the **PC/Mosaic** directory. If you want to use the **16-bit version**, look in the **PC/Mosaic/old** directory. You'll also find the last *released* version in that directory (currently version 1.0).

☞ **Cello** is also free, and you can find it at the **ftp.law.cornell.edu** FTP site, in the **/pub/LII/Cello** directory.

☞ **WinWeb** is freeware (for noncommercial use). Currently, it's in its first "alpha" phase, so the software may be unstable. You can find it at the **ftp.einet.net** FTP site, in the **/einet/pc/winweb** directory.

Gopher Tools

A good place to find gopher tools is the **boombox.micro.umn.edu** FTP site, in the **/pub/gopher/Windows** directory. You'll also find a few in the **ftp.cuhk.hk** site in the **/pub/gopher/PC** directory. You'll find most or all of the gopher tools we looked at in these two sites.

☞ **PC Gopher** is a shareware program from the University of Minnesota. You can find it in the **boombox.micro.umn.edu** FTP site, in the **/pub/gopher/PC_client** directory. I looked at PC Gopher II in this book, but PC Gopher III has recently been released.

☞ **BCGopher** is free. For the latest version, check the **bcinfo.bc.edu** FTP site, in **/pub/bcgopher**. (At this FTP site, you will use the username **anonymous**, but you must use **guest** as the password.)

☞ **Gopher Book** is freeware. For the latest version, check the **ftp.cnidr.org** FTP site, in the **/pub/NIDR.tools/gopher/pc/ windows** directory.

☞ **HGopher** is freeware. For the latest version, check the **lister.cc.ic.ac.uk** FTP site in the **/pub/wingopher** directory.

☞ **WGopher** is freeware. For the latest version, check the **ftp.cuhk.hk** in the **/pub/gopher/PC** directory.

☞ **WSGopher** is freeware. For the latest version, check the **boombox.micro.umn.edu** FTP site in the **/pub/gopher/Win-dows** directory, or the **sunsite.unc.edu** FTP site in directory **pub/ micro/pc-stuff/ms-windows/winsock/apps**.

Viewers

To make the most of the WWW and Gopher, you need viewers, programs that display or play files you find in cyberspace—programs that display .GIF and .JPG graphics, play video, play music, and so on.

You may already have some of the programs you need. For example, Windows comes with Media Player and Sound Recorder, and you may have installed other such programs. However, you can find lots of shareware and public domain viewers online, too. Check out the **www.law.cornell.edu** FTP site and look in the **/pub/LII/Cello** directory. You can also download them from the NCSA's WWW server, at **http:// www.ncsa.uiuc.edu/SDG/Software/WinMosaic/viewers.html**, or from the **ftp.ncsa.uiuc.edu** FTP site in the **/Web/Mosaic/Windows/viewers** directory. Another good site is the FTP site, in the **/pc/win31/util/viewers** directory. Within this directory, you'll find four more subdirectories: one for programs that will display animations, display graphics, play sounds, and capture whatever's displayed on your screen and save it in a file.

FTP

Looking for an FTP program? Here's where to look.

☛ **WS_FTP** is freeware. WS_FTP's "home" site is **ftp.usma.edu**. You should be able to find it in the **/pub/msdos/winsock.files** directory.

☛ **Wftpd** is shareware ($15). You can find it in the **ftp.wst.com** FTP site, in the **/pub/winsock/wftpd** directory.

☛ **WSArchie** is freeware. I haven't been able to track down the "home site" of this program, but you can find it in a number of places. Try the **ftp.demon.co.uk** FTP site in the **/pub/ibmpc/winsock/apps** directory; the **oak.oakland.edu** FTP site in the **/pub/msdos/winsock** directory; and the **ftp.uni-stuttgart.de** FTP site in the **/pub/org/nda/gfi** directory. If you use Archie to search on WSARCHIE, you'll find this file all over the place.

☛ **WinFTP** is freeware. Its home is the **mica.chrr.ohio-state.edu** FTP site in the **/WINSOCK** directory. You'll find several different versions of the program here.

News & Mail

Here are the sources for the many fine shareware and freeware Newsgroup and Mail programs we looked at.

☛ **Trumpet** is a shareware newsreader for DOS. You can find it in the **ftp.utas.edu.au** FTP site in the **/pc/trumpet/dostrump** directory.

☛ For **Trumpet for Windows**, check the **ftp.utas.edu.au** FTP site in directory **/pc/trumpet/wintrump**.

☛ **WinVN** is freeware. Look in the **ftp.ksc.nasa.gov** or **titan.ksc.nasa.gov** FTP site in the **/pub/win3/winvn** directory. (This is a VMS host, where the FTP rules work a little differently. If you use WS_FTP, though, you should have no trouble.) This product is in the public domain. There's also a separate ZIP file containing a huge documentation file for this program (many pictures).

☛ For **WinElm**, look in the **lister.cc.ic.ac.uk** FTP site in the **/pub/winelm** directory. For the MIME support files, look in **/pub/winmime**. You must install ELM-PC first. You can find that in **/pub/elm-pc**.

☛ **Eudora** is a free program used by QUALCOMM Incorporated to promote their commercial version (which costs about $65). You can find this in the **ftp.qualcomm.com** FTP site in the **/quest/windows/eudora** directory. This directory contains a subdirectory with the number of the Eudora version (currently 1.4), so the full directory path is, currently, **/quest/windows/eudora/1.4**. There may also be a **beta** subdirectory in which you can find the latest beta version of Eudora (currently version 1.4.2b16). You can get more information about Eudora from **eudora-sales@qualcomm.com**, or call 800-238-3672. The commercial version is much stronger and full function.

☛ **RFD Mail** lets you connect to a dial-in terminal account and grab your e-mail. It's shareware ($29.95). You can find it at the **ftp.std.com** FTP site in the **/customers/software/rfdmail** directory. It comes with a few scripts to make it run on some service providers' systems. You can also check the **/customers/software/rfdmail/scripts/beta** directory for more scripts, or write your own.

Multiple Application Program

Looking for a Swiss army knife of a program? Try this:

☛ **WinQVT** is a shareware program ($40, $20 for students). It handles e-mail, Telnet, FTP, and newsgroups. Try the **biochemistry.cwru.edu** FTP site in the **/pub/qvtnet** directory, or **ftp.cica.indiana.edu** in **/pub/pc/win3/uploads**.

WAIS

Finding your WAIS around? (Would you believe me if I said "no pun intended?") Check out these:

☛ **EINet winWAIS** is a shareware program. It's $35, and comes with a couple of graphics-viewing programs: WinECJ and gfxVIEW. You can find it at the **ftp.einet.net** FTP site, in the **/einet/pc** directory.

☛ **WAIS for Windows** (WinWAIS) is freeware from the U.S. Geological Survey. It includes Trumpet Winsock, which you can install during the WinWAIS installation program. You can find the program at the **ridgisd.er.usgs.gov** FTP site in the **/pub/wais** directory (perhaps in the **winwais** subdirectory of that directory).

Other Stuff

A few other gems:

☞ **Finger** is a free Windows finger facility. It's currently in version 3.1, though another version should be out by the time you read this. See the **sunsite.unc.edu** FTP site in the **/pub/micro/pc-stuff/ms-windows/winsock/apps** directory.

☞ **WSIRC** is a Windows Internet Relay Chat program. There are several versions available, a freeware version (2 channels), a shareware version (5 channels), and a version that is distributed to people who register their shareware version (up to 255 channels). It costs $29.95 to register. Its author initially uploads it to these sites: the **cs-ftp.bu.edu** FTP site (try in the **/irc/clients/pc/windows** directory); and the **ftp.demon.co.uk** FTP site (try **/pub/ibmpc/winsock/apps/wsirc**). He also says he puts it in the **undernet.org** FTP site, though I've no idea where.

☞ **WinTalk** is freeware. You can find it in the **ftp.elf.com** FTP site, in the **/pub/wintalk** directory.

☞ **Internet VoiceChat** lets you talk—literally—with other VoiceChat users around the world. It costs $20 to register. The home site is the **ftp.cica.indiana.edu** FTP site in the **pub/pc/win3/winsock** directory. The current version (1.0) doesn't work with Trumpet Winsock, but the next one will.

☞ **Com***t* Com*t* lets you connect any telecommunications program to your WINSOCK.DLL connection, so you can use it for a Telnet session. It's shareware ($15.95). You can find it at the **ftp.std.com** FTP site in the **/customers/software/rfdmail** directory.

☞ **NCSA Telnet for MS Windows** can be found by doing an Archie search for **wintelb3.zip** (that's the current file name; you may prefer to search for **wintel** in case the name changes). You'd think that you could find this at the NCSA's own site (**ftp.ncsa.uiuc.edu**), but I couldn't—they've reorganized and this program seems to have gone missing.

☞ **Trumpet Telnet's** home site is the **ftp.utas.edu.au** FTP site in the /**pc/win31/netstuff/apps** directory. Get the **winapps.zip** file, which contains the Trumpet FTP, Telnet, chat, Archie and ping clients.

Lots More Goodies

There are many other programs available on the Internet. We're going to keep adding programs to the Macmillan FTP site, so check there periodically.

You may also take a look at the document called *Windows Internet ("WINTER") Software Packages*, distributed by Ed Sinkovits. This lists all sorts of programs. We've looked at most of the ones that Ed put in his original document, but if he keeps it updated, you should see new and interesting apps appear in this list. You can find it at the **ftp.cica.indiana.edu** FTP site, in the /**pub/pc/win3/misc** directory, in a file called **WINTER01.ZIP**. (The 01 will change with later editions, of course.) This FTP site is very busy, so you may want to do an Archie search on the word **WINTER**, or look in one of this site's *mirror* sites if you can't get in. (A mirror site is one that is exactly the same as another—when you try to connect to the **ftp.cica.indiana.edu** site, it will show you a list of mirrors.)

Do You Write Software?

If you've written some Internet software and would like us to include it at the Macmillan FTP site, please contact me at pkent@lab-press.com.

Get some crayons and draw a nice picture with some trees and mountains and birds and flowers on this page. It'll make you feel good, I bet.

Speak Like a Geek: The Complete Archive

alias   A name that is substituted for a more complicated name. For example, a simple alias may be used instead of a more complicated mailing address or for a mailing list.

America Online   An online information system. America Online is in the process of adding full Internet access.

anonymous ftp   A system by which members of the Internet "public" can access files at certain FTP sites without needing a login name; they simply log in as anonymous.

Archie   An index system that helps you find files in thousands of FTP sites.

archive file   A file that contains other files, generally compressed files. Used to store files that are not used often, or files that may be downloaded by Internet users.

ASCII   The American Standard Code for Information Interchange, a standard way for computers to use bits and bytes to represent characters. An ASCII file contains simple text without any special formatting codes.

backbone   A network through which other networks are connected.

baud rate   A measurement of how quickly a modem transfers data. Although, strictly speaking, this is not the same as bps (bits per second), the two terms are often used interchangeably.

BBS   See *bulletin board system.*

beta test   A program test based on the premise that "this program's virtually finished, we just need a little help getting the rough edges off—let's give it to a few more people."

BIND   Berkeley Internet Name Domain, a UNIX version of the *DNS.*

BITNET   The "Because It's Time" network (really!). A large network connected to Internet.

bits per second   A measure of the speed of data transmission; the number of bits of data that can be transmitted each second.

bps   See *bits per second.*

bulletin board system   A computer system to which other computers can connect so their users can read and leave messages, or retrieve and leave files.

chat   Similar to talk programs, except that chat systems let large numbers of users chat together. Where a talk program is like a phone call, a chat system is like a party, sometimes with different "rooms" known as channels or groups.

client   A program or computer that is "serviced" by another program or computer (the server). For example, a Gopher client program requests information from the indexes of a Gopher server program.

CSLIP   Compressed SLIP. See *SLIP.*

Cyberspace   The "area" in which computer users travel when "navigating" around on a network.

daemon   A UNIX server (pronounced "DEE-mon"), a program running all the time in the background (that is, unseen by users), providing special services when required.

dedicated line   A telephone line that is leased from the telephone company, and used for one purpose only. In Internetland, dedicated lines connect organizations to service providers' computers, providing dedicated service.

dedicated service   See *permanent connection*.

dial-in service   A networking service that is used by dialing into a computer through a telephone line.

dial-in direct connection   An Internet connection that is accessed by dialing into a computer through a telephone line. Once connected, your computer acts as if it were an Internet host. You can run client software (such as Gopher and WWW clients), and can copy files directly to your computer. This type of service is often called SLIP, CSLIP, PPP, or TCP/IP. See also *dial-in terminal*.

dial-in terminal connection   An Internet connection that is accessed by dialing into a computer through a telephone line. Once connected, your computer acts as if it were a terminal connected to the service provider's computer. This type of service is often called Interactive or dial-up. See also *dial-in direct*.

dial-up service   A common Internet term for a dial-in terminal connection.

dig   Domain information gopher, a program that provides information about hosts on the Internet.

direct connection   See *permanent connection*.

Domain Name System (DNS)   A system by which one Internet host can find another, so it can send e-mail, connect FTP sessions, and so on.

domain name   A name given to a host computer on the Internet.

download   The process of transferring information from one computer to another. You *download* a file from another computer to yours. See also *upload*.

Elm   An e-mail program.

e-mail or **email**   Short for electronic mail, this is a system that lets people send and receive messages with their computers. The system might be on a large network (such as Internet), on a bulletin board, (such as CompuServe), or over a company's own office network.

emoticon   The techie name for a smiley.

encryption   The modifying of data so that unauthorized recipients cannot use or understand the data.

FAQ   Frequently-Asked Questions. A menu option named FAQ will lead you to a document that answers common questions. You may also find text files named FAQ.

File Transfer Protocol   See *FTP*.

finger   A UNIX program used to find information about a user on a host computer.

flame   An abusive newsgroup message.

Free-Net   A community computer network, often based on the local library, which provides Internet access to citizens, from the library or sometimes from their home computers. Free-Nets also have many local services, such as information about local events, local message areas, connections to local government departments, and so on.

freeware   Software that can be freely used, though it still belongs to someone. The owner often defines certain conditions on its use; it may be used for noncommercial purposes, for instance. See also *shareware*.

FTP   File Transfer Protocol. A protocol defining how files are transferred from one computer to another. FTP is also the name of a program used to move files. FTP can be used as a verb (often in lowercase) to describe the procedure of using FTP. As in, "ftp to **ftp.demon.co.uk**," or "I FTPed to their system and grabbed the file."

gateway   A system by which two incompatible networks or applications can communicate with each other.

GML   Generalized Markup Language, a way in which a simple text document can be marked using various codes, so a special reader can format the document. This allows different programs to display the document in different ways, and, perhaps more importantly, to display the document to be used on different computer types. See *SGML*.

Gopher   A system using Gopher clients and servers to provide a menu system used for navigating around the Internet.

GUI   Graphical User Interface (pronounced "GOO-ee"). The GUI provides tools, such as menus, icons, scroll bars, borders, toolbars, and so on, all designed to make working with the program easier. The GUI, in effect, provides graphical "prompts" to remind you how to do things and let you do them more quickly using a mouse.

host   A computer connected directly to the Internet. A service provider's computer is a host, as are computers with permanent connections. Computers with dial-in terminal connections are not; they are terminals connected to the service provider's host.

host address   See *IP address*.

host number   See *IP address*.

HTML   HyperText Markup Language. A collection of codes that are entered into a document to denote certain WWW components, such as links between documents. See *SGML* and *GML*.

Hypertext   A text document containing "links" between pages, chapters, or topics. Users can "navigate" through such a document, usually by clicking on colored or underlined text.

HYTELNET   A directory of Telnet sites. A great way to find out what you can do on hundreds of computers around the world.

internet   The term internet spelled with a small i refers to networks connected to one another. "The Internet" is not the only internet.

internet address   See *IP address*.

Internet Protocol   The standard protocol used by systems communicating across the Internet. Other protocols are used, but the Internet Protocol is the most important one.

IP address   A 32-bit address that defines the location of a host on the Internet. Such addresses are normally shown as four bytes, each one separated by a period (such as 192.156.196.1).

IRC   Internet Relay Chat, a popular *chat* program. Internet users around the world can chat with other users in their choice of IRC channels.

Jughead   Jonzy's Universal Gopher Hierarchy Excavation And Display tool; a new gopher search tool, similar to Veronica. The main difference between Veronica and Jughead is that Jughead searches a specific gopher server, while Veronica searches all of gopherspace.

Kermit   A file transfer system from Columbia University.

Knowbot Information Service (KIS)   An experimental system that helps you search various directories for a person's information (such as an e-mail address).

LAN   See *Local Area Network*.

LISTSERV lists   Mailing lists—using mail reflectors—that act as newsgroups. Messages sent to a LISTSERV address are sent to everyone who has subscribed to the list. Responses are sent back to the LISTSERV address.

Local Area Network (LAN)   A computer network that covers only a small area, often a single office or building.

logging on   Computer jargon for getting permission from a computer to use its services. A "logon" procedure usually involves typing in a username (also known as an account name or userID) and a password. This procedure makes sure that only authorized people can use the computer. Also known as *logging in*.

logging off   The opposite of logging on, telling the computer that you've finished work and no longer need to use its services. The procedure usually involves typing a simple command, such **exit** or **bye**.

login   The procedure of logging on.

mail gateway   A computer connecting different e-mail systems, so the systems can transfer messages.

mail reflector   A mail address that accepts e-mail messages and then sends them on to a predefined list of other e-mail addresses. Such systems are a convenient way to distribute messages to a group of people.

mailing list   A list of e-mail addresses to which a single message can be sent by entering just one name as the To address. Also refers to discussion groups based on the mailing list. Each message sent to the group is sent out to everyone on the list. (LISTSERV groups are mailing list groups.)

megabyte   A measure of the quantity of data. A megabyte is a lot when you are talking about files containing simple text messages, not much when you are talking about files containing color photographs.

MIME   Multipurpose Internet Mail Extensions, currently a little-used system that lets you send computer files as e-mail.

mirror site   An FTP site that is a "mirror image" of another FTP site. Every week or two, the contents of the other FTP site are copied to the mirror site. So if you can't get into the original site, you can go to one of the mirror sites.

MUD   A type of game popular on the Internet. MUD means Multiple User Dimensions, Multiple User Dungeons, or Multiple User Dialogue. MUDs are text games; each player has a character. Characters communicate with each other by the users typing messages.

netiquette   Internet etiquette, the correct form of behavior to be used while working on the Internet. Can be summed up as "Don't waste computer resources, and don't be rude."

Netnews   See *USENET*.

newbie   A new user. The term may be used to refer to a new Internet user, or a user who is new to a particular area of the Internet.

newsgroup   The Internet equivalent of a BBS or discussion group (or "forum" in CompuServe-speak) in which people leave messages for others to read. See also *LISTSERV*.

newsreader   A program that helps you find your way through a newsgroup's messages.

news server   A computer that collects newsgroup data and makes it available to *newsreaders*.

nslookup   A program that provides detailed information about a host on the Internet.

online   Connected. You are online if you are working on your computer while it is connected to another computer. Your printer is online if it is connected to your computer and ready to accept data.

packet   A collection of data. See *packet switching*.

packet switching   A system that breaks transmitted data into small *packets* and transmits each packet (or package) independently. Each packet is individually addressed, and may even travel over a route different from that of other packets. The packets are combined by the receiving computer.

permanent connection   A connection to the Internet using a leased line. The computer with a permanent connection acts as a host on the Internet. This type of service is often called direct, permanent direct, or dedicated service, and is very expensive to set up and run.

permanent direct   See *permanent connection*.

Pine   An e-mail program.

ping   A simple program that sends a message to another host and waits for a response, in order to analyze the connection between the two hosts.

Point Of Presence   Jargon meaning a local telephone number in a particular area. If a service provider has a POP in, say, Podunk, Ohio, people in that city can connect to the service provider by making a local call.

Point-to-Point Protocol   A method for connecting computers to Internet via telephone lines, similar to SLIP (though, at present, less common).

POP   See *Post Office Protocol* and *Point Of Presence*.

Post Office Protocol (POP)   A system for letting hosts get e-mail from a server. This is typically used when a dial-in direct host—which may only have one user and may only be connected to the Internet periodically—gets its e-mail from a service provider. The latest version of POP is POP3.

port Generally, port refers to the hardware through which computer data is transmitted; the plugs on the back of your computer are ports. On the Internet, port often refers to a particular application. For example, you might telnet to a particular port on a particular host. The port is actually an application.

posting A message (article) sent to a newsgroup, or the act of sending such a message.

postmaster The person at a host who is responsible for managing the mail system. If you need information about a user at a particular host, you can send e-mail to **postmaster@*hostname***.

PPP See *Point-to-Point Protocol*.

PRODIGY A computer information service.

protocol A set of rules that defines how computers transmit information to each other, allowing different types of computer and software to communicate with each other.

public domain software Software that does not belong to anyone. You can use it without payment, and even modify it if the source code is available. See also *shareware* and *freeware*.

Qwkmail A system by which e-mail and newsgroup messages are compressed, transferred to your computer, and then opened by a Qwkmail program (usually public domain, freeware or shareware). Useful for dial-in terminal accounts, though Qwkmail can be a hassle to set up on the host end (easy to set up on the terminal end).

remote login Another term for Telnet.

rlogin See *remote login*.

rot13 Rotation 13, a method used to encrypt messages in newsgroups, so you can't stumble across an offensive message. If you want to read an offensive message, you'll have to decide to do so.

router A system used to transmit data between two computer systems or networks using the same protocol. For example, a company that has a permanent connection to the Internet will use a router to connect its computer to a *leased line*. At the other end of the leased line, a router is used to connect it to the service provider's computer.

Serial Line Internet Protocol (SLIP)   A method for connecting a computer to Internet using a telephone line and modem. (See *dial-in direct*.) Once connected, the user has the same services provided to the user of a permanent connection.

server   A program or computer that "services" another program or computer (the client). For instance, a Gopher server program sends information from its indexes to a Gopher client program.

service provider   A company that provides a connection to Internet. Service providers sell access to the network, for a variety of prices. Shop around for the best deal.

shareware   Software that can be freely distributed and used, though it requires the payment of a registration fee if you decide to use it beyond a certain time (usually 30 days). See also *public domain software* and *freeware*.

shell   In UNIX, a shell is a program that accepts commands that you type and "translates" them for the operating system. In DOS, a shell is a program that "insulates" you from the command line, providing a simpler way to carry out DOS commands.

signature   A short piece of text transmitted with an e-mail or newsgroup message. Some systems can attach text from a file to the end of a message automatically. Signature files typically contain detailed information on how to contact someone—name and address, telephone numbers, Internet address, CompuServe ID, and so on.

Simple Mail Transfer Protocol (SMTP)   A way to transfer e-mail between computers on a network.

SLIP   See *Serial Line Internet Protocol*.

smiley   The term given to those goofy little pictures made out of letters and characters that people use in e-mail, such as :-). The correct term is emoticon.

talk A program that lets two or more UNIX users, on the same host or different hosts, type messages to each other. As a user types a character, that character is immediately transmitted to the other user. There are several common talk programs: **talk**, **ntalk**, and **YTalk**.

TCP/IP Transmission Control Protocol/Internet Protocol. A set of protocols (communications rules) that control how data is transferred between computers on the Internet.

Telnet A program that lets Internet users log into computers other than their own host computers, often on the other side of the world. Telnet is also used as a verb, as in "telnet to **debra.doc.ca**."

telneting Internet-speak for using Telnet to access a computer on the network.

TLA Three Letter Acronym. What would we do without them? See also *EFLA*.

tn3270 A Telnet-like program used for remote logins to IBM mainframes.

Token Ring A system used for creating small local area networks. Such networks may be connected to the Internet.

UNIX A computer operating system. Most hosts connected to the Internet run UNIX.

upload The process of transferring information from one computer to another. You upload a file from your computer to another. See also *download*.

URL Uniform Resource Locators. Used by the WWW to specify the location of files on other servers.

USENET The "User's Network," a large network connected to the Internet. The term also refers to the newsgroups distributed by this network.

UUCP UNIX to UNIX Copy Program, a system by which files can be transferred between UNIX computers. The Internet uses UUCP to provide a form of e-mail, in which the mail is placed in files and transferred to other computers.

uudecode   If you use uuencode, you'll use uudecode to convert the ASCII file back to its original format.

uuencode   A program used to convert a computer file of any kind—sound, spreadsheet, word processing, or whatever—into an ASCII file so that it can be transmitted as a text message.

Veronica   The Very Easy Rodent-Oriented Net-wide Index to Computerized Archives, a very useful program for finding things in Gopherspace.

VT100   The product name of a Digital Electronics Corporation computer terminal. This terminal is a standard that is "emulated" (duplicated) by many other manufacturer's terminals.

WAIS   See *Wide Area Information Server*.

whois   A program that lets you see who is currently logged onto a host.

Wide Area Information Server   A system that can search databases on the Internet for information in which you are interested.

World Wide Web   A hypertext system that allows users to "travel through" linked documents, following any chosen route. World Wide Web documents contain topics that, when selected, lead to other documents.

WWW   See *World Wide Web*.

X.500   A standard for electronic directory services.

XRemote   A rarely used type of dial-in direct connection.

Ytalk   Currently one of the best UNIX talk programs. Unlike the basic **talk** program, **YTalk** lets several users talk together at once. It can also communicate with other types of talk programs.

Index

Who cares what you think? WE DO!

We take our customers' opinions very personally. After all, you're the reason we publish these books. If you're not happy, we're doing something wrong.

We'd appreciate it if you would take the time to drop us a note or fax us a fax. A real person—not a computer—reads every letter we get, and makes sure that your comments get relayed to the appropriate people.

Not sure what to say? Here are some details we'd like to know:

- ☛ Who you are (age, occupation, hobbies, etc.)
- ☛ Where you bought the book
- ☛ Why you picked this book instead of a different one
- ☛ What you liked best about the book
- ☛ What could have been done better
- ☛ Your overall opinion of the book
- ☛ What other topics you would purchase a book on

Mail, e-mail, or fax it to:

Faithe Wempen
Product Development Manager
Alpha Books
201 West 103rd Street
Indianapolis, IN 46290

FAX: (317) 581-4669
CIS: 75430,174

Special Offer!

Alpha Books needs people like you to give opinions about new and existing books. Product testers receive free books in exchange for providing their opinions about them. If you would like to be a product tester, please mention it in your letter, and make sure you include your full name, address, and daytime phone.

Everyone's talking about
The Complete Idiot's Guides!

The Complete IDIOT'S GUIDES

"Thanks for helping me get started."
Jim Ellars, Greenfield, IN

"It is written in plain, old English and tells me what I need to know to do what I want to do."
Craig Connolly, Lincoln, NE

"I've made friends with my computer."
Marjorie Bock, Slidell, LA

"...quite helpful in gaining familiarity and confidence in various computer topics."
Martin Bondy, New York, NY

"...most of all, the books helped build a much-needed confidence."
Bill Shepson, Sacramento, CA

"I could hardly put it down—anxious to find out a little more and more."
June Littlejohn, Irving, TX

"...covered the basics of the entire program without getting too bogged down in details."
Robert Matson, New York, NY

"...one of the best introductory computer books that I have come across in the past few years. It's refreshing to have instructional material written at the level of the beginner and not making many assumptions regarding prior computer ability."
Daniel Green, Saratoga Springs, NY

"It teaches in such a simplified, straightforward manner."
Richard Boehringer, Miramar, FL

"This book taught me that I'm in control."
Greg Wright, Ashmore, Australia

"...simple, easy to read, and enjoyable. I felt like someone was talking to me."
Jon Marshall, Dover, OH

"The best thing about the book is the readability."
Gerard van Os, The Netherlands

"I appreciate material that assumes me to be lacking in information rather than lacking in intelligence."
Holly Waldrop, Nashville, TN

"I have to say that this is THE book for teaching in this area."
Richard Caladine, University of Wollongong, Australia

"After really close review, I have found it to be superb. The concepts are as clear as I have seen."
Barry Owen, San Juan, CO

"Lest I forget, your bright orange cover and cheat sheet proved to be invaluable amongst a cluttered desk."
Darryl Pang, Honolulu, HI

The Complete Idiot's Guides—For People With Better Things To Do

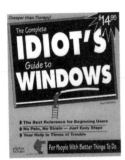

Also Available!

Yes, it's true!
Computers and computer programs don't
have to make you feel like a complete idiot!

**The Complete Idiot's
Guide to the Mac**
ISBN: 1-56761-395-0
$14.95 USA

**The Complete Idiot's
Guide to Buying
& Upgrading PCs**
ISBN: 1-56761-274-1
$14.95 USA

**The Complete Idiot's
Guide to Multimedia**
ISBN: 1-56761-505-8
$19.95 USA

**The Complete Idiot's
Guide to CD-ROM**
ISBN: 1-56761-460-4
$14.95 USA

**The Complete Idiot's
Guide to CorelDRAW!**
ISBN: 1-56761-429-9
$16.95 USA

**The Complete Idiot's
Guide to Photoshop**
ISBN: 1-56761-527-9
$19.95 USA

**The Complete Idiot's
Guide to QuarkXPress**
ISBN: 1-56761-519-8
$19.95 USA

**The Complete Idiot's
Guide to Access**
ISBN: 1-56761-457-4
$14.95 USA

**The Complete Idiot's
Guide to Computer Terms,
Second Edition**
ISBN: 1-56761-506-6
$10.95 USA

**The Complete Idiot's
Guide to Modems
& Online Services**
ISBN: 1-56761-526-0
$19.95 USA

**The Complete Idiot's
Guide to UNIX**
ISBN: 1-56761-511-2
$19.95 USA

**The Complete Idiot's
Guide to 1-2-3,
New Edition**
ISBN: 1-56761-404-3
$16.95 USA

**The Complete Idiot's
Guide to 1-2-3 for
Windows, Second Edition**
ISBN: 1-56761-485-X
$16.95 USA

**The Complete Idiot's
Guide to Excel**
ISBN: 1-56761-318-7
$14.95 USA

**The Complete Idiot's
Guide to Works
for Windows**
ISBN: 1-56761-451-5
$14.95 USA

**The Complete Idiot's
Guide to WordPerfect,
Second Edition**
ISBN: 1-56761-499-X
$16.95 USA

**The Complete Idiot's
Guide to WordPerfect
for Windows**
ISBN: 1-56761-282-2
$14.95 USA

**The Complete Idiot's
Guide to Word for
Windows, New Edition**
ISBN: 1-56761-355-1
$14.95 USA

**The Complete Idiot's
Guide to Ami Pro**
ISBN: 1-56761-453-1
$14.95 USA

**The Complete Idiot's
Guide to QBasic**
ISBN: 1-56761-490-6
$19.95 USA

**The Complete Idiot's
Guide to Visual Basic**
ISBN: 1-56761-486-8
$19.95 USA

*If you're new
to computers,
you need
these books!*

Congratulations!

By buying this book, you have become the proud owner of the handsome diskette strapped cleverly to the inside back cover of this book. On that disk, you'll find everything you need to connect to The Pipeline, a hot new Internet service for Microsoft Windows that makes access as easy as point and click.

Follow this procedure to install the software:

1. Place the disk in your floppy disk drive.

2. In Program Manager, select **File ¦ Run.**

3. Type **b:\setup** or **c:\setup** (use the appropriate one for the disk drive you are using) and press **Enter.**

4. Follow the instructions on-screen to complete the installation procedure.

5. When installation is complete, double click on The **Pipeline** icon in Program Manager to start the program.

6. Follow the instructions on the screen to configure the Pipeline (it's not too difficult), or check out Chapter 22 for full details.